The Ways Of God
A Yearly Devotional

Allen E. Shepherd, MD

TEACH Services, Inc.
P U B L I S H I N G
www.TEACHServices.com • (800) 367-1844

World rights reserved. This book or any portion thereof may not be copied or reproduced in any form or manner whatever, except as provided by law, without the written permission of the publisher, except by a reviewer who may quote brief passages in a review.

The author assumes full responsibility for the accuracy of all facts and quotations as cited in this book. The opinions expressed in this book are the author's personal views and interpretations, and do not necessarily reflect those of the publisher.

This book is provided with the understanding that the publisher is not engaged in giving spiritual, legal, medical, or other professional advice. If authoritative advice is needed, the reader should seek the counsel of a competent professional.

Copyright © 2021 Allen E. Shepherd MD
Copyright © 2021 TEACH Services
ISBN-13: 978-1-4796-1296-3 (Paperback)
ISBN-13: 978-1-4796-1297-0 (ePub)
Library of Congress Control Number: 2021904256

All Scripture quotations, unless otherwise indicated, are taken from the New International Version. Copyright © 1973, 1978, 1984, 2011 by Biblica, Inc®. Used by permission. All rights reserved worldwide.

Scripture quotations marked NIV 1988 are taken from the New International Version. Zondervan Publishing House, Grand Rapids, Michigan. 1988.

Scripture quotations marked KJV are taken from the King James Version® of the Bible. Public domain.

Scripture quotations marked NKJV are taken from the New King James Version®. Copyright © 1990 by Thomas Nelson. Used by permission. All rights reserved.

Scripture quotations marked NLT are taken from the New Living Translation. Copyright © 1996, 2004, 2015 by Tyndale House Foundation. Used by permission of Tyndale House Publishers, Inc., Carol Stream, Illinois 60188. All rights reserved.

Scripture quotations marked ESV are taken from the English Standard Version. Copyright © 2001 by Crossway, a publishing ministry of Good News Publishers. Used by permission. All rights reserved.

Published by

TEACH Services, Inc.
P U B L I S H I N G
www.TEACHServices.com • (800) 367-1844

TABLE OF CONTENTS

Endorsements... iv

Preface..v

Section 1. The Foundations....................................7

Section 2. The Trinity.......................................32

Section 3. The Creation: Thinking about the Creation.........57

Section 4. The Creation: The Wonders of the Creation.........89

Section 5. The Fall and the Flood...........................127

Section 6. Abraham, Isaac, and Jacob........................149

Section 7. The Way of Grace.................................162

Section 8. God and the Jews.................................181

Section 9. God in Human Form Comes to Earth.................234

Section 10. The Installation of King Jesus..................290

Section 11. Women...323

Section 12. God and the Church..............................346

Section 13. Satan and the Angels............................368

Section 14. The End and the Consummation of All Things......378

Endorsements

"Dr. Allen Shepherd's *The Ways of God* is devotional writing that comes from his heart and is filled with thoughtful insights. The fact that it is a labor of love is evident on every page. You will be blessed as you read in both your spirit and in your intellect as you wrestle with ideas and glimpse more fully the God of love who so cared for the world that He gave His one and only Son. This is a book not merely to be read, but to be prayed through. Happy reading."
—**George R. Knight**, Emeritus Professor of Church History, Andrews University and the author of many books on Adventist history and theology

"Dr. Shepherd's observations about God, the world and life in general never cease to inspire and challenge me. His gift for drawing profound lessons from everyday experiences and simplifying deep spiritual truths are sure to touch an answering cord in your heart and deepen your love for God. *The Ways of God* represents the distillation of the wisdom and experience of a lifetime, offered to the world by a man whose life continues to be a blessing to all who have the privilege of coming within his circle of influence, as I have."
—**Bryce Bowman**, Pastor, Michigan Conference of SDA

"Dr. Allen Shepherd served as a pastor in the Indiana Conference for 12 years, and was loved and appreciated by those in his congregations. Upon retirement he was led to write this devotional book, carefully integrating science and scripture. His daily readings are challenging and thoughtful. He covers a variety of themes, which build over several days. This is a devotional book that you will look forward to reading each day."
—**Pastor Vic Van Schaik**, President, Indiana Conference of Seventh-day Adventists

"If you are looking for a devotional book with deep insights into the character of God, this is the devotional book for you. As I read, I saw more clearly the mind of God in the Great Controversy and plan of redemption. It also left me looking forward to the next day's reading longing to know more about the wonderful God we serve."
—**Eric Freking**, Indiana Conference Evangelist and doctoral student at Andrews University

Preface

"For my thoughts are not your thoughts, neither are your ways my ways," declares the LORD. "As the heavens are higher than the earth, so are my ways higher than your ways and my thoughts than your thoughts" (Isa. 55:8–9).

Although God's ways are beyond ours, and His thoughts above ours, He has graciously chosen to reveal Himself in His Word. And as a skillful craftsman cannot hide his skill, but discloses himself in his work, so the Bible and the Creation speaks to those who will listen to the voice of His artistry.

As I contemplated these things, I felt it a duty to share my thoughts on the Master and His methods. Thus, this small volume.

My prayer is that the words here would be a blessing to those seeking to know the Master of earth and sky and sea, the Savior of our souls.

Oh, the depth of the riches of the wisdom and knowledge of God!

How unsearchable his judgements, and his paths beyond tracing out!

"Who has known the mind of the Lord? Or who has been his counselor?"

"Who has ever given to God, that God should repay them?"

For from him and through him and for him are all things.

To him be the glory forever! Amen. (Rom. 11:33–36)

Section 1

The Foundations

Before the beginning, God laid a foundation that is unshakable. On this foundation, He built all that has come after.

"For no one can lay any foundation other than the one already laid, which is Jesus Christ" (1 Cor. 3:11).

> How firm a foundation, ye saints of the Lord,
> Is laid for your faith in His excellent Word!
> What more can He say than to you He hath said,
> To you who for refuge to Jesus hath fled?[1]

---

[1] Rippon's A Selection of Hymns, "How Firm a Foundation," *The Seventh-day Adventist Hymnal* (Hagerstown, MD: Review and Herald, 1985).

THE FOUNDATION OF THE WORLD

January 1

Revelation 13:8, "[T]he book of life of the Lamb slain from the foundation of the world" (KJV).

We must start at the beginning at the very foundation of the world.

Most would think the beginning would mean the Creation, perhaps the Big Bang, or at least the beginning of our world itself. But that is not what is at the foundation. There is something else there.

At the foundation we find God. But He is not creating. He is not thinking of what He will do to bring about the universe, or of the necessary elements of the periodic table, the stuff of the stars, the carbon and oxygen and hydrogen that He must assemble so that the universe might be able to sustain the creatures He will speak into existence. No, He is doing something else. Something startling, unnerving and completely unexpected, and at once seemingly out of character of a Creator, of One who is all-powerful.

He is dying.

Surprisingly it is the last book of the Bible that reveals the very, very beginning. In Revelation 13:8, Jesus the Lamb is described as having been slain from the foundation of the world, or from the Creation. That is, the very first act of God that is told to us is this act of dying. Before God even spoke or began the process of Creation, Christ tasted death. The Life-giver died on Calvary, but He experienced death before then, before time and space had taken form. Before the sun or stars or galaxies had been shaped by God's mighty hand, Christ knew death. It has been a fact of His existence from eternity past. How strange that He would begin the universe with death!

But, in His acting, He assuredly laid such a foundation that it could not be shaken by the entrance of sin or the failings of His created beings. He had already taken it all into account so that what He built was so sure that nothing could destroy it.

So, Christ is the Lamb slain from the foundation of the world. That is the firm foundation and none could have been found surer.

THE CHOICE
January 2

1 Peter 1:18–20, "For you know that it was not with perishable things such as silver or gold that you were redeemed ... but with the precious blood of Christ, a lamb without blemish or defect. He was chosen before the creation of the world."

This choosing was not a simple or easy matter. Ellen White gives us an inkling of the process:

> The plan of salvation had been laid before the creation of the earth; for Christ is "the Lamb slain from the foundation of the world" (Revelation 13:8); yet it was a struggle, even with the King of the universe, to yield up His Son to die for the guilty race. But "God so loved the world, that He gave His only-begotten Son, that whosoever believeth in Him should not perish, but have everlasting life." John 3:16.[2]

How did the choice of such a magnitude come about? How did the Father and Son and Holy Spirit come to the agreement on what would be done to assure the very foundation of all things?

The conversation and act are shrouded in the darkness of eternity past. But in it was the life and light of all and the agreement to die was made by Christ so that all could be saved.

Fathers have given their lives for their children, but in this case, the Father could not intervene. The choice was the universe or His Son. How the struggle played out we are not told except that the Father yielded because of love.

The plan of salvation was laid before a single atom was created, or a single world or angel had come into being. As Ellen White has said, every loaf of bread is marked with the cross.[3] Our lives are dependent still on that death. We live because He chose to yield the One that is life itself.

---

[2] Ellen G. White, *Patriarchs and Prophets* (Mountain View, CA: Pacific Press, 1890), p. 63.
[3] Ellen G. White, *The Desire of Ages* (Mountain View, CA: Pacific Press, 1898), p. 660.

THE EMPTYING

January 3

Philippians 2:5–8, "Christ Jesus: Who, being in very nature God, did not consider equality with God something to be grasped, but he made himself nothing, taking the very nature of a servant, being made in human likeness. And being found in appearance as a man, he humbled himself by becoming obedient to death—even death on a cross!"

These verses describe the act of Jesus in coming to our dark world. It was an act of utter humility.

He was of the God class; above all, the Creator of everything made—galaxies, the stars and planets and nebulae we see through the Hubble. All were made by Him. And the earth we live in was made by Him as well, with all its delights and delicacies, the plants, animals and we ourselves. And He made love and compassion, and all the powers we have to do good and excel. All this was His by creative power. He owns the cattle on a thousand hills (Ps. 50:10).

And He set it all aside to come and visit with us here as a man. An unbelievable act of descent into the lowlands of our existence!

But He did not come as a king. He came as a simple man. Not of royal parentage, but Son of a laborer and a teenage girl, born in the rudest of buildings—an animal shed.

And He endured all the indignities that we endure here: the awkwardness of youth, the rejection by peers and the difficulties of being born in a place where the evil one, not God is ruler.

He was thought an illegitimate Child and faced the ridicule that often occurs with that situation. He lived as you and I do, not as One from a heavenly throne.

And I am thankful for His descent to our place. We may glory in His humility.

WHEN THE FULLNESS OF TIME WAS COME PART 1
January 4

Galatians 4:4, "But when the time had fully come, God sent his Son."

God's purposes know no haste and no delay. He had revealed to Daniel when the Anointed One would arrive on earth (Dan. 9:25). And the timetable was true and sure. Ellen White says this:

> Providence had directed the movements of nations, and the tide of human impulse and influence, until the world was ripe for the coming of the Deliverer. The nations were united under one government. One language was widely spoken, and was everywhere recognized as the language of literature. From all lands the Jews of the dispersion gathered to Jerusalem to the annual feasts. As these returned to the places of their sojourn, they could spread throughout the world the tidings of the Messiah's coming.[4]

The subtlety of God's timetable is beyond our ken. How could the things noted above have been manipulated so that the arrival of Jesus had been prepared for? Any student of history can see that the back and forth of human passion and impulse is irrational, erratic and completely unpredictable. The Romans overcame the Carthaginians only with great difficulty. It could have gone the other way ... And yet, when the time had fully come ....

In our own time, the message has also gone out as predicted by Daniel, "Unto two thousand and three hundred days: then shall the sanctuary be cleansed" (Dan. 8:14, KJV).

So too, the antitypical day of atonement began, as announced, in 1844, and the message to the world began (Dan. 8:14), "Fear God and give him glory, because the hour of his judgement has come. Worship him who made the heavens, the earth, the sea and the springs of water" (Rev. 14:7).

God has a timetable. It has extended to our day. We can look up and say, "Hallelujah, God reigns!" Let us accept the privilege to be part of that proclamation.

---

[4] Ibid., p. 32.

WHEN THE FULLNESS OF TIME WAS COME PART 2
January 5

Jeremiah 31:3, "The Lord appeared to us in the past, saying: 'I have loved you with an everlasting love; I have drawn you with loving kindness.'"

Satan had studied the prophecies, and knew that the time was near, and had put into motion a plan to counteract that of God. Ellen White saw the utter hopelessness of human ability to save itself, and the circumstances that faced the Christ at His arrival. She says this:

> The deception of sin had reached its height. All the agencies for depraving the souls of men had been put in operation .... The bodies of human beings, made for the dwelling place of God, had become the habitation of demons .... With intense interest the unfallen worlds had watched to see Jehovah arise, and sweep away the inhabitants of the earth. And if God should do this, Satan was ready to carry out his plan for securing to himself the allegiance of heavenly beings .... Had the world been destroyed, he would have claimed that his accusations were proved true. He was ready to cast blame upon God, and to spread his rebellion to the worlds above. But instead of destroying the world, God sent His Son to save it .... At the very crisis, when Satan seemed about to triumph, the Son of God came with the embassage of divine grace. Through every age, through every hour, the love of God had been exercised toward the fallen race. Notwithstanding the perversity of men, the signals of mercy had been continually exhibited. And when the fullness of time had come, the Deity was glorified by pouring upon the world a flood of healing grace that was never to be obstructed or withdrawn till the plan of salvation should be fulfilled.[5]

---

[5] Ibid., pp. 36–37.

AN ALIEN INVASION
January 6

Isaiah 7:14, "The virgin will conceive and give birth to a son, and will call him Immanuel."

Hollywood has made many movies depicting the invasion of earth by aliens. The aliens have nefarious designs. They will kill everyone and rule the planet, take all the women, suck the air or water from the earth or do some other deed that will destroy the human race. The aliens have advanced technology, or some sort of superpower that renders them almost impregnable.

However, some hero among us (usually a Sylvester Stallone type) appears and saves the day by destroying the alien ship, discovering their weakness or managing to find some power that they had not anticipated. Earth is saved from the dread invaders.

But when God invaded, He came as the most defenseless of aliens. There was nothing to fear from Him at all. He was, since Jesus had emptied Himself of all power, the most harmless and helpless of aliens. He came as a baby. Who's afraid of a baby?

He was in more danger from us than we were from Him. He was sucking up nothing except the nutrient milk from His mother's breast and taking no captives whatsoever. He could not even walk and was in more danger of being killed by the ruling King Herod than He was of killing anyone. A Stallone-type savior was not necessary to stop this invasion.

That is how God came to us. As a baby, harmless and helpless and depending on His mother for sustenance. How could He have been less threatening?

He came to serve—not to be served. And so, He came as the weakest of all, a child just born, a babe in a manger. That He came like this reveals the character of God, a God who has no wish to kill or destroy, but only to love. He did this for us.

THE ACT OF ONE HAVING ALL POWER
January 7

John 13:3–5, "Jesus knew that the Father had put all things under his power, and that he had come from God and was returning to God; so he got up from the meal .... and began to wash his disciples' feet."

Power. A heady tonic that befuddles the mind and stifles our more generous impulses. The rich lust after it that they might control wealth. The ambitious long for its blessing, that they might realize their dreams. Idealists seek it to change the world. And those that do not have it yearn to possess this amazing potion that they may sit with those they so envy. Power. If only we had more power!

Satan himself wanted power. All power. "I will ascend above the tops of the clouds; I will make myself like the Most High" (Isa. 14:14). His passion for power led to his downfall. He became the prince of the air and has ruled here for 6,000 years. He offered the power of the kingdoms of this world to Jesus, and knew he could deliver, if only Christ would worship.

But Jesus, knowing power's intoxicating charm, refused to be controlled by it. So, when He knew He had *all* power and that *all* things were His, He knelt on the dusty floor, took a towel and basin and began to wash dirty feet.

As the universe looked on, they saw One who could be trusted with power. No one else had demonstrated such an ability. The angels had failed to understand it and a third had lost their place in heaven. Adam had grasped it and lost his garden home. Who could be trusted?

Only God. The Creator with all power, knew that it could only be used safely by One who was willing to empty Himself of it. Such a One could then take the reins of power without becoming corrupted by it.

And He calls us to surrender ourselves to Him that we too may use it safely.

"Oh, the depth of the riches of the wisdom and knowledge of God! How unsearchable his judgements, and his paths beyond tracing out!" (Rom. 11:33).

ABSOLUTE POWER CORRUPTS ABSOLUTELY
January 8

Isaiah 14:13, "I will ascend to the heavens; I will raise my throne above the stars of God."

We have a saying that most would accept as truth: "[P]ower tends to corrupt and absolute power corrupts absolutely."[6]

That power does corrupt is apparent. That absolute power might do so absolutely does not seem a stretch, especially when we observe those who hold the reins of power in our own governments. Power does something to a person.

This saying also gives voice to the fear we have of power. Power can be frightening. We know that the exercise of it can bring pain and suffering and loss. Those in power have fallen to its allure, even the righteous. The example of King David and his willingness to use power to take what he wanted and to even kill to do it disturbs any confidence we might feel as to our own ability to resist the temptations of power. After all, if one who was a man after God's own heart fell so completely, what chance do we have?

Noble Frodo (*Lord of the Rings*) resists the power of the ring to the very end, but then refuses to surrender it to the flames, assuming its power instead as his own.[7]

> *But God has absolute power. Omnipotence. Is He absolutely corrupt? Can He be trusted? We would not know if it had not been for Jesus. God on the cross is an astounding revelation. He is found there because He loves us more than He loves power. He surrendered all power so that He might save us.*

But God has absolute power. Omnipotence. Is He absolutely corrupt? Can He be trusted? We would not know if it had not been for Jesus. God

---
[6]Lord Acton, "Lord Acton writes to Bishop Creighton …," ONLINE LIBRARY OF LIBERTY, https://1ref.us/1g7 (accessed December 1, 2020).
[7]"Did Frodo fail at Mt. Doom by putting on the ring and refusing to destroy it?" Quora, https://1ref.us/1g8 (accessed December 1, 2020).

on the cross is an astounding revelation. He is found there because He loves us more than He loves power. He surrendered all power so that He might save us.

And He calls us to take up our own cross of humility. It is a call to turn from power to service. Will you heed the call? It comes from God Himself.

THE SUPPER PART 1

January 9

1 Corinthians 11:26, "For whenever you eat this bread and drink this cup, you proclaim the Lord's death until he comes."

The Lord's Supper, or Communion, is one of the two ceremonies Jesus enjoined on Christians, the other being foot washing. Baptism was borrowed from John the Baptist, so is not original to Jesus, although He made it part of His teachings.

But this meal memorializes Jesus' death. Why not the resurrection? Why dwell on this dark event rather than the bright one that occurred a very short time later? Why does Jesus tell us to remember His death, and doesn't say a word about the resurrection?

Because His death was the most important thing He did.

Jesus went about healing the sick, forgiving sin and raising the dead. Whole villages were free of disease after He came. And death had no power when He was present. The sisters of Lazarus said, "If you had been here, my brother would not have died" (John 11:21). So, resurrection was easy. He was the God of life, its Creator, so giving life was as natural as breathing. Easy as pie, you might say.

But dying? The King of life dying?? How can the One at whose face death fled, die? It is an alien act. It is a seeming repudiation of His life, a Life that gave life.

So, Jesus asks us to memorialize it for it is the most important thing that has ever happened in the universe. That day when the Lord of life died, taking death to Himself, and surrendering the thing that was His natural endowment ….

There is nothing we could better do than proclaim the Lord's death. It was His greatest and God's greatest act.

THE SUPPER PART 2

January 10

Luke 22:19, "And he took bread, gave thanks and broke it, and gave it to them, saying, 'This is my body given for you; do this in remembrance of me.'"

When I was younger, Communion was celebrated in a very solemn manner. There was no real celebration, because it was felt that the death of Jesus was such a serious and sad thing that celebration was inappropriate.

More recently, the rite has been done with more joy. Which is the right way to do this? What is the right attitude?

There are two sides to this memorial. One is the memory of the horror endured by Jesus on the cross, and the giving up of the Lord of life of His birthright—Life itself. He surrendered His life, who being the very Author of life, had a natural right to it. But for us, He laid it down.

And that act reveals the second characteristic of the meal. It is a memorial of the attitude of God towards us. We are so valuable to Him, and He is the One who ultimately determines the *real* value of a thing, that He gave up His life that we might have eternal life. We are the most valuable thing to Him. He laid down that very valuable thing, His life, that He might gain us, something He considers of even greater worth.

And this is cause for great joy and celebration. That our God would do that because of our value should convince us of our true worth.

The world does not think people are of much value. They are deceived, sold, abused and killed for little gain. But Jesus saw how valuable we really are!

Rejoice then and be exceeding glad, for you are of surpassing worth! Jesus showed it by His death. Let's celebrate!

THE GLORY BEFORE THE WORLD BEGAN
January 11

John 17:5, "And now, Father, glorify me in your presence with the glory I had with you before the world began."

Jesus prayed these words just before He left the upper room. What was this glory that had not been manifest until this time?

Jesus is about to be tried and crucified, and He asks God to glorify Him. Was the cross and His suffering a manifestation of the glory that He had with the Father before the world began?

As you recall, the first act of God recorded in Scripture is this dying that Christ partook of from the foundation of the world (see January 1). Here again He speaks of an act that occurred before the Creation. But of course, no one was there except the Trinity, so no one knew of the dying that had begun at that time.

But now it is to be revealed. Jesus asked the Father to glorify Him with the glory that They both partook of at that time.

And what is that glory revealed by the crucifixion story?

It is the length to which the love of God will go to save the ones He loves. This love could not have been known before this day, for there was no opportunity for its revelation. But now, God can show the world and the whole universe the depths of His love. The cross will plumb the abyss of that love, showing the sacrifice of Himself that He would make for those He had created, even those who had rebelled against Him, the race He had knelt over at the Creation, giving the breath of life with His own lips.

And that was the highest glory that God could reveal, the death of His beloved Son on this dark and evil place for the universe He had made. Oh, the depths of the love of God!

IN THE GARDEN PART 1
January 12

Matthew 26:39, "Going a little farther, he fell with his face to the ground and prayed, 'My Father, if it is possible, may this cup be taken from me. Yet not as I will, but as you will.'"

What was this cup, and why did Christ struggle so to drink it?

The Old Testament mentions the cup in several passages. God calls the nations to drink it and even Judah must drink to the full. It is the cup of God's wrath (Ps. 75:8; Isa. 51:17; Jer. 25:15).

When the Zebedee brothers and their mother came to Jesus asking for the best seats in the kingdom, Jesus inquired if they could drink from His cup (Matt. 20:20–22). He knew what lay just in the future, and yet in the garden He was reluctant to take it. He asked to be excused if possible.

What is this cup of God's wrath?

Wrath seems a thing alien to God's character. Why would He be wrathful? The Bible is clear that His wrath can be aroused by sin. And the horror of His wrath is that it means separation from Him. And if we are separated from Him, we are separated from Life itself. He is the Author of life, and no other being can bestow it.

And now Jesus shrinks from embracing and absorbing that wrath.

Must the Author of life take the cup of separation from life? How can it be? His hand trembles at the horror of night now to descend on Him. Is there not another way?

Three times He prays, but at each prayer He is willing to do the Father's will. Will the Trinity be shattered by disunity in Itself? Can God bear the sins of the whole world that we might be free?

IN THE GARDEN PART 2
January 13

Matthew 26:42, "He went away a second time and prayed, 'My Father, if it is not possible for this cup to be taken away unless I drink it, may your will be done.'"

This is the crisis moment. It is now that the plan instigated before time began hangs in the balance.

Hitherto, Jesus and the Father had agreed on every aspect of Creation and the character of the universe. They had carried out Their work as a team, a team to bring the universe into existence and to populate it with creatures that loved Them and on whom They bestowed Their unfailing love.

But now, *but now*, a difference has arisen between them. There had been war in heaven, now was there to be war within the Trinity who had created it all? This was a crisis for the whole of the universe. The foundation was tested. What would be the result? Was it sure enough to hold everything together, or would the universe be shattered into atoms and shaken to destruction? That is what was at stake.

Jesus noted the will of the Father, the agreement They had made at the beginning. But the separation that had been anticipated so long ago was now to be a reality. This was an experience that Jesus, and no man, not even God the Father, nor even, surprisingly, Satan had even realized. No being had been so separated from God as Jesus was to be in these moments.

The cup trembled in His hand. Ellen White says that Jesus, when seeing the horror of that great darkness about to descend on Him, thought of the human race and that He would not let some of His beloved creation suffer eternal loss.[8]

He took the cup and drained it to the dregs.

---

[8]Ibid., pp. 690–693.

THE EMPTYING

January 14

Philippians 2:8, "And being found in appearance as a man, he humbled himself by becoming obedient to death—even death on a cross!"

Jesus, when He became man, put aside His divine attributes becoming like one of us in all things except sinfulness. He entered the world as One who had never sinned, but did have the weaknesses of the flesh that had deteriorated over the millennia since Creation.

This was a great humiliation, but it was not the end of humiliation. He died a death of utter humiliation. On a cross naked between heaven and earth!

Artists are reluctant to picture that kind of shame. So, they always add a loin cloth. But that is not how it was when He died. The soldiers gambling for His seamless inner robe show that all His clothes were taken from Him. He was there naked before all, and the priests and scribes came, taunting Him: "'He saved others,' they said, 'but he can't save himself! Let this Messiah, this king of Israel, come down now from the cross, that we may see and believe'" (Mark 15:31–32). And the thieves mocked Him as well. Everyone there was making fun.

And the Father was silent.

Think of it, the holy God naked, being mocked by those He came to save! If this does not show the lengths to which God was willing to go to redeem, nothing will. He did not retaliate in anger or frustration. He did not use His power to torture those persecutors with a painful affliction like Satan did with Job, but endured it all that we might have life.

That was what emptying was. We know nothing of such emptying, no matter how humiliated we may have been. And He was God!

THE SEPARATION
January 15

Luke 23:33, "When they came to the place called the Skull, they crucified him there."

The trial and crucifixion were terrible, but Ellen White says that they were hardly felt by the Son of God:

"The withdrawal of the divine countenance from the Saviour in this hour of supreme anguish pierced His heart with a sorrow that can never be fully understood by man. So great was this agony that His physical pain was hardly felt."[9]

Jesus had spent His life doing the will of His Father. He had fulfilled it perfectly, as a dutiful Son. He had done all His Father's will. But now there was a change. He had accepted the cup that had trembled in His hand and now drank it to the very bottom, the dregs of human sin were completely consumed. And when all of the sin of the world was placed on Him, He cried out in the agony of separation: "My God, my God, why have you forsaken me?" (Matt. 27:46).

This forsaking of Jesus by the Father was the final separation of the Two before the death of Christ. It was as if Jesus, looking at His life and what He had done could not understand why the Father was withdrawing. "Why are you leaving Me alone to die as the sinner dies, without God or hope? I have not sinned! My life has been perfect before You, and yet You have left Me, alone to die forsaken!" (See Ps. 22:1, 2, 7, 8.)

This is the cry of humanity when left to ourselves. But this Human had not forsaken God. He had lived in God's presence and according to His will His whole life long. God had even said that with Him He was well pleased (Matt. 3:17). And yet, *and yet*, He is forsaken. What is the nature of sin that it tears the Trinity asunder?

---

[9]Ibid., p. 753.

THE NATURE OF SIN
January 16

Romans 6:14, "For sin shall no longer be your master."

What is sin that it tore the Trinity asunder and brought the Son to the cross?

Sin seems like such a small thing to us. We indulge in it, often on a whim, falling into temptations that do indeed easily beset us (Heb. 12:1). We are used to it. The world lives in a state of sin and notes the dissonance when One who is holy intrudes. It reacts with cruel rejection, eventually being even willing to destroy such a One.

Why is that?

Sin is the rule of self. Love is the rule of selflessness.

We are afraid of selflessness. We are afraid we will be taken advantage of or abused or beat into submission. We have to stand up for ourselves.

But Jesus showed that it is selflessness that is the answer to all these fears, and it is the most attractive characteristic of the Godhead. They gave of Themselves to make the world, and even gave the creatures freedom to rebel. And when that rebellion came to fruition, They gave of Themselves to bring it to an end by sending a Member of the Godhead to die. That is selflessness of the highest order—real, costly selflessness. Jesus died that we might be free when we were in slavery to our selfishness. And since He has done all that is necessary for salvation and eternal life, we can rest in Him, and quit worrying about ourselves. We can then become selfless as well and reveal to others the love that God has for us all.

Without the death of Jesus, we would not have an idea of the dead-ended-ness of sin. Selfishness is naturally attractive to us.

But the cross shows its utter worthlessness and deadly nature. There was no other way to show that characteristic of sin.

JESUS CHRIST, CHIEF OF SINNERS PART 1
January 17

2 Corinthians 5:21, "God made him who had no sin to be sin for us, so that in him we might become the righteousness of God."

Isaiah tells us that God laid on Christ the iniquity of us all (Isa. 53:6), but Paul is starker in his analysis. He says Jesus was made sin for us—He actually became sin. This is a most terrible insight. That God, the One who had rejected sin at the beginning and excluded it from His universe, would actually become what was completely repulsive to Him is astounding. But by becoming sin He was able to save us from it.

He took sin—all sin—unto Himself. He absorbed it so to speak, as a sponge absorbs water. It became His, He suffered the punishment for it, and can now claim it all as His own by right. There is no sin that is not His. And if we think that we are being punished by God for our sins, we deny the ownership that Jesus has asserted by His death on the cross.

He became sin for us! To what depths was He willing to descend that He might lift us up to the heights of heaven and salvation? He is able to save to the utmost because He became sin to the utmost.

There is a peace and rest that comes with the realization that Jesus has borne all my sin. He is so identified with it that Paul, the great New Testament theologian, tells us that Jesus became sin for us. He could not have expressed the thought more forcefully and clearly.

He became sin for us! To internalize that truth is to be free from its power to ensnare. Let us submit to Him that all may go well with us.

JESUS CHRIST, CHIEF OF SINNERS PART 2
January 18

2 Corinthians 5:21, "God made him who had no sin to be sin for us, so that in him we might become the righteousness of God."

There is another aspect of this verse that requires comment. Jesus became sin for us that WE might become the righteousness of God.

How by Jesus' taking to Himself our sin do we become the righteousness of God? How can sinners become the very righteousness of God? How can that be?

One could argue that God reveals HIS righteousness by doing what He has done for us. His goodness and mercy, generosity, grace, and long suffering, and all His other attributes become clear because of what He did for us. The universe then sees His character more clearly because of this revelation.

But that is not what the verse is saying. It says WE BECOME the righteousness of God. That is, we—His people—become His righteousness.

Now the above thought is part of it, but it is bigger than that.

He identifies US as His righteousness. It is not His attributes that He is pointing out, but us. WE are His righteousness.

God seems to delight in revealing Himself through concrete demonstrations rather than abstract assertions. We can speak of His goodness and mercy, but to see it actuated in a living being, a creature who has become an example of such an attribute who can testify to its reality, that is so much more convincing.

So we are then the righteousness of God. We are what He points to when He wants to demonstrate His righteousness. That rank sinners can become such a thing is amazing beyond words. Our sins would seem to excuse us from righteousness, but God can make US His righteousness. *Wonder of wonders.*

THE TRIUMPH OF THE CROSS
January 19

Colossians 2:15, "And having disarmed the powers and authorities, he made a public spectacle of them, triumphing over them by the cross."

This verse is a great paradox. How is it that Christ disarmed the powers of evil and made them a spectacle by His cross? The cross was an utter humiliation. Jesus hung naked before all His enemies who challenged Him to come down. Instead of coming down, He died in their presence. How could that possibly be a triumph? And how were the powers of evil made a spectacle?

Satan had won the allegiance of man in the garden, and so had become the ruler of this world (Eph. 2:2, Job 1 and 2). But that rule appeared to be an appalling thing. There was pain and death, tears and sickness and all manner of evil. As the universe looked on, his rule was clearly inferior to God's rule of light and peace.

But Satan had an answer to the problem of appearances. He used God's omnipotence against Him. He said, "God is manipulating the situation here on earth. He is all-powerful, you know, and is making me look bad by interfering behind the scenes. You cannot believe what you see."

How could God answer such an accusation? He is all-powerful after all and could be doing just as Satan said.

There was one way: give up all power.

And so Christ emptied Himself as Philippians 2:7 says. He set aside His divinity and became a man, the least powerful being in the universe, a creature with weakness as his inheritance. It was clear that godly power had been set aside.

Then Satan, having Christ in his grip, revealed his true nature. He killed Him in a most cruel fashion—the cross. And Christ did not retaliate, but died, exposing Satan for the evil creature he was. Christ took the nature of the weakest of the weak, and Satan showed what he would do with such a One—utterly destroy Him.

The universe knew that God, being all-powerful, could destroy Satan. But He had not done so. Satan, however, when he had God in his grasp, did not hesitate, murdering Christ by torture.

The cross tore away Satan's deceptive mask before the entire universe. His accusations were proved utterly false. So, Christ triumphed over the powers of darkness and defeated them completely. It only remains for Him to come and claim His own and destroy sin. We may be part of the victory by giving our loyalty to Him who loved us and gave Himself for us.

SATAN IS CAST DOWN
January 20

Revelation 12:7–9, "Then war broke out in heaven. Michael and his angels fought against the dragon, and the dragon and his angels fought back. But he was not strong enough, and they lost their place in heaven. The great dragon was hurled down—that ancient serpent called the devil, or Satan, who leads the whole world astray. He was hurled to the earth, and his angels with him."

It is clear from Colossians that Jesus defeated Satan at the cross (Col. 2:15). And with that defeat, he lost his place in heaven. Apparently, he had access to heaven as did his fellow wicked angels up until that time. But with the crucifixion, they lost all sympathy with the angelic host. There was no one who would listen to their accusations, and Satan was cast out by a total revulsion of the angels. He lost his place as the accuser of the brethren and was banished.

Satan had had the sympathy of some of the angelic host before the crucifixion. But with his action toward Jesus as He hung on the cross, all that sympathy evaporated.

And an amazing thing happened. Satan was cast out of heaven, and now there is no one there to accuse us! The accuser has been banished to earth and no longer accuses us day and night before God and the universe. So, at the judgement bar of God, there is only the Father—the Judge—Jesus our advocate and the books of heaven themselves. No prosecutor is there (1 John 3:20).

The books show all of the heavenly family that belongs to God. And Jesus pleads His blood for them and is a thoroughly adequate Savior.

Although Satan is now among us, and full of wrath, it is heaven to which we should look. Our Savior is there representing us and He will be successful.

A GIFT FROM BEFORE TIME
January 21

2 Timothy 1:8–9, "So do not be ashamed of the testimony about our Lord .... [Who] has saved us and called us to a holy life—not because of anything we have done but because of his own purpose and grace. This grace was given us in Christ Jesus before the beginning of time."

Grace, that wonderful characteristic of God that meets the profound needs of His wayward children, was also conceived in the beginning.

Paul tells us that the grace of God was given to us before time began. At the meeting of the Godhead before time began, grace was devised. Grace was put in place then, before the world and before sin.

When we understand through our own experience our need for grace, that is, that we need it every day, and even every moment, it is wonderful that God provided for our deficiency way before He even created us.

History seems to be chaotic and unplanned. Time and chance happen to us all as Solomon says (Eccles. 9:11). There appears to be no rhyme nor rhythm. Yet, before the world took form and anyone walked the globe, God had made provision for our weaknesses and sinfulness by providing grace.

Amazing grace! How sweet the sound! And this sound reverberated silently through time even before there were human ears to hear it. God saw and provided for us before we even existed. Amazing grace indeed.

Let us then relax in His arms, a place of grace for all our deficiencies.

THE KINGDOM PREPARED FROM THE FOUNDATION OF THE WORLD

January 22

Matthew 25:34, "Then shall the King say unto them on his right hand, Come, ye blessed of my Father, inherit the kingdom prepared for you from the foundation of the world" (KJV).

At the beginning, God laid a firm foundation on His own suffering and dying. This was done before time began and before a single creature had come from His creative hand. This act allowed for all His acts that followed and anchored all of His creation in Himself and the unyielding bedrock of His own character.

He did another thing at that time as well: He laid the foundation for His kingdom, prepared before time began.

It was not only His death that was conceived from the foundation of the world, but His kingdom as well. And the astonishing thing about that kingdom is that we were part of it, from the foundation of the world.

Evolution would tell us that we are an act of chance—an accident of time and fortune. There is no purpose, there is no design, no intention, no will that brought us into being. One could even say we are freaks of nature.

But Jesus, when contemplating the great assize, remembers the thinking of His Father at the very beginning. His kingdom, the thing He came to establish with His death, contains not only the kingdom itself, but the citizens of that kingdom, you and me. We were included in the mind of God before a single atom was brought into being.

We are not flukes, afterthoughts or accidents, but beings brought on the stage of life by purpose and the will of the Creator Himself. God had us in mind before He put a single star in place.

We should value ourselves as God does, creatures loved by a loving God who gave all for us from the very beginning. We were not an afterthought or accident, but an act of love. Let us never forget that.

Section 2

The Trinity

Who is this God in three Persons? How might we understand Him?

"Holy, holy, holy! Lord God Almighty!
All Thy works shall praise Thy name in earth and sky and sea;
Holy, holy, holy! merciful and mighty!
God in three persons, blessed Trinity!"[10]

---

[10]Reginald Heber, "Holy, Holy, Holy," *The Seventh-day Adventist Hymnal* (Hagerstown, MD: Review and Herald, 1985).

THE TRINITY AS CREATOR
January 23

Genesis 1:1–3, "In the beginning God created the heavens and the earth. Now the earth was formless and empty ... and the Spirit of God was hovering over the waters. And God said ...."

At the beginning, in Genesis 1, the Trinity appears in Its role as Creator. God the Father is mentioned first, then the Spirit is seen brooding over the face of the waters. Then the Word of God, Jesus, speaks and brings everything into being.

All the Godhead worked to create the heavens and earth; each had a part in creating and organizing the world and its systems. By including the "heavens" in the Creation story, the whole universe, the galaxies, the stars and all the planets, nebulae and every atom that is present in this vast domain are included. When the Bible says on the fourth day that He made the stars also (Gen. 1:16), these other suns, which may not have been created at this instant, are named. They, nevertheless, are the works of the Trinity, in concert with One another.

That the Trinity can be seen in these first verses attests to the fundamental truth of this concept, though it is not so well developed until the New Testament where the issue became more necessary and more clear. The hints of Its existence can be seen in various places in the Old Testament.

These verses (Gen. 1:26; 3:22; 11:7; Isa. 6:8) where God speaks of Himself in the plural number, give a hint to us of this reality. But this first revelation is most important. The Trinity worked from the very beginning, the One God doing His will.

WHY THE TRINITY?
January 24

John 10:30, "I and the Father are one."

Why has God manifested Himself as a Trinity? Many have discussed why they believe in the Trinity, but few have pondered the why. So why is God a Trinity?

Phillip Fuller makes the argument from perfection and love. Here is its outline:

1. God is Perfect
2. God is Love
3. Because God is perfect He doesn't need the world—He is perfect in Himself
4. But since God is love—and love requires an object or person of its affection—God requires an object/person to share His love
5. In order for God to be love and remain perfect—without need of the world—He finds within Himself another Person to love (the Son) [Note: He does not *create* a lover, but He finds Him there.]
6. The Holy Spirit embodies the love that the Father and the Son share; He is the "spirit" of that Relationship, the joy and generation of that ecstatic union[11]

A perfect Being would have no lack and would need nothing. But a loving Being must have an object of His love. Thus, the above argument.

C. S. Lewis wrote: "[T]he words 'God is love' have no real meaning unless God contains at least two Persons. Love is something that one person has for another person. If God was a single person, then before the world was made, He was not love."[12]

Although the Bible does not make such arguments as these, it allows us to ferret out the truths hidden therein. The statements above do not exhaust the reasons for God's taking this form, but give a reasonable explanation. He is above and beyond our thinking, but desires to reveal Himself to us. The Trinitarian doctrine helps explain the mystery He is.

---

[11]Mike Duran, "Why God Exists in Trinity," Mikeduran.com, https://1ref.us/1g9 (accessed December 1, 2020).

[12]C.S. Lewis, *Mere Christianity* (New York, NY: Collier Books, MacMillan Publishing Co., 1952), pp. 135–136.

THE REALITY OF THE TRINITY
January 25

John 1:1–3, "In the beginning was the Word, and the Word was with God, and the Word was God. He was with God in the beginning. Through him all things were made; without him nothing was made that has been made."

John begins his Gospel with the above statement about the relationship of Jesus with God the Father. The Greek construction was very carefully done to signify that Jesus was God, was with God and a different Person from God, but God nevertheless.[13]

The book of John shows Jesus taking the name and prerogatives of God. He calls Himself the I AM (John 8:58). The Jews understood His claim and took up stones to kill Him for committing what they supposed to be blasphemy.

In Mark 2:1–12, Jesus heals a paralytic and then forgives his sins, the prerogative of God alone.

In John 17:5, Jesus prays that He might have the glory He had with God in the past, but God says in Isaiah 48:11 that He will share His glory with no one.

In John 20, Jesus accepts the name of God without rebuking the man who said so (John 20:28). He even acknowledged He was God (John 20:29).

Jesus thus claims to be equal to God. To deny this is to ignore His own words on the subject.

If Jesus is God, and He spoke to the Father, and admitted that He always followed the will of the Father, and claimed to be His Son, then there is more than one Person in God or rather the Godhead. The God of one purpose is composed of more than one Person.

The Jews condemned Jesus for blasphemy (Matt. 26:65–66) and said He deserved death. It was clear what His claims were and how the people who had received the law saw it. Jesus claimed to be God and the Jews acknowledged that claim by killing Him. It is thus a truth that Jesus was Emmanuel, God with us.

---

[13]James White, "John 1:1—Meaning and Translation," Alpha and Omega Ministries, https://1ref.us/1ga (accessed December 1, 2020).

THE SUBORDINATION OF JESUS PART 1
January 26

Philippians 2:5–7, "[H]ave the same mindset as Christ Jesus: Who being in very nature God ... made himself nothing by taking the very nature of a servant, being made in human likeness."

While on earth, Jesus subordinated Himself to the Father. He says so on several occasions:

- John 5:19, "Jesus gave them this answer: 'Very truly I tell you, the Son can do nothing by himself; he can do only what he sees his Father doing, because whatever the Father does the Son also does.'"
- John 6:38, "For I have come down from heaven not to do my will but to do the will of him who sent me."
- John 7:16, "Jesus answered, 'My teaching is not my own. It comes from the one who sent me.'"
- Matthew 20:23, "Jesus said to them, 'You will indeed drink from my cup, but to sit at my right or left is not for me to grant. These places belong to those for whom they have been prepared by my Father.'"
- Mark 14:36, "'*Abba*, Father,' he said, 'everything is possible for you. Take this cup from me. Yet not what I will, but what you will.'"

It is clear from these verses that Jesus did not do His own will, but that of the Father. He prayed that the cup might pass from Him, but took it from the Father's hand and drank it as His own because that was the Father's will.

Why was it so important that Jesus do only the Father's will and not His own? Was Jesus not allowed to think on His own?

Jesus is our example. He lived a life submissive to God and calls us to follow in His steps. We thus become like Him as He is.

THE SUBORDINATION OF JESUS PART 2
January 27

Philippians 2:6–7, "Who, being in very nature God, did not consider equality with God something to be grasped, but made himself nothing, taking the very nature of a servant, being made in human likeness."

What exactly happened when Jesus became a man and died here on earth? This verse says that though He was God, He became nothing.

Now, later in the chapter, Paul says God exalted Him and made it such that every knee should bow and every tongue should confess that Jesus is Lord (Phil. 2:10). But nowhere in Scripture is a mention made that the qualities that were laid aside were restored. Revelation tells us of Jesus in heaven and calls him the Man, Jesus Christ (Rev. 1:13; 1 Tim 2:5).

So, the God-like characteristics that Jesus laid off when He came here have not been returned to Him. He is still a man. A human like you and me. He sits at the right hand of God as a man. Now He has a glorified body, but it still bears the scars from the crucifixion. Ellen White says this: "No other one bears these evidences that He is the crucified Lord. And these wounds witnessed then, as they will to all eternity, to the love that gave its all on Calvary."[14]

Is Jesus still God, part of the Godhead? Although He has laid aside God-like characteristics, He remains God indeed.

We can worship Him without sin.

Peter says we may "participate in the divine nature" (2 Peter 1:4). Jesus, by becoming a man, brought us so close to Him that we, in a sense, become part of the Godhead! This is a great gift—amazing that we should have such potential!

We will plumb the depths of the subordination of Christ throughout eternity. It will never be completely understood—only by Jesus Himself. It is our privilege to enjoy the fruits thereof.

---

[14]Ellet J. Waggoner, "Studies from the Gospel of John. Christ Risen. John 20:11–20," *The Present Truth*, June 1, 1899.

JESUS AND THE FATHER'S WILL PART 1
January 28

John 6:38, "For I have come down from heaven not to do my will but to do the will of him who sent me."

Why did Jesus so conscientiously follow the will of the Father? Was He not capable of following His own will, and yet accomplishing the way of salvation? It's almost as if He did not trust Himself.

There is a reason for this.

Satan had initiated his rebellion by acting in an independent manner from God. One of Satan's main principles was that the creatures God had created should be able to act and decide for themselves. He based his government on this principle: we creatures have the ability and the right to be and think independently. It is unfair and demeaning that God requires such condescending servitude. This is real freedom and submitting to God is real slavery. "Let us break their bands asunder," as the psalmist says (Ps. 2:3).

But in truth, it is just the opposite. Submission to God is true freedom and self-rule abject slavery. How can this be? How can submission be freedom and apparent freedom, slavery?

We, and yes, even the angels, do not have the ability to control ourselves. Our passions and desires, our wants and even needs, unless submitted to God, are so powerful they will run riot and destroy us. They need to be controlled by a will that we do not possess.

Our passions and desires are like powerful stallions. Unless under the mastery of a skilled rider, these horses are extremely dangerous. But when a competent horseman has the reins, riding becomes a delight. And such a ride can be an exhilaration.

God desires for us this thrilling ride. And Jesus showed us how we might have such a life: submit in all things to the Father.

Jesus lived as an example of such a life. If we emulate Him, we will have such a one as well.

JESUS AND THE FATHER'S WILL PART 2
January 29

Isaiah 14:14, "I will ascend above the tops of the clouds; I will make myself like the Most High."

There is another reason why Jesus followed the Father's will explicitly.

It was important that the universe understand that whatever happened in His life here on earth, the Two, the Father and He, were always in agreement with One another. That is, Jesus was not acting independently from God.

Satan had made independence the bedrock of his rebellion. He wanted to set up a rule where each of us could be a god unto himself. We could call the shots. We could act in a way that we saw fit and rule our own selves. We did not need a God to rule over us.

And so, Satan rebelled. But that rebellion has led to great suffering, death and destruction. Satan cannot even rule himself without causing the universe and even God to suffer.

So, when Jesus came, He came not only to save mankind, but to demonstrate that the will of God and submission to it would result in great good and the best possible outcome for the universe as a whole.

And this was true even when God's will was that Jesus die on a cross in the most humiliating of ways, naked and apparently under the control of evil men!

Jesus on several occasions spoke about His submission to His Father, so that His intentions were abundantly clear. "[N]ot my will, but yours be done!" was His way of life (Luke 22:42). There was never a time when He was living on His own.

He thus showed that self-rule was the reign of death.

And so the Father exalted Him to the highest place, to be worshiped by all, that all might know that following the will of God was the best the universe could choose.

GOD AND OUR PASSIONS
January 30

John 10:10, "I have come that they may have life, and have it to the full."

But some may ask, "Why did God make us this way? If we cannot control ourselves, is it not His fault when we fall afoul of our own passions? Should He not have made us differently so that we can be in control ourselves? Was He not setting us up for failure?"

God's desire was for creatures of consequence. We are not like the lower animals that are ruled by the laws of instinct, influences that they have no power to resist. Our powers are not under the control of instinct but the will, a will that we freely exercise and can exercise for good or ill.

In paradise, while submitted to God's rule and with a sinless nature, our wills were strong and able to control our passions. But with the fall, our wills became weakened to such an extent that we no longer have the power to rule over them. Even positive feelings like mother love or sympathy for others can become warped and deformed so that they cause great harm.

It was not God's will that such a situation develop here on earth. But there was that potential because He made us in His image, and He gave us free will.

As long as man was obedient, his passions were under the control of a power that could allow their full expression without evil consequences. But with the fall, and the loss of control, our passions can lead us to terrible sin. And we are prone to following them wherever *they* lead!

There was a risk in making us as we are with such passions that can both drive us to great evil or, when under the control of God when we submit to Him, to great good. We can have an influence over others around us that can have an eternal impact for either good or evil.

God did not make junk, but creatures with amazing potential, creatures that could make Him proud. Let us submit that we may not fall short.

OUR WILL OR HIS
January 31

Matthew 11:28–29, *"Come to me, all you who are weary and burdened, and I will give you rest. Take my yoke upon you and learn from me, for I am gentle and humble in heart, and you will find rest for your souls. For my yoke is easy and my burden is light."*

"For all sad words of tongue and pen,

The saddest are these, 'It might have been'."[15]

Ellen White describes the thoughts of Moses as he stood on Mt. Nebo:

> Though his trials had been great, he had enjoyed special tokens of God's favor; he had obtained a rich experience during the sojourn in the wilderness, in witnessing the manifestations of God's power and glory, and in the communion of His love; he felt that he had made a wise decision in choosing to suffer affliction with the people of God, rather than to enjoy the pleasures of sin for a season.[16]

Moses looked back without regret. He had taken the yoke of Christ and endured the trouble of forty years of wandering in the wilderness, leading stubborn people. But it was the shrewdest of choices.

We need experience no regret either. Jesus bids us take His yoke. It may seem hard, filled with the toil of service for others. But it is a yoke of satisfying labor, full of the pleasure of a job well done. The alternative is a life of regret at not doing the best one could have done by following Jesus.

> *We need experience no regret either. Jesus bids us take His yoke. It may seem hard, filled with the toil of service for others. But it is a yoke of satisfying labor, full of the pleasure of a job well done.*

Do not, dear reader, choose to ignore the call of God to you to come up higher and be a follower of the One who is altogether lovely (Song of Sol. 5:16), and the Giver of everlasting pleasure (Ps. 16:11). May God bless your decision.

---

[15] John G. Whittier, "John Greenleaf Whittier Quotes," Brainy Quote, https://1ref.us/1gb (accessed December 1, 2020).

[16] Ellen G. White, *Patriarchs and Prophets* (Mountain View, CA: Pacific Press, 1890), p. 472.

THE SUBORDINATION OF THE SPIRIT
February 1

John 16:13, "But when he, the Spirit of truth, comes, he will guide you into all the truth. He will not speak on his own; he will speak only what he hears."

Throughout the history of Christendom there has been great debate about the Spirit. Is He (It?) a force, a being, an emanation from the Father or Jesus? Does He even exist at all, being really just part of the Father? Does He have a will? And on and on.

Why all this confusion? Why is there not a clear understanding about who He is and what He does among us? Does He not care about our knowing His actual reality?

He has something bigger in mind than His own reputation or even the fact of His existence.

The Spirit has emptied Himself in a fashion similar to the emptying that Jesus did. He has subordinated Himself to Jesus. He will not speak on His own, as John says, but will speak what Jesus says to Him. His mission is to make Christ known to us rather than making Himself known.

And this subordination is so complete that there is confusion about His very existence! He has made Himself of none effect that Christ may be all in all. He has put Himself in the background, pushing Christ forward, giving Him priority of place. It is important that there be no confusion about who is the representative of God to man. It is Jesus.

The Spirit thus hides Himself, acting as the wind, blowing where He pleases, but whose place of origin and destination are imperceptible. This hiddenness is His glory. He is the third Person of the Godhead.

THE SUBORDINATION OF THE FATHER
February 2

Philippians 2:9–11, "Therefore God exalted him to the highest place and gave him the name that is above every name, that at the name of Jesus every knee should bow ... and every tongue acknowledge that Jesus Christ is Lord."

Most know that Jesus took human nature, humbling Himself, taking the form of a creature and even going so far as to die on a cross. But few see the subordination of the Father. It is an unusual kind of subordination, but it is subordination nonetheless.

In 1 Corinthians 15:20–28, Paul tells of the relationship between the Father and Jesus. God puts all things under Jesus. This means all look to Him for leadership, solace and rule. The act is similarly described in Philippians 2.

So, God exalts Jesus to an all-powerful position leaving Himself at the top, alone, giving Jesus rule over all with reception of all homage. It is as if He has handed everything to Jesus and the whole creation looks to Him.

Why does the Father do this? Because the actions of Jesus, this emptying of Himself, this laying off His divinity, this making of Himself nothing and becoming a servant is the most complete revelation of the divine character given to the universe. It is exactly what the Father would have done if He were in Christ's place. Such an act must be recognized as the very essence of divinity. God gives Jesus the highest place and all worship so that all may know that the Father and Jesus are in complete agreement on the importance of this revelation.

Now, with the whole universe worshiping Jesus, what of the Father? There is a certain sense that He has surrendered His place to Christ that Jesus may be all in all. Yes, the Father still rules, and Jesus is subordinate, but it is clear the Father is doing just as Jesus did as recorded in Philippians 2:7, He has emptied Himself.

And we are called by His Word and example to have the same mind as He does.

THE IDEA OF INCARNATION
February 3

Hebrews 1:1–2, "In the past God spoke to our ancestors through the prophets ... but in these last days he has spoken to us by his Son."

God has spoken to us in various ways. He sent the prophets to us and angels have spoken to men as well. Besides these messengers, God speaks to our minds, bringing conviction on us through the Word of the Bible, or through visions or dreams.

But He also communicates with His creatures in a special way, called incarnation. That is God becomes a being like the ones He wishes to commune with. This was not a way unique to Jesus' visit to earth, for God had come in human form before this, several times in the Old Testament.

One example is the story of Abraham and the visitors (Gen. 18). There Jehovah comes as a man, accepting the hospitality of Abraham and giving the promise personally to him and his wife of the soon-to-be-born son of promise. In these verses, the Visitor is several times called Jehovah and Abraham calls Him the judge of the earth. The incarnation is thus confirmed before the New Testament (See John 8:58). God walked among men to give a glimpse of His will.

Michael the archangel, in some passages, seems to be Jesus seems to be Jesus embodied as an angel, so that it is not only humans that have been blessed by God incarnating among them, but the angels as well. This way of communication is the most intimate that God uses when visiting with His creatures, becoming like one of them.

So, Jesus' incarnation was not a new thing. It had been done before (Gen. 16:7–13; 18:1; Judges 13:3–21). What was different about Jesus' visit was that He went on to die while incarnated. That was a new thing, a radical departure from the usual.

WHY DID GOD BECOME MAN?
February 4

John 1:14, "The Word became flesh and made his dwelling among us. We have seen his glory, the glory of the one and only Son, who came from the Father, full of grace and truth."

Since the beginning of Christianity, there have been those who do not believe in the Trinity. They believe that Jesus was not actually God, but less than Him. There are two problems with this position and these two problems are another reason why the doctrine of the Trinity is necessary to vindicate God.

• Issue 1: If Jesus is not God, then we do not really know what God is like. The prophets and Moses were sent by God to explain His ways to us. But they were humans and could have misunderstood or made some errors in transmitting the knowledge of God to us. How would we know? They claim to have heard from God, and appear to have His endorsement, but because of the weakness and sinfulness of humanity, perhaps they cannot be completely trusted. Hebrews 1:1–2 says that we now not only have the prophets, but the words of a Son, one with the Father—One so intimate with Him, He is called God by God the Father (Heb. 1:8).

• Issue 2: God had set up the universe, and then a terrible problem arose: sin. He was in a sense responsible, for He had created it all in the first place. Who was going to take care of this seeming oversight? Would He take responsibility Himself, or delegate it to another? God does not shirk His duty when it comes to His creatures. So, He came to right the wrongs Himself.

These reasons are why He alone is worthy of worship. He has stepped into the breach when no one else could and taken the work onto Himself.

THE STERN AND UTTER REALITY OF THE INCARNATION

February 5

John 1:14, "The Word became flesh and made his dwelling among us."

When Jehovah visited Abraham, He came as an adult, a fully-grown man with all the faculties of an adult human. He was self-possessed, able to care for Himself and decided for Himself in all things. He was a man, but a man who had not become a man in the usual fashion.

When Jesus became a man, He partook of all that it meant to be human. He was born a baby, developing in the womb as all babies do. His mother went into labor and delivered Him, as all babies are that are born on this planet.

He learned to walk and to talk as we do. He babbled as all babies do and learned by experience. Hebrews 5:8 says, "Son though he was, he learned obedience from what he suffered." So, He learned as we do, through suffering and the pain that we learn from.

He experienced the trials of childhood and youth, the awkwardness of those periods of life. He became a creature in every way, as we are creatures in every way. So, God knows what the creaturely problems and difficulties are firsthand. No one can say that He has remained aloof from our experiences. He knows them intimately.

And then He died as one of us, with all that such a death entailed. He was abandoned by His friends, even the "beloved disciple" fled when the mob came to take Him away. No one stood with Him at the trial. He had no friend who understood. He trod the winepress alone in the fullest sense of the term.

Then He died, not as a righteous man, but as a sinner, abandoned even by God. Even Satan stood speechless at its reality. Yes, God knows what it means to be human. He knows like no one but us.

IT'S GOD'S FAULT
February 6

2 Samuel 6:8, "Then David was angry because the LORD's wrath had broken out."

God is blamed for everything that can go wrong. People just naturally attribute their problems to Him. He is the boss after all, and the Creator, so could He not have done a better job of it? Even our insurance policies speak of "Acts of God," meaning destructive events such as floods, tornadoes and hurricanes.

We did not ask to be born here. And now horrible things have happened to us. It certainly can't be *our* fault. If God had not set up things the way they are, none of these things would have happened.

David's anger was directed toward God who had interfered with a celebration that he had planned for Him after all. He was mad.

Isaiah 53:6 says that "the LORD has laid on him the iniquity of us all." The text is usually interpreted to mean that God graciously took our sin on Himself so that we would not have to suffer for it. He bore the sin for us.

But there is another way to look at this. God *did* create this world and is ultimately responsible for what happens here. And the situation has not turned out well. One could argue that He is therefore to blame, especially when we did not ask to be here or have the characters we have inherited.

Surprisingly, God does not argue the point, but takes responsibility. All the iniquity is laid on Him, and He suffers for all of it. There is no one that can say that God has not received punishment for the mess that has developed here on this planet. And He is willing to take that responsibility and was duly condemned and punished.

Wicked men blame God. But at the judgment they will see that He bore the punishment for any "wrongdoing" that He had done, and then graciously offered them eternal life, in spite of *their* sin. The torture and death of Christ answers every question that we can ask. Even this issue of blame.

THE POWER OF DIVINATION
February 7

Isaiah 45:21, "Who foretold this long ago, who declared it from the distant past? Was it not I, the LORD? And there is no God apart from me, a righteous God and a Savior; there is none but me."

How can anyone who is actually able to see the future be trusted?

One with such power would certainly manipulate it. And would it not be to their advantage to do so? Who or what could stop them if they so wished? With such power in their hands could anyone else be truly free? Are we all just puppets being played by the Master Puppeteer?

And how could we know that was not the case when there was excellent evidence that such a One could indeed see the future (Dan. 2, 7 and 9)?

Such questions show the dilemma God faced with Satan's rebellion. God could be accused of manipulation, and how would we, the angels or any created beings be able to know if, in fact, God could do with the future as He saw fit? Satan could say, "You are the One in charge, I am just doing what You are making me do. All this evil is Your fault!"

But God had anticipated such difficulties and had a way to show He was not the Grand Manipulator. As is the case in all God's dealings with questions of His character, the answer was Jesus and the cross.

Jesus laid aside all power, lived as a creature rather than God, and most importantly was crucified on a cross, not an experience anyone who controlled the future for his own benefit would have allowed. Then and there it was Satan who was clearly in control. God thus showed that He did not manipulate the future but lived freely in it as you and I do and could be trusted with it.

We can rest in this knowledge. The future is open and free; the One who died on the tree has it in His hands. Hallelujah!

THE WRATH OF GOD PART 1
February 8

Romans 1:18, "The wrath of God is being revealed from heaven against all the godlessness and wickedness of people, who suppress the truth by their wickedness."

There has been much controversy about the wrath of God. Why would He be angry anyway? What is He mad about? We moderns see "wrath" as a more primitive idea, and most dismiss it as a proposition rejected by those of us who are the more enlightened ones.

But Paul, surprisingly, starts his grand dissertation on righteousness by first mentioning wrath. It is the next sentence after his thesis statement in Romans 1:17.

So, what is this wrath?

In his reasoning on faith, Paul first shows what the wrath of God is. It is not what many think—some angry tantrum on God's part, but something much more profound.

God's wrath is His handing over of a creature to his own sinful desires. Paul states this clearly in verses 24, 26 and 28 of Romans 1. Verse 24 says it this way, "Therefore God gave them over in the sinful desires of their hearts to sexual impurity." In verse 26, "God gave them over to shameful lusts." And in verse 28, "God gave them over to a depraved mind."

So, it is not some capricious pique, but a sad allowing of a creature to have his own way and to follow his own sinful desire. Careful consideration reveals this a terrible fate. Our own passions will most surely destroy us if allowed free reign. God would keep us from ourselves, but if we are determined to ignore and slight His Spirit, He will allow us our own way.

That is His wrath.

THE WRATH OF GOD PART 2
February 9

Isaiah 53:10, "Yet it was the LORD's will to crush him and cause him to suffer, and though the LORD makes his life an offering for sin, he will see his offspring and prolong his days, and the will of the LORD will prosper in his hand."

There is another aspect to the idea of wrath that must be discussed.

When Jesus was dying on the cross, he cried out, "My God, my God, why have you forsaken me?" (Matt. 27:46).

This is the cry of dereliction, the cry of abandonment. At this moment, God had let Jesus go. He had withdrawn in the same way that God withdraws from a sinner that has fully decided to follow sin.

But of course, Jesus had not been sinning but was perfect in all His ways. God had even said of Him, "This is my Son, whom I love; with him I am well pleased. Listen to him!" (Matt. 17:5).

But now Jesus is abandoned to death. God hands Him over, treating Him as sin and laying on Him the iniquity of us all. Since that iniquity is there, and the sin of the whole world, God can only do one thing, turn away from Jesus and hand Him over.

Jesus thus absorbed the wrath of God for us. We need not face it or be under it ourselves.

By laying all our sins on Jesus, God could be just and justifier of those who believe on Jesus (Rom. 3:26). The sins had been taken care of so God could gather us into His arms and still be a righteous God.

So, instead of abandoning us as He must do for all who have sinned, He can justify us and still be righteous. Psalm 85:10 says, "righteousness and peace kiss each other."

HIDDEN OR REVEALED?
February 10

Hebrews 1:1–2, NKJV, "God, who at various times and in various ways spoke in time past to the fathers by the prophets, has in these last days spoken to us by His Son."

There is controversy about whether God is a God of revelation or a hidden God. In the verses above, the author of Hebrews says that God spoke to us through many voices, but finally sent His Son. In this, He states that God is ever trying to make contact with His people in various ways: by prophets, priests, kings, ceremony and ritual. Finally, the ultimate revelation has been made, God speaks through His Son. It is as if God determined to give one last try as the other methods had not given the desired response. Then God was satisfied.

However, there is another idea on God's knowability. He is the hidden God, the God who is incomprehensible and inscrutable, whose ways are past finding out (Rom. 11:33). He hides Himself in the clouds (Ps. 97:2; 18:11). His ways are so deep and dark that we cannot know them. Men seem to be searching in a fog and at the end cannot make out what God is trying to do, or what His basic characteristics are. Agnostics would argue so.

In fact, God is both a God of revelation and a hidden God. In John 7:17 Jesus said, "Anyone who chooses to do the will of God will find out whether my teaching comes from God." Surprisingly, to those who choose to follow, God comes into focus.

But to those who do not wish to obey, God and His will are shrouded in darkness. 2 Thessalonians 2:10–11, "They perish because they refused to love the truth and so be saved. For this reason God sends them a powerful delusion so that they will believe the lie."

This seems a bit unfair. Why would God send delusion to anyone?

THE HIDDEN GOD
February 11

2 Thessalonians 2:11, "For this reason God sends them a powerful delusion so that they will believe a lie."

To those who do not wish to obey, God hides Himself. The verse above says He even sends delusion to them, even strong delusion. Is that completely fair? Why would God do that?

This verse is a terrible warning to those who do not wish to follow God's will.

It is about the nature of sin and the results of believing a lie. Our minds are quite malleable. They conform to the thoughts with which we fill them. If we fill them with lies, then lies will become the basis for all action and the truth will become foggy and unclear. Our decision to follow a lie—a way more amenable to our desires—will, to us, look more and more like the truth. We will become convinced more and more, even though it is untrue.

The saying, "A man convinced against his will, is of the same opinion still,"[17] describes that process. We all know what that proverb means. People who do not want to be convinced, will not be convinced. There is often such a strong bias in us that reason will mold itself to the will of a man who will not see the truth because of his preference. It is a powerful process.

God recognizes this process and describes it in the verse above. He would have us be free from the lies that so often hinder us from a full and free life in Him. But if we will not abandon them, He allows for them, and even lets Satan send more. He cannot defend us, for we have chosen to ignore any advice He would give us.

Such is the state of the wicked. They will not be convinced, for they have embraced a lie. As God said in Hosea 4:17, "Ephraim is joined to his idols; leave him alone!"

---

[17]Dale Carnegie, *How to Win Friends and Influence People*, revised ed. (New York, NY: Simon and Schuster, 1981), p. 145.

DOES GOD PUNISH? PART 1
February 12

Exodus 32:34, "However, when the time comes for me to punish, I will punish them for their sin."

If God does not punish us, but our punishment for sin was borne by Jesus, how is it that there is so much trouble in the world? And what about the Old Testament where God specifically states that He is going to punish the Israelites or the Ammonites for their sin?

I assert that Jesus did bear the punishment for our sins. And He bore it all, for if He did not, then there remains some that I must bear. But the Bible says God "laid on him the iniquity *of us all*" (Isa. 53:6, emphasis added). There are two answers to the above objection.

1. The difficulties and problems we suffer now are consequences and not punishments. Our acts bring on us the problems that we face. Although He may use them to mold and hew our characters, they are not His will, and He would spare us these experiences. My patients often demonstrate this. They bring all manner of trouble on themselves. We have no one to blame but ourselves.
2. But what about the calamities God sent on Israel and the surrounding nations? Were they not God's punishments?

No, they were not punishments.

They were God's acts of discipline. Now is that not punishment? The motive here was not to punish, but to correct. A father may say, "I had to punish my child for his disobedience." What he really means is that he did something to prevent a recurrence of the child's act. It is not retribution, but discipline, and there is a difference. God's disciplines are always remedial.

But there are other things that seem more like punishments, such as the flood. We will discuss that tomorrow.

DOES GOD PUNISH? PART 2
February 13

Genesis 6:5–7, "The LORD saw how great the wickedness of the human race had become on the earth, and that every inclination of the thoughts of the human heart was only evil all the time. The LORD regretted that he had made human beings on the earth, and his heart was deeply troubled. So the LORD said, 'I will wipe from the face of the earth the human race I have created.'"

So, was this an act of punishment? Again, I would say it was not. This was rather an act to allow the human race to continue to survive. The antediluvians had become so wicked that they only thought evil continually. In verse 11, God notes that the earth had become full of violence. They had perfected evil to such an extent that men were unable to resist the evil that was pervasive on the earth. The culture caused men, weakened by sin, to be unable to discern the Holy Spirit's voice. It had become stilled in their souls. God had to act so as to allow for future generations to exist. He destroyed the evildoers of that day and shortened the lifespan of men, that they could not bring evil to perfection. It was an act of mercy for generations to come.

It was thus not an act of punishment, but a surgical procedure to remove a cancer that would have destroyed all future generations. The destruction of Sodom and Gomorrah was along those lines as well. Some evil has to be dealt with in such a way that it does not corrupt a larger group and make salvation impossible for others.

These acts look terrible, but they prevent wickedness from becoming a universal phenomenon and the human race irredeemable.

DOES GOD PUNISH? PART 3
February 14

Genesis 7:21, "Every living thing that moved on land perished ... all mankind."

God took a great risk in doing this.

Satan threw in His face the failure of the men He had created. Enoch had lived among them, so godly he was translated to heaven before seeing death (Gen. 5:24). Adam had given his testimony for well-nigh 1,000 years, and yet all of this was not enough to save the human race from destruction. Noah had preached for 120 years without any results whatsoever, except his own family, and even one of them was corrupt. And Noah embarrassed himself by becoming drunk and naked (Gen. 9:20–27).

Satan had triumphed. He had the whole human race on his side save the eight that entered the ark when the door closed. What a disaster!

And Satan would say, "You are destroying my people, the ones who have chosen to follow me! That is not fair."

He turns to the angels as they fly back and forth from heaven. "Look what has happened! God has failed to save men, and now He is wiping out the whole earth! What does that say about His rule? He makes a mistake, cannot remedy it, so destroys it, thinking we won't see. What a joke His rule is! If He was better at this, He would have solved it by now. Why do you continue to obey Him? Can't you think for yourself?"

How could God answer? It did appear to be a failure. God was pained that this had been the result. He does not want anyone to be lost (2 Peter 3:9). He hated to do what He did but He had no choice but to do so to save the greater number.

God is not afraid of losing a battle so as to win the war. He could take the criticism, for He had laid a plan long ago. Thank God for His sacrifice to save us!

DOES GOD PUNISH? PART 4
February 15

Luke 13:1–3, "Now there were some present at that time who told Jesus about the Galileans whose blood Pilate had mixed with their sacrifices. Jesus answered, 'Do you think that these Galilean were worse sinners than all the other Galileans because they suffered this way? I tell you, no! But unless you repent, you too will all perish.'"

There are other events, seeming capricious tragedies, that appear to have no purpose. Jesus mentioned two brought up during His stay on earth, a massacre by Pilate, and the collapse of a tower (Luke 13:4). Childhood leukemia and great natural disasters fall into this same category—terrible events that have no apparent remedial value.

What are we to make of these things?

It is noteworthy that Jesus did not try to resolve the issue but warned that failure to repent would bring the same on those who spoke to Him.

He had no obligation to explain these events, for they were not His or God's responsibility. Humankind had rebelled, accepting Satan as Lord. All humans had joined the rebellion and were under Satan's rule. There were none righteous, not even one (Rom. 3:10). And Satan is a capricious ruler, and his kingdom is based on chaos, disorder and lawlessness. We can thus expect things like a massacre or the collapse of a tower or other inexplicable events to happen rather regularly. The book of Job shows that God is constantly restraining him (Job 1:9–10). But it would be unfair for God to keep him constantly in check, as he would then be unable to demonstrate the nature of his rule or do as he has a right to do in his own kingdom.

Jesus' advice was good. An attitude of repentance is the only answer to Satan's control. It is our duty to take His words seriously.

Section 3

The Creation: Thinking About The Creation

God created the world, but what were His methods and His motives? Did He use evolution? Was He free? Why suffering and sin?

> This is my Father's world, O let me ne'er forget
> That though the wrong seems oft so strong,
> God is the Ruler yet.
> This is my Father's world; Why should my heart be sad?
> The Lord is King; let the heavens ring!
> God reigns; let the earth be glad.[18]

---

[18] Maltbie Babcock, "This Is My Father's World," *The Seventh-day Adventist Hymnal* (Hagerstown, MD: Review and Herald, 1985).

IN THE BEGINNING GOD MADE THE HEAVENS AND THE EARTH
February 16

Read all of Genesis 1.

The Creation story of Genesis 1 is the most elegant story of Creation from the ancient world. There is nothing to compare with it in power and form. Yet it is a simple account. In Genesis 1, God takes a dark chaotic world of water and molds it into a home for humankind that is full of blessings.

God hovers over the water before His creating, seeming to contemplate the acts He is about to perform to bring the world into being (Gen. 1:2).

He then takes six days (or seven if the rest day is included) to make the world and populate it with creatures. Each act takes one day and is complete at the end of that day. As God looks over the things He has made, at the end of the day, He proclaims satisfaction with His work, as a master craftsman might do after he has finished a project taking great effort and skill.

There is a progression to the Creation: three days are used to create the things over which the entities made on days four through six will rule. The sun and moon rule the day and night, the fish and birds rule the water and air, and the land creatures and man rule the land and vegetation. There is a hierarchy of sorts.

God moves in a deliberate fashion, seeming to know no haste nor delay, going about His work in a way He sees fit. There is a certain joy and pleasure in His proclamations as He marshals the elements to do His will. He seems happy to be doing what He is doing, and brings forth a Creation celebration at the end of each day, ending it with a day of rest. It is also clear that He had had a plan all along and worked His plan.

At the end, all is done, and all is very, very good.

And yet, He has created a being who will rebel, and a race that will crucify His Son! How could He?

THE FREEDOM OF GOD PART 1
February 17

Matthew 19:26, "Jesus looked at them and said, 'With man this is impossible, but with God all things are possible.'"

Is it really true that with God all things are possible? Or is it just an exaggeration? Is God free to do as He pleases, or is He constrained in some way?

The Creation of man shows just how free God is.

The problem here is that God knew that man was going to rebel but created him anyway. He made him despite any conflict in His mind about what such an act might entail. Man would rise against Him and sin, taking the forbidden fruit. There would be misery and death spread throughout the world, and millions and billions would die, often with great suffering and pain. Mental anguish would plague the race as many lived without hope or help. Men would curse the God of heaven. "Oh, my God," would become a trite and common oath rather than a statement of wonder.

And in the end, the Trinity Itself would be rent by death, the death of the most beloved Son. And yet He creates this creature anyway?

Yes, He creates him anyway, because He is free. There is nothing that constrains Him, for He is complete in Himself, but longs for the companionship of the creatures of His hand. If He did not create man, He would have been untrue to Himself. He would have made a mental reservation about what He was doing, manipulating the Creation to avoid any problems that would bring suffering to Himself. It would have been an act of selfishness not to create man, just so He could avoid some difficulties.

Instead He created, you could say, with abandon, with no consideration for Himself.

Some have said Adam's taking of the fruit so he would not be separated from Eve showed the foolishness of love. But God had already done such an act in creating Adam in the first place.

THE FREEDOM OF GOD PART 2
February 18

Genesis 2:16–17, "And the LORD God commanded the man, 'You are free to eat from any tree in the garden; but you must not eat from the tree of the knowledge of good and evil.'"

The previous essay would seem to implicate God in the origin of evil. If God's freedom to act led to all sin and suffering, cannot all of it be laid at His feet? Is not He to blame? Could He not have done it a different way?

God is not to blame in any way whatsoever. Adam and Eve brought sin into the world by their choice. They did not have to eat of the tree, and God had warned them in no uncertain terms about the consequences of eating from it. "You will certainly die" (Gen. 2:17). There was no mystery in that.

But Eve was deceived and Adam decided to join her in rebellion. If God had not stepped in, they would have died then and there. And there would have been no argument that such a death was improper. They had been warned, they had clearly taken the fruit in rebellion.

The question here is whether God was amiss in giving the creatures the freedom of choice in the first place. Could He have made creatures that made all the right choices without them being some sort of machine rather than a living, choosing human being?

And could that being have been the same as one who did have the power to choose? Just what does being able to choose add to a human that he would not have without it?

It is good to think on these things, as we are thinking God's thoughts after Him. God had a good reason for endowing us with choice.

THE PROBLEM OF SIN AND SUFFERING PART 1
February 19

Gen 2:16–17, "And the LORD God commanded the man ... 'you must not eat from the tree of the knowledge of good and evil.'"

The problem of evil has troubled men since the beginning. Why did God allow a place for Satan in the garden? And why were Adam and Eve able to perform an act that brought all sin and suffering into the world? It is one of the strongest arguments against theism. How could an all-powerful and all-good God allow for such a situation as this?

The simple answer, surprisingly, is love! Yes, love.

How can that be?

There was an older couple in the church I pastored, Gene and Eloise. They were still in love with one another even though in their eighties. One day as we were talking about life, he said to me, "She chose me!" The fact still caused wonder in his soul. He was the one, among many, upon whom she chose to bestow her affections, and to whom she gave herself fully with all the implications that entailed. He still stood in awe of her selection. "She chose me!"

Adam and Eve were given the power of choice. It was not just the power to choose, but the power to commit, to give one's whole self. And in order for that gift to have full expression, there had to be an actual choice. There had to be an alternative to God. To whom would the pair give their hearts and their very selves?

And so there was the tree. The choice was not a difficult one, in fact it was so easy it is almost laughable. That is why the fall was so serious and the consequences so horrendous. Failing this trial called into question all of Adam's virtue.

But Love found a way even then and was prepared for the crisis. Jesus stepped into the gap and gave the pair and us a second chance.

THE PROBLEM OF SIN AND SUFFERING PART 2
February 20

Deuteronomy 5:29, "Oh, that their hearts would be inclined to fear me and keep all my commands always, so that it might go well with them and their children forever!"

There is another reason why God allows evil. It was to show the utter inadequacy of creaturely independence. Creatures independent of God, in the end, wreak havoc with the universe. They cannot see the end from the beginning and make horrible judgements that result in great harm. We cannot even govern ourselves. One example is Stalin.

As a youth he was enrolled in a Christian school. He excelled but was mischievous, causing quite a bit of trouble for himself. But his grades were so good he was allowed in the seminary run by his town. He absorbed the radical thinking of the day and became an atheist. How could he know the ultimate horror of the results of those decisions? He joined the communist party and quickly rose to a leadership position. Lenin did not trust him and as his grip on power was slipping, advised those around him to keep the ambitious Stalin in check. They could not, and he became the head of the Soviet Union.[19] Ultimately, he filled some 10–12 million graves. He signed a pact with Hitler that betrayed his country and led to terrible death and suffering.[20]

None of us can see the ultimate consequences of our actions. Our "free acts" will never lead to peace, fulfillment or even good. There will always be collateral damage.

God told Adam that choosing his own way would lead to death. God's admonition was to submit to the God of love. But he would not, so brought on our world the curse of independence. As Jesus said of the Jewish leaders, "[T]hey know not what they do" (Luke 23:34, KJV).

---

[19]"Joseph Stalin," Wikipedia, https://1ref.us/1gc (accessed December 1, 2020).
[20]"German-Soviet Nonaggression Pact," HISTORY, https://1ref.us/1gd (accessed December 1, 2020).

DEATH BEFORE SIN
February 21

Genesis 1:2, "[A]nd the Spirit of God was hovering over the waters."

The Bible states that the primordial earth was covered with water. It does not tell how the water came to cover the earth, it merely makes a simple statement of the fact.

It should be noted that there was something here at that time when God began His creative work. He did not call the earth into existence from nothing but shaped a watery world present at the time (Gen. 1:2).

Therefore, if He is the Creator of all things, He must have put this orb in place at some time prior to the beginning of His seven-day work of Creation. This is also implied by the statement on the fourth day that "He also made the stars" (Gen. 1:16). He did not make them then but had made them in a previous creative act.

Does this allow for an evolutionary theory of life? Ruin-restoration theories postulate just that, as do some theistic evolution theories. They teach that the world was destroyed or moved through various periods where organisms died and were replaced by others. The final period is the one in which we now live. Evidence of these previous periods is said to be found in the fossil record.[21]

The problem with these theories is that death would then be present before sin. And the days become great eons of time, not consistent with the text. Even more importantly, death would have been God's plan for life, and He would be dependent on it to create the diversity in life we see today. It is a terribly cruel method.

Those who accept such theories need to realize the implications of these processes. Death is an enemy to be defeated, not a means of creation. God has done better than that.

---

[21]"NINE VIEWS OF CREATION," BLUE LETTER BIBLE, https://1ref.us/1ge (accessed December 1, 2020).

CREATION AND MATERIALISM (EVOLUTION) PART 1
February 22

Hebrews 11:3, "By faith we understand that the universe was formed at God's command."

It is important for us who live in this age of doubt and skepticism to understand the stark differences between the two Creation accounts most often accepted by modern men. One, the biblical account of God creating in seven literal days, is countered by the materialist/evolutionist view that the world is an accident of the universe, and that the diversity of life is a result of Darwinian processes: chance and necessity (natural selection [necessity]) working on random mutations [chance] requiring millions or billions of years to occur). Although there are other views on the "reasons" for the world, life and the universe, these two are the most widely held.

The foundations of these two views will be discussed subsequently. However, their philosophical differences are deep and profound, and must be understood prior to examining the basis for these two theories.

1. The idea of deliberate creating versus chance.
2. The waste of evolution and the frugality of the seven-day Creation.
3. The role of death.
4. The place of man.

Deliberation vs. Chance: There can be no greater difference than between these two theories. The Genesis account shows God acting intentionally, where He intimately shapes the material He uses to create. He animates the elements, creating a wonderful world of light and life. He then stoops to mold from common clay, a being of amazing power, one who can even resist His will!

In the materialistic approach, there is no deliberation whatsoever. All that we see is the result of an astounding cosmic accident. There is no purpose, no will, no intention. Where the Bible envisions active design, materialism sees only the workings of chance. This characteristic of materialism is one of its greatest weaknesses.

Waste vs. Frugality: The materialist view also postulates great waste. Since there is no purpose, there is no thought of the destruction of vast numbers of creatures or material to bring our present world into being. The waste is astonishing. Billions of creatures live, suffer and die.

A seven-day Creation, on the other hand, requires a minimum of waste. Things come into being immediately on the Creator's command. No great expenditure of time or resources is necessary.

CREATION AND MATERIALISM (EVOLUTION) PART 2
February 23

John 10:10, "I have come that they may have life, and have it to the full."

Besides the issues of chance in contrast to design, and the great waste of evolution, there are two other philosophical issues that separate the two ideas, creationism and materialism.

The role of death: Death and time are the heroes of materialistic evolution. It is Creator Death that allows for the progression of living things to more and more survivability and complexity. Without the replacement of the weak, the strong could not prosper. The fit survive. That the sparrow should fall is a positive good and a necessary part of progress.

The place of man: Man is an accident of evolution that could very well not have existed if things had gone differently. He is not the Son of the Most High made in God's image, but a glorified ape. A naked ape at that, who covers himself to hide his nakedness. Since he is an accident, he too has no purpose.

> *In the Creation story, each creature has its niche, its proper place of existence, a place made for it to live and prosper. God has planned for each one and has His eye on that sparrow (Luke 12:6). His intention is a characteristic of His love for the creation.*

In the Creation story, each creature has its niche, its proper place of existence, a place made for it to live and prosper. God has planned for each one and has His eye on that sparrow (Luke 12:6). His intention is a characteristic of His love for the creation.

The place of man in the Creation story could not be more different. To be made in God's image is the complete opposite of being an accident.

Many argue that it is not the philosophy of each idea that makes the difference, but whether one or the other is true. What is the foundation of each idea? How does each support itself as credible?

Is unsupported faith the basis of one, and reason and science the basis of the other? Hardly ….

CREATION AND MATERIALISM (EVOLUTION) PART 3
February 24

2 Corinthians 6:14, "[W]hat fellowship can light have with darkness?"

Before discussing the foundations of each of the main theories of the origin of the universe, mention should be made of the attempts to meld the two into one unified whole.

The motivation for such efforts is to reconcile modern scientific discoveries with the assertions of Scripture. The Bible is not a scientific text, but a book of encounters between God and men. It thus does not attempt to answer questions of a scientific nature, especially those posed by modern scientific methods. It just records the acts of God without explanation, taking certain underlying assumptions for granted.

Attempts to combine science and Scripture most often overlook the violence done to basic biblical teachings. The theory of evolution is an example.

If God has created the diversity of biological life through evolution's processes, He is a wasteful and evil Creator. In fact, an ogre. How could He possibly state that He values sparrows when His process of creating means the death of billions of them, often by cruel means? And since death lies at the very heart of evolution's creative power how does it make any sense for Him to be working to defeat it, as if it were an enemy (1 Cor. 15:26)?

If evolutionary doctrine is true, the story of the fall is nonsense, and any theory of sin and death as an intruder is nonsense as well.

These are basic Bible doctrines, not just vague theories of Creation. The idea of salvation is intimately intertwined with the first chapters of Genesis and the whole of Scripture is based on their veracity. To destroy them or explain them away is to destroy the foundations of faith.

This is not to say that men cannot hold to two contradictory ideas and live with them. It happens all the time. But if one takes Scripture seriously, one must realize that marrying materialist and creationist theories leads to internal contradictions.

MATERIALIST FAITH
February 25

Psalm 19:1, "The heavens declare the glory of God."

Many materialists feel that their system of belief is based solely on scientific evidence and that their thinking does not require faith, but only reason. However, there are several areas where faith is required even of them.

The origin of the universe is one such area. How is it that there is a universe rather than nothing at all? Our experience is that all things have ultimate causes of some type. It is a real act of faith to believe that something like the universe came from nothing.

The universe seems to be exquisitely designed for life to exist—a trait called the anthropic principle (the observation that the universe has stringent characteristics that allow for life).[22] Certain physical constants require careful fine tuning for life to exist.[23] It is a great act of faith to believe that this could have happened by mere chance.

Abiogenesis is the idea that life can come from inanimate things. Materialists postulate that in a warm pond filled with the right chemicals, it arose spontaneously. After life occurred, the process of evolution could bring forth the myriad of creatures we see today. But there is no evidence that life arose this way, and all attempts to create life from non-life have utterly failed. Such thinking that a process will be discovered in the future is an act of faith.[24]

And life is so amazingly complex! Belief that it could have emerged by chance alone is a very long stretch. If one came upon a table of pennies all heads, one would not think there had been a random toss, but that someone had arranged them.

God has given much evidence for design in the universe. We do not have to exercise any more faith than materialists do when we believe in God.

---

[22]"Anthropic principle," Wikipedia, https://1ref.us/1gg (accessed December 1, 2020).
[23]"ID's Top Six—The Fine-Tuning of the Universe," Evolution News, https://1ref.us/1gf (accessed December 1, 2020).
[24]Jerry Bergman, "Why Abiogenesis Is Impossible," *Creation Research Society Quarterly* 36 (2000).

THE FOUNDATIONS OF MATERIALISM
February 26

Proverbs 14:12, "There is a way that appears to be right, but in the end it leads to death."

Materialists' faith is not without basis. They have evidence that supports their view of things. To believe they are unthinking and foolish doubters is going a step too far.

Their main supporting evidence is as follows:

1. The geologic column. This is a table of the layers of the sediments found in various places around the earth. It is never complete at any one area. It is actually a construct. The column always seems to have the more primitive organisms at its base, and the more complex at the top. This implies that there was progressive development over time from less complex to more complex. There are some difficulties with this interpretation, but it is one of the main supports for their theories. If the bone of a modern animal turned up at the bottom, it would disprove this evidence. So far, no such bone has materialized.[25]

2. Radiometric dating. Although the fossils themselves cannot usually be dated, intrusions into the column have contained material that can be dated using radioactive means. These dates seem to indicate increasing age as one descends the column. Again, there are some issues with this, but this is probably the strongest evidence for the materialist position.[26]

3. Evidence for evolution. Vestigial organs, various relationships of animals and other findings in the biological sphere seem to indicate that evolution did take place. This evidence is much less compelling then the two cited above and can often be explained. But issues here do remain.[27]

4. The problem of suffering and sin. These philosophical problems counter the belief in a beneficent Creator and are used to discredit the Creation theory. They are probably the easiest to meet.[28]

This and some others are the main support for the materialists' view. Do theists have any support for their views?

Yes.

---

[25]Paul M. Karabinos and Thomas E. Krogh, "Dating," Encyclopædia Britannica, https://1ref.us/1gh (accessed December 1, 2020).
[26]"Radiometric dating," Wikipedia, https://1ref.us/1gi (accessed December 1, 2020).
[27]"Evidence Supporting Biological Evolution," *Science and Creationism*, https://1ref.us/1gj (accessed December 1, 2020).
[28]"Problem of evil," Wikipedia, https://1ref.us/1gk (accessed December 1, 2020).

THE FOUNDATIONS OF FAITH
February 27

Hebrews 11:3, "By faith we understand that the universe was formed at God's command, so that what is seen was not made out of what was visible."

Do those who believe in the Bible have any support for their thinking like the materialists have?

Yes, but it is of a different nature. Theists first point to their relationship with the Creator. This is subjective evidence, but is very powerful when combined with a life changed by that relationship. There is nothing more persuasive than a loving and lovable Christian. Against such a life, scientific arguments have little power.

But there is more than just subjective evidence. It can be divided into two broad categories: scientific and biblical.

Scientific evidence:

1. The argument from design. The universe and life itself have the look of design. Even evolutionists admit this but say it is only an appearance. However, the design is so exquisite that chance seems an inadequate explanation.
2. The beauty of the Creation attests to a wonderful Creator. When one is confronted with the utter beauty seen in all creation, from simple organisms to the vastness and beauty of the universe, a benevolent Creator comes naturally to mind.

Biblical evidence:

1. The Bible meets the needs of the human soul and speaks to us in ways no other book does. It reveals a Savior of amazing compassion and care who meets the needs of our innermost being.
2. The fulfilled prophecies tell of One who can see the end from the beginning. They are powerful evidence for God.

Two of these prophecies are examined in tomorrow's entry.

ABRAHAM AND MARY—TWO PROPHECIES
February 28

Genesis 12:2, "I will make your name great, and you will be a blessing."

Luke 1:48, "From now on all generations will call me blessed."

These two predictions show how God's knowledge of the future has anchored our faith in the present.

Abraham, a rich herder from the twentieth century BC, has become the most revered man of ancient history.

In fact, Abraham is the most respected man from any historical era, even surpassing Jesus. He is considered father of the faithful by half the world's population (Jews, Christians, and Muslims). That is more than 4.3 billion people![29] No one even comes close to Abraham.

If any verse in Scripture has been fulfilled, this one has! Abraham, a man living 4,000 years ago, has outshone all the great kings and men of ancient history, and his name is indeed great. No conqueror from Greece, Rome, or Babylon, or any other kingdom can compare with him.

Mary is the world's most respected woman. She is revered among Christians and Muslims, who refer to her as the greatest woman who has lived.[30] Some Catholics have even considered giving her a place next to Jesus as a Co-Redemptrix, though this has been rejected by the Vatican.[31] She is universally held up as a pure woman given the utmost of respect.

She has eclipsed all others.

God has given us this prophetic evidence on which to found our faith. It is not vague or unsure, but real. It is not science, but is even more compelling than that category of evidence.

There is one more piece that shows the veracity of faith. It is a most unusual evidence that materialists are mistaken in their assertions. I will discuss this in the next two entries.

---

[29] "List of religious populations," Wikipedia, https://1ref.us/1gl (accessed December 1, 2020).
[30] "Mary in Islam," Wikipedia, https://1ref.us/1gm (accessed December 1, 2020).
[31] "Co-Redemptrix," Wikipedia, https://1ref.us/1gn (accessed December 1, 2020).

THE PROBLEM OF THE SELF PART 1
February 29

Jeremiah 31:3, *"I have loved you with an everlasting love; I have drawn you with loving-kindness."*

There is another argument in favor of faith that is surprising on its face. It is the materialists' view of the self.

Materialists believe that all we see and experience arises from matter, energy or some combination of these two. There is no supernatural aspect to nature or any part of the universe or ourselves. It is only atoms and energy that are real. Humans are then just a very complex bag of chemicals that react in various ways.

Our minds are a consequence of the actions of these elements and have no basis in actual reality. Our sense of self, our feeling that we are conscious beings who can will this or that is a mere illusion. Although we may feel that we are real persons, this sense is a byproduct of chemistry and not reality itself.[32]

Here are quotes from two materialists:

"You can let go and just accept that it's just the universe doing its stuff. It's not me against the world because there really isn't any me at all. Death has no sting, because there never was a 'you' to die."[33]

Daniel Bennett, philosopher at Tufts University:

"[O]ur conception of a self is an illusion created by our experience of the world."[34]

Materialism robs us of our very personhood! Instead of sons and daughters of God, we are nothing but illusions.

But to live as if your beloved daughter, that little creature who runs to greet you with hugs and kisses, is a mere bag of chemicals is impossible, even for them. They assert that self is an illusion, but they cannot live as if it were so.

And if a confirmed materialist cannot live his own system of belief, how can it possibly be taken seriously?

---

[32] See also: Ross Douthat, "Opinion," *New York Times*, January 6, 2014.
[33] Robert L. Kuhn, "Is Your 'Self' Just an Illusion?" Live Science, https://1ref.us/1hk (accessed January 18, 2021).
[34] Ibid.

THE PROBLEM OF THE SELF PART 2
March 1

John 8:32, KJV, *"And ye shall know the truth, and the truth shall make you free."*

Further mention must be made of this weakness in the materialistic worldview.

Materialists often accuse creationists of refusing to face scientific reality, but they ignore the difficulties of their own worldview.

Richard Dawkins noted when asked about his materialistic worldview and determinism (the idea that we have no free will and are merely a package of molecules following the laws of physics): "[W]e don't feel determined. We feel like blaming … or giving people the credit for what they do. We feel like admiring people for what they do …. it is an inconsistency [that we are determined, but feel free] that we sort of have to live with otherwise life would be intolerable."[35]

From: "The Heretic" on March 25, 2013:

> Fortunately, materialism is never translated into life as it's lived …. [M]aterialists never put their money where their mouth is. Nobody thinks his daughter is just molecules in motion and nothing but …. A materialist who lived his life according to his professed convictions—understanding himself to have no moral agency at all, seeing his friends and enemies and family as genetically determined robots—wouldn't be just a materialist: He'd be a psychopath.[36]

A strictly materialistic viewpoint is impossible to square with the lives we live and the value we place on our fellow humans. To postulate that we are illusions, a trick of some deeper reality cannot be lived as a reality.

This shows the bankruptcy of materialist thinking and axioms. One can live as a Christian. One cannot live as a materialist. In a sense, it is as simple as that.

---

[35] William Dembski, "Repeat After Me: "This Has Nothing To Do With My Views On Religion," UNCOMMON DESCENT, https://1ref.us/1hl (accessed January 18, 2021).
[36] Andrew Ferguson, "The Heretic," *Washington Examiner*, https://1ref.us/1hm (accessed January 18, 2021).

AND MAN BECAME A LIVING SOUL
March 2

Genesis 2:7, "God formed a man from the dust of the ground and breathed into his nostrils the breath of life, and the man became a living being."

It may be useful at this point to discuss the two main theories of self that the present world believes, and suggest a third more logical view.

The first, as noted yesterday, is the materialist view that self is an illusion. We are real in the sense that a table is real. We are a complex set of chemical reactions that produce an illusion of an actual self. Man then is actually nothing. The illusion of reality ceases at death but was never actually in existence even when alive.

The second is called dualism. This belief, developed by Greek thinkers several centuries before Christ, is held by most Christians.

This view asserts that man is a combination of two things, a body and a spirit, or soul. The soul is immortal, living only temporarily in the body from which it is freed at death to live in a different sphere forever. Souls are immortal, and cannot be destroyed, even by God.[37]

There is an intermediate view. In this view, man is a combination of the breath of life and the body. They are an indivisible entity that only exists when the two are together. There is no living thing that exists outside the body, but both are required for there to be an actual man.[38]

When death comes, the breath returns to God. It is not a conscious thing, but a life principle. The body disappears in decay.

At the resurrection, bodies are remade and the breath is returned to them by God. We are thus made anew to live forever with Christ. And Jesus said we would be like Him when we arose (1 John 3:2). Then we are real people as He was a real person at His resurrection, eating and doing other bodily things.

---

[37] "Mind-body dualism," Wikipedia, https://1ref.us/1hn (accessed January 18, 2021).
[38] *Seventh-day Adventists Believe* (Hagerstown, MD: Review and Herald, 1988), pp. 79–96.

REAL AT THE RESURRECTION
March 3

1 John 3:2, "Dear friends, now we are children of God, and what we will be has not yet been made known. But we know that when Christ appears, we shall be like him, for we shall see him as he is."

An objection has arisen concerning the resurrection.

If we are made new, are we really ourselves or are we a mere copy of the person we were? Those that bring this up are skeptical that we can be resurrected because when we die, we disappear. A human is just too complex, and even if God could make us over in exactly the same way, it would actually be a copy of us, but not really us.

This idea destroys hope. If it is so, once I am gone, I will never reappear. John's friends were concerned about this as they mourned for those that died among them. They saw it as an eternal loss.

But God had an answer for them. It is found in our verse for today: We shall be like Jesus when we arise.

When Jesus arose, the disciples did not believe it was Him.

Luke tells us in Luke 24:38–39: "He said to them, 'Why are you troubled …? Look at my hands and my feet. It is I myself! Touch me and see; a ghost does not have flesh and bones, as you see I have.' Then He asked for something to eat" (Luke 24:41).

Jesus appeared as Himself and claimed to be the very same Jesus that had died on the cross. He even showed the wounds that He had received at the time. Those were wonderful evidence that it was the same One they had seen on the cross.

We need not trouble ourselves with doubts as to the nature of our resurrection. We will be ourselves, just as Jesus was His very Self.

SOMETHING FROM NOTHING
March 4

Psalm 33:9, "For he spoke, and it came to be; he commanded, and it stood firm."

Why is there something instead of nothing? That is, why is there a universe—a cosmos—instead of nothing?

Our experience tells us that things do not come to be without something causing them to come to be. It is called the law of cause and effect. How then is there a universe? What was its cause?

In the mid-twentieth century, there were two ideas about the origin of the universe: the steady-state theory and the Big Bang theory. With the discovery of background radiation and other observations, the steady-state theory fell out of favor. The Big Bang theory points to a beginning for the universe. The earth was not eternal but came to being at some point in the past. So, what caused it?

To avoid the obvious, materialists have cast about for a means other than God.

Among the most commonly accepted is Stephen Hawkins' no boundary theory that postulates a smooth exponential inflation of a small quantum disturbance right at the Big Bang. There is no evidence for such nor source for such a powerful field that could do such a thing. In other words, an outside force, with no known source, appeared and caused the expansion. It just happened.[39]

Something from nothing. Theists should not be anxious over the criticisms of materialists. Their imaginary forces explain nothing. Anyone can make up something but the order of the cosmos and life itself point to a Designer. Believers in God need not be ashamed of their faith.

---

[39] Natalie Wolchover, "Physicists Debate Hawking's Idea That the Universe Had No Beginning," *Quantamagazine*, https://1ref.us/1ho (accessed January 18, 2021).

THE BIG BANG PART 1
March 5

Hebrews 11:3, "By faith we understand that the universe was formed at God's command, so that what is seen was not made out of what was visible."

There is controversy among creationists about the Big Bang theory. How could the universe be 13.5 billion years old if the Genesis account is true? The genealogies of Genesis 5 can account for a couple thousand years at most, but 13.5 billion? Hardly.

However, some argue that there was material here before Creation week: "the Spirit of God was hovering over the waters" (Gen. 1:2). The formless void was something, not nothing. So, there was something here before the account of God shaping the world into a home for man.

But the Big Bang theory shows two amazing things that agree with Scripture which is grudgingly accepted by scientists.

First, the universe was made from nothing. Hebrews 11:3 tells us that by faith we understand that what is seen was not made by what is visible. The Big Bang theorizes the same, that the universe originated from a singularity, and before that, nothing, just as Hebrews says.

Second, the theory teaches that the universe had a beginning. It came into being at a point in time and was nonexistent before that time.

Both of these ideas are compatible and in fact support the Bible's assertions about the Creation of the universe: that it came from nothing and that it had a beginning.

Many scientists realize the implications of this theory and have made efforts to come up with another explanation for the universe such as the multiverse theory, or some sort of ever vibrating universe.

These, however, have no evidence to support them, and actually have grave weaknesses.

But the Big Bang? There must be something behind the Bang—the everlasting God.

THE BIG BANG PART 2
March 6

Jeremiah 10:12, "But God made the earth by his power; he founded the world by his wisdom and stretched out the heavens by his understanding."

The Big Bang theory gives evidence for God in its order and action.

Although it was the most powerful explosion ever, it contained a subtle order that was present from the very beginning.

Big Bang theorists believe that three or four minutes after the initial event, some hydrogen atoms combined to form helium and a little lithium as well. These three are the lightest elements on the periodic table. But their very existence shows something amazing about this "Big Bang."[40]

The laws governing the elements, the laws that make the periodic table periodic and describe the various characteristics and intersections of atomic nuclei were present at the very beginning of the universe.

The formation of these three elements implies the whole of the table and the complex laws governing matter that make possible the elements in all their array.

If these laws had not been in place at the very beginning, at the moment of the expulsion, the three could not have formed so early, nor could they be like they are today.

God in His wisdom brought the universe into being that His creatures might have a place to enjoy and study—a place of delight and wonder.

The Big Bang was not a chaotic explosion, but just the opposite; a quite carefully planned event, with all the laws of the universe in place even before it occurred.

It gives evidence of His great power and love for order as well. It is a monument to His wisdom and might.

---

[40]"Chronology of the universe," Wikipedia, https://1ref.us/1hp (accessed January 18, 2021).

THE ANTHROPIC PRINCIPLE
March 7

Isaiah 45:18, "[H]e is God; he who fashioned and made the earth, he founded it ... to be inhabited."

Over the last several decades, scientists have become aware of an unusual characteristic of the universe. In order for life to exist, certain fundamental characteristics called constants must be within very precise parameters. That is, the universe has been very—and that is very, very—carefully crafted so that life may exist.[41] As astrophysicist Fred Hoyle noted, "A common sense interpretation of the facts suggests that a super intellect has monkeyed with physics, as well as with chemistry and biology, and that there are no blind forces worth speaking about in nature."[42] Hoyle's work on stellar fusion led to the discovery that the element carbon's structure was very finely tuned as well.[43] A discussion of this involves fairly complex physics. I will give a few examples of the fine tuning of the universe.

1. The proton/neutron mass ratio. The proton must be nearly equal in mass to the neutron or the nuclear reactors in the cores of stars could not operate. At its core, a star slams protons together and one becomes a neutron and they adhere together, making deuterium, an isotope of hydrogen. Two deuterium atoms combine to make helium, which releases a large amount of energy. If the two were not so equal in mass, this reaction could not occur and there would be no stars.[44]
2. The proton/electron charge ratio. If there was a difference of one in a billion between the charge on these two particles, atoms would have a net charge and not be neutral and would not be able to combine as they do.[45]
3. The strong nuclear force. If this force were not in a narrow range, protons would either stick together well, reducing their ability to form larger atoms, or atoms would not form at all.[46]

---

[41]"What is the best evidence or argument for intelligent design?" compelling truth, https://1ref.us/1hr (accessed January 18, 2021).
[42]"Fred Hoyle," Wikipedia, https://1ref.us/1hq (accessed January 18, 2021).
[43]"Triple-alpha process," Wikipedia, https://1ref.us/1hs (accessed January 18, 2021).
[44]Jay Richards, "LIST OF FINE-TUNING PARAMETERS," Discovery, https://1ref.us/1ht (accessed January 18, 2021).
[45]Ibid.
[46]Ibid.

These are just a few of the characteristics necessary for life. To believe that the universe is the creation of a skillful Designer is not a baseless act of faith, but the commitment of one accepting the evidence.

ICONS OF EVOLUTION PART 1: DARWIN'S FINCHES
March 8

Genesis 1:20–21, "And God said, 'Let the waters teem with living creatures, and let birds fly above the earth across the vault of the sky.' So God created the great creatures of the sea and every living thing with which the water teems according to their kinds, and every winged bird according to its kind. And God saw that it was good."

In 1831, Charles Darwin set sail on the *HMS Beagle,* a ship sent to survey and map the coast of South America for the British admiralty. It spent several years at the task, arriving in the Galápagos Islands off the coast of Ecuador in September 1835.[47] There Darwin collected specimens of the famous finches that bear his name, which his followers claim show evolution in progress.[48]

However, further study has cast doubt on that proposition.

The finches can mate among themselves, indicating that this group of birds, thought to be some sixteen different distinct types, are really just one species with great ability to adapt to different environments. In other words, instead of evolution, there is merely adaptation.[49]

This bird has been cited extensively as a prime example of what Darwinian evolution can do, but the genetics, studied extensively, show the interrelatedness of the birds rather than their differences.

Ornithologist, Robert Zink, from the University of Minnesota noted that "Sequences of their nuclear and mitochondrial DNA show little variation and none of the telltale signs that suggest distinct species."[50]

God has not left us to struggle with doubt about His Word but has allowed the purported evidence against it to fail. There will always be cause for doubt, but there is much to suggest faith. We can hold to these if we will.

---

[47]"Second voyage of HMS *Beagle*," Wikipedia, https://1ref.us/1hu (accessed January 18, 2021).
[48]"Darwin's finches," Wikipedia, https://1ref.us/1hv (accessed January 18, 2021).
[49]Greg Breining, "Are Darwin's Finches One Species or Many?" Discover, https://1ref.us/1hw (accessed January 18, 2021).
[50]Ibid.

ICONS OF EVOLUTION PART 2: THE PEPPERED MOTH
March 9

John 20:27, "Then he said to Thomas, 'Put your finger here; see my hands. Reach out your hand and put it into my side. Stop doubting and believe.'"

Every student of biological evolution learns about peppered moths. During the Industrial Revolution, the dark ("melanic") forms of this moth, *Biston betularia*, became much more common than light ("typical") forms, though the proportion of melanics declined after the passage of pollution-control legislation. When experiments in the 1950s pointed to cryptic coloration and differential bird predation as its cause, "industrial melanism" became the classical story of evolution by natural selection. Subsequent research, however, has revealed major flaws in the classical story.[51]

It turned out that the moths did not normally land on lichen-covered tree trunks as the original scientist, Kettlewell, thought. Not only that, in other places in England and in the United States, where the moth lived, the differences in coloration did not have a significant relationship to the decline or increase in the numbers or colors of moths in the wild.[52]

Although cryptic coloration and selective predation have not been ruled out, one recent review concludes that "there is little persuasive evidence, in the form of rigorous and replicated observations and experiments, to support this explanation at the present time."[53]

Yet, as Jonathan Wells has noted, textbooks continue to present the classical story of industrial melanism in peppered moths as an example of evolution in action. Clearly, this is misleading.[54] But why would those who write science texts attempt to mislead us?

Even the best of us have weaknesses and difficulty abandoning a good story. But we must not be misled. Jesus has an answer to our doubts. It is He Himself.

---

[51] Jonathan Wells, "Second Thoughts about Peppered Moths," Discovery Institute, https://1ref.us/1hx (accessed January 18, 2021).
[52] Ibid.
[53] Ibid.
[54] Ibid.

ICONS OF EVOLUTION PART 3: ANTIBIOTIC RESISTANCE
March 10

Hebrews 12:1, "Therefore, since we are surrounded by such a great cloud of witnesses, let us throw off everything that hinders and the sin that so easily entangles. And let us run with perseverance the race marked out for us."

Evolutionists have presented bacterial resistance to antibiotics as evidence of modern evolution, especially to those synthetic antibiotics developed by humans rather than nature.

This, however, is not the case:

> The first clinically useful antibacterial agent that was safe and effective was prontosil rubrum, a sulfa drug synthesized in 1931. However, prontosil was not the first antibacterial agent to be invented, and humans were not the initial inventors …. Bacteria have been killing each other with these weapons, and using resistance mechanisms to protect themselves against these weapons, for 20 million times longer than we have even known that antibiotics exist. To underscore the point, in 2011, a study was published in which investigators explored a deep cave in the Carlsbad Caverns system in New Mexico …. The section of the cave that they explored had never before been accessed by humans. The investigators cultured many different types of bacteria from the walls of the caves. Every strain of bacteria was resistant to at least one modern antibiotic; most were multidrug-resistant. Not only was resistance found to naturally occurring antibiotics, it was also found to synthetic drugs that were not created until the 1960s–980s (including fluoroquinolones, daptomycin, and linezolid).[55]

Again, resistance was not something modern bacteria developed, but something they have possessed all along. It had not developed via evolutionary mechanisms.

---

[55] "Myths about antibiotics, resistance," Awesome Investors, https://1ref.us/1hy (accessed January 18, 2021).

ICONS OF EVOLUTION PART 4: SUMMARY
March 11

Hebrews 10:35, "So do not throw away your confidence; it will be richly rewarded."

When I first became aware of the claims of evolutionists, I was troubled by the implication they had for the Bible and belief in God. I had to come to terms with Darwinism, for his theory has been accepted by most scientists and they believe it correctly describes the facts of biology. They believe that God is not really involved in its workings to any meaningful extent. That He would care if sparrows fell was explained as mere sentimentalism and wishful thinking.

As I hope to have shown, many of the reasons that they have used to persuade students of science have fallen short. They really cannot be presented as evidence to support their theory.

Those that believe the Bible, however, cannot answer all the objections to their thinking either. Radiometric dating and the details of the geologic column remain problems. They are things that creationists cannot adequately explain.

An act of faith, without complete knowledge, is still part of Christianity. But the followers of Darwin and materialism must also make leaps of faith because their theories are not supported by incontrovertible evidence. Life could not have arisen by chemical evolution. Evolution itself has not been proved.

They cannot claim that their thinking only involves the realm of reason while believers are credulous accepters of fairytales.

God has not left us orphans to struggle with doubt. Even in our day there is evidence for His Word and reason to trust it. Yes, faith is required. But it is not an unreasonable faith. Thank God for His mercy in these last times.

ABIOGENESIS: LIFE FROM NON-LIFE
March 12

Genesis 1:24, "And God said, 'Let the land produce living creatures according to their kinds ....' And it was so."

I must speak of one more thing before leaving this topic. That is the idea of abiogenesis, the thought that at some point, in a little warm pond or some other special place, life came into being spontaneously. Such thinking is pure speculation without any basis in chemistry, biology or science at all. It is wishful thinking in its purest form.

How can I say such a thing? Because life has never been observed arising from non-life in any situation. Not one. It cannot even be imagined without wishful thinking. The problem is the utterly astounding complexity of life.

Let me give a simple example. One of the three hypotheses for abiogenesis is the "RNA First" model. In this scenario, RNA (as a ribozyme) forms in the "primordial soup" and begins to catalyze the chemical actions of the cell. Here are four (of the several) objections to this model:

1. The co-formation of two components of RNA, (the bases, adenine, cytosine etc., and the sugar, ribose), are not possible. They interfere with one another.
2. The ribonucleic bases tend to join in the wrong conformation, altering the geometry of the molecule.
3. "The Molecular Biologists Dream:" The RNA only duplicates itself, no other nearby molecule. This is not how chemistry works.
4. The RNA would have to have multiple catalytic abilities. This is just too unlikely.

If there were not a commitment to materialism, the idea would be rejected out of hand as impossible.[56]

This is just one example of the complexity required. The other hypotheses have similar fatal flaws. Nothing works. Only an intelligent Agent could make the cell.

It is only God, the Author of life who can bring life from non-life.

---

[56] Dean Kenyon and Gordon Mills, "The RNA World: A Critique," Access Research Network, https://1ref.us/1hz (accessed January 18, 2021).

PANPSYCHISM
March 13

Psalm 102:25–26, "In the beginning you laid the foundations of the earth, and the heavens are the work of your hands. They will perish, but you remain; they will all wear out like a garment. Like clothing you will change them and they will be discarded."

From Wikipedia:

> In philosophy of mind, **panpsychism** is the view that mind or a mind-like aspect is a fundamental and ubiquitous feature of reality .... Contemporary academic proponents hold that sentience or subjective experience is ubiquitous ... they ascribe a primitive form of mentality to entities at the fundamental level of physics but do not ascribe it to most aggregates, such as rocks or buildings .... Panpsychism is one of the oldest philosophical theories, and has been ascribed to philosophers including Thales, Plato, Spinoza, Leibniz, William James, Alfred North Whitehead, and Galen Strawson.[57]

Some, seeing the order revealed in life, ascribe it to a natural quality of the matter itself. They assert that matter can organize itself. It has a "mind" of its own, and thus can arrange itself to form the complex functions needed so that life may exist. And the adherents are notable, Plato, etc.[58]

Objections to the theory include that it cannot be tested, it is just plain bizarre and that there is no good explanation for how an aggregate of atoms or molecules could combine to form a conscience entity.

The psalmist separates God from His creation. He wears it as a garment, but it is not part of Him, nor does He address it as a conscious thing. He manipulates it in a way that suits Him (Ps. 102:5–27).

This theory is an attempt to sidestep evidence of a Creator in the creation, taking glory from Him. At base, it is a form of idolatry.

---

[57]"Panpsychism," Wikipedia, https://1ref.us/1i0 (accessed January 18, 2021).
[58]Ibid.

GOD AND LAW

March 14

Psalm 119:89–90, "Your word, LORD, is eternal; it stands firm in the heavens. Your faithfulness continues through all generations."

God is a God of law. He governs by the rule of law and to break or ignore those laws is to put oneself in jeopardy. Our sinful natures hate to be under law; we would prefer to be a law unto ourselves. But this rebellion ignores the stability that God's insights regarding law have given us.

The laws of nature allow us to work and play. Gravity keeps us on the planet—a wonderful thing. The astronauts have to deal with a gravity-free environment and must take special measures just to perform simple tasks. Not only that, they gradually lose muscle mass, even if they exercise. The law of gravity even allows us to enjoy the thrill of the rollercoaster.

The sun comes up each day; we can depend upon it. The atmosphere is governed by the laws of gaseous movement and pressure, and God uses these to give us the wonderful variety of weather and climate. We can enjoy the pleasure of four seasons, the constant sunshine of the desert or the stormy power of the mountain fastness.

Light and sound obey strict laws that we can depend on. The atoms of our being are governed by the laws of quantum mechanics, a mysterious almost miraculous set of principles that seem, while keeping the atoms stable, to allow for free will. The laws of electricity that hold the electrons in orbit around the nucleus are cleverly employed by inventors to give us the labor-saving devices that make our lives free of much drudgery. These laws are unvarying, the same, day after day.

But the most important thing we can learn from God's use of law is the insight it gives into His character. The laws show how faithful He is. He has built it into the creation. What He says, He will do. It is as sure as the sunrise. We can trust Him, He has written it on our very being.

THE ABOLITION OF THE LAW
March 15

Ephesians 2:14–15, "For he himself is our peace, who has made the two ... one ... by setting aside in his flesh the law with its commands and regulations."

Ephesians 6:1–3, "Children, obey your parents in the Lord, for this is right. Honor your father and mother—which is the first commandment with a promise—so that it may go well with you and that you may enjoy long life on the earth."

Some Christians feel that the law has been abolished, that it was nailed to the cross. They cite various verses including the verses above in Ephesians. And a simple reading would seem to indicate that they are correct. Ephesians 2:15 even uses the term "commands."

But there has to be a more nuanced way to interpret this.

Chapter four and five in the book are recommendations for Christian living, and Paul includes there a "Household Code," a set of rules for home life, common in that culture.

Paul admonishes children to obey their parents. And to bolster his point, he quotes from the fifth commandment, where children are to honor their parents, noting that it is the *first* commandment with a promise (with the implication that there are others that should be observed).

Now it is the fifth among ten, and indeed *does* contain a promise.

But how silly would it be for Paul to refer to this commandment if he had just argued a few paragraphs prior that the commandments had been abolished?

"Children obey your parents because, well, the commandment says so, but, yes, you're right, it has been abolished ...."

His simple comment confirms the endurance of the Ten Commandments. If they were gone, it would be foolish to refer to them for the support of his argument.

Section 4

The Creation: The Wonders of the Creation

God has revealed Himself in the amazing things He has made. His handiwork speaks to us of His majesty and power.

> "All things bright and beautiful,
> All creatures great and small.
> All things wise and wonderful.
> The Lord God made them all."[59]

---

[59]Cecil Alexander, "All Things Bright and Beautiful," *The Seventh-day Adventist Hymnal* (Hagerstown, MD: Review and Herald, 1985).

THE CREATION OF MAN
March 16

Genesis 1:26, 28, "Then God said, 'Let us make mankind in our image, in our likeness, so that they may rule over the fish in the sea and the birds in the sky ... and over all the creatures that move along the ground ....' God blessed them and said to them, 'Be fruitful and increase in number.'"

Artificial intelligence enthusiasts speculate about the ability of their creations to govern themselves and to become autonomous. Hollywood has created movies about robots taking over the world to rule the humans.

What about God? He appears to have had no compunction about creating man. He does not have the slightest fear that He would be threatened by this creature that came from His hand. The creature is much more than a robot. This man is able to rule the world and be master of his domain.

But God, instead of worrying about usurpation, rejoices at His creatures' abilities.

What motivated Him to create this amazing creature, who is indeed autonomous, made after His own image, and is able to make new creatures at will?

He was certainly not afraid. He gives the humans a place to rule, encouraging them to produce more like themselves. There is not a whiff of insecurity.

God desires someone like Himself to share the universe with Him. His creatures have His own image. He even calls them sons as a proud father might call his offspring, and He honors them with His own abilities, the power to think and to do.

What a gift is ours! Both like God and desired by Him, so that He would sacrifice Himself for us. It is a profound compliment.

THE FORCE OF THE WILL
March 17

Revelation 22:17, "Let the one who is thirsty come; and let the one who wishes take the free gift of the water of life."

John 7:17, "Anyone who chooses to do the will of God will find out whether my teaching comes from God or whether I speak on my own."

God has made us in His image and so we have godlike characteristics. Particularly we have a will. We can analyze, think and plan, and then carry out those plans. These attributes are of the very nature of divinity and He has graciously made us like Him in this respect.

Our wills determine what we will be and do. We have amazing power to act and to resist any influence on us. Even God can be resisted.

God has not just given us this wonderful gift, self-determination, He respects our wills so that He will not violate them, but only woos and draws us. We have free use of our wills

Thus, it is important to understand its power. As Ellen White says, "We need to understand the value of willpower …. Everything depends on the right use of this power. God has given the power of choice to each person, and it is theirs to use."[60]

It is this power given to God, by the surrender of self to Him, that can overcome the world. God will not allow even the weakest saint to be overcome if they will choose to follow Him in all things.

Our wills, respected by God, and surrendered to Him will bring us to heaven. By choosing Christ we become His, and He can work His will in us.

He will answer the prayer of one who reaches out to Him to give himself to His will. It is His pleasure to make us His.

---

[60] Ellen G. White, "Steps to Jesus," Ellen G. White Writings, https://1ref.us/1i1 (accessed January 18, 2021).

THE VULNERABILITY OF GOD
March 18

Genesis 2:7, "Then the LORD God formed a man from the dust of the ground and breathed into his nostrils the breath of life, and the man became a living being."

How can we explain the creation of Adam and Eve?

If God could see the future, and knew that the two would prove to be rebellious, why not just move on and let it be? No one would have known, after all, and the problem of evil would not have arisen.

It would have been the same with Satan. Why create him? Leave a blank there and let Gabriel be the leader of the angelic hosts.

But God's character would not allow it. His inner Being is the standard of honesty and freedom and He would not eliminate a creature in His plan for His own convenience. His convenience was never the issue, but His love and freedom were.

His love made Him vulnerable. Love always makes one vulnerable. When you love, you are committing. And if you are the greatest of lovers, it is the greatest of commitments. And when you commit in love, which will not use force, there is the possibility of rejection.

God could not have had a reservation in His mind, else the whole of the universe would have been tainted by dishonesty and God would have taken on the character of the deceiver. And it all would have happened in His own mind!

The universe was founded on the honesty of God. It is a real thing, built on a solid rock—His own character which is transparent and free. He bids us be the same that we may enjoy the freedom that such being brings.

FEARFULLY MADE PART 1
March 19

Psalm 139:14, "I praise you because I am fearfully and wonderfully made; your works are wonderful, I know that full well."

The human mind is the most complex thing that we know in the universe. Nothing else even comes close. Think on this one small task that the mind is capable of:

When I sit down at the piano to learn a piece of music, my memory, with the practice, becomes "branded" with the various moves that my fingers must make so that each note is struck with the right finger. It is not just the movements of the fingers that are necessary for each note, but the tension in my arms and shoulders must be just right to anchor them as a platform for my hands. The pressure that I am going to put on each key must be just right in order for it to be of the proper intensity. And with each passage, there is a movement, or a phrasing as the notes are strung together as a group. As I learn the piece, the whole of these movements and actions are stored in my memory, in a small part of my brain.

When I have learned the piece well, I can sit down and exactly reproduce each movement required and press each note with the intensity with which I learned it, along with the phrasing that the piece requires. And if I have learned it well, the action is nearly automatic. And if I have learned it really well, I can vary the movements at will, changing the way I play it, either louder or softer, slower or faster, etc.

A single piece can involve thousands of muscular actions and great coordination so that the piece is reproduced with passion, beauty and flow. Some pieces can last for up to an hour, and can be completely memorized, and in some, an orchestra or other instruments play along and must also be integrated into the action.

But this is just the beginning. Concert pianists have several such pieces stored in their memories, each with its own set of movements. And I have learned, even though I am older and not able to so well absorb such things, that my memory is never full. I do not have to stop and unlearn something so that room may be made for more. In fact, the files seem to be infinite!

Not only that, each piece is filed in such a way that it is immediately available so that once the pianist chooses to play it, there is no hesitation.

Indeed, we are wonderfully made.

Thank You, Father, for such skill in creating us, and gifting us with such talent. May we use it for Your glory.

FEARFULLY MADE PART 2
March 20

Psalm 40:5, "Many, O Lord my God, are the wonders you have done. The things you planned for us no one can recount to you."

Most all of us are given by God a set of instruments with which we may explore our world. And these are such a fine set of instruments that their value is beyond calculation. A lab would have to have an unlimited budget to afford such as we have for free.

First, we are able to detect certain electromagnetic waves in a narrow spectrum called "light." All substances emit electromagnetic waves of various wavelengths, but we can see only those in a certain small range, so that our minds might be used efficiently. Our eyes, however, can detect the smallest particle of light—the single photon.[61]

But our world is not just light and dark, it is colorful. This sensor is capable of detecting about 10 million different shades, making the world a riot of color for our enjoyment.[62]

We can also sense vibrations. Anything can be made to vibrate, from the smallest mite to the earth itself, and we can hear a range of these. They are not just sensed as different amplitudes of the same character, but our ears can pick up the timbre of each and recognize not just the musical instruments of men's devising, but even more importantly, the voices of those we love.

We can also sense the world chemically. Our noses, though not as sensitive as the canine family, can detect thousands of chemical signals, both pleasant and unpleasant. And God has filled the world with pleasant smells and tastes for our pleasure.

Finally, we have special nerves that can sense pressure, pain and heat. These sensors are placed strategically on movable arms that are able to probe and maneuver in amazing ways—yes, this is referring to our hands. Although this skill seems less important than the others, it is a great blessing. Visualize the caress that a mother can give to a child or a lover to his beloved in such a sensitive, delicate manner that great emotion is communicated without a word being said. And think when you receive such

---

[61]"Visual perception," Wikipedia, https://1ref.us/1i2 (accessed January 18, 2021).
[62]"Color vision," Wikipedia, https://1ref.us/1i3 (accessed January 18, 2021).

a signal from one you love. This stimulation is so important to newborns that those who do not receive it cannot survive.[63]

It may be surprising to realize that our God is a God of pleasure, far outstripping Bacchus of the Greek myths. One could almost consider our bodies one great pleasure machine!

Thank You, Lord for the delights our bodies give for our enjoyment.

---

[63] Maia Szalavitz, "Touching Empathy," *Psychology Today*, https://1ref.us/1i4 (accessed January 18, 2021).

MOLECULAR MACHINES
March 21

"Although Darwin was able to persuade much of the world that a modern eye could be produced gradually from a much simpler structure, he did not even attempt to explain how the simple light sensitive spot that was his starting point actually worked."[64]

It is not just the universe that shows the skill of God as Creator. The innermost workings of our bodies, the activities of the cells are truly amazing.

In Darwin's day, scientists thought the cell was a loose bag of jelly-like substance with little form. The microscopes at that time could not resolve the organelles of the cell. It was thought that for cells to do what they did, that small bag of jelly could just do it.

But now we know better. And the knowledge is astounding. The cell is a complex mixture of molecules that performs amazing feats. It is full of microscopic molecular machines that are wonderful to behold.

An example, used by Behe in his book, *Darwin's Black Box*, is the flagellum.

This is a little tail-like organelle that emerges from the cell membrane of bacteria allowing them to move. It acts like a corkscrew, rotating in a sweeping fashion that moves the organism in a direction it wishes. It can rotate clockwise, or counterclockwise, changing almost instantaneously. When a flagellum is broken it can self-regenerate.

The thing has several parts made of various proteins. There is a rotor, the part that rotates, a stator, the part that remains stationary and propels the rotor, and a mechanism to provide power to rotate the tail for motivation. Most bacteria use a hydrogen ion system that is extremely efficient. It is imbedded and anchored to the cell membrane so that it can be stabilized.

The design is exquisite. Many scientists have attempted to show how the thing could have emerged by chance and random mutations. No one, for over twenty years now, has come up with an evolutionary explanation.[65]

---

[64] Michael J. Behe, "Molecular Machines: Experimental Support for the Design Inference," Pitt.edu, https://1ref.us/1i5 (accessed January 19, 2021).
[65] Michael J. Behe, *Darwin's Black Box: The Biochemical Challenge to Evolution* (New York, NY: Free Press, 1996), pp. 51–73.

HAIR PART 1
March 22

"The hair is the richest ornament of women."[66] ~ Martin Luther

Hair does not seem like something that would inform us of God's dealings with His creatures, but in fact hair is an amazing gift, and shows God's desire to give us the freedom to be individualistic and creative.

Women and men have differing hair distributions. Women have hairless faces, but men at maturity can grow facial hair in more or less large quantities, covering most of the lower face, chin, cheeks and neck. Both sexes have hair covering the scalp, an area of rich blood supply that our hair helps keep warm.

Hair is a wonderful appendage. It grows continually, but is nonliving, so can be trimmed in any manner of ways without permanent harm. One can even shave it all off and it will regrow.

This characteristic of hair allows humans to shape it without irreparable disfigurement and to change their appearance at will. Women can style the hair on the tops of their heads into large coiffures or allow it to hang in flowing tresses, dramatically changing the feeling others experience in their presence, whether formal, casual or elegant. It allows for amazing changes in a woman's appearance, even at different times of day or night.

Men's beards, or facial hair, can be worked into a limitless number of styles, radically changing their faces, the thing that is presented to their peers daily. Again, styles can be rugged, formal, bushy, chaotic or distinguished.

> *Some think of God as rigid and stern, but our hair tells us otherwise. He gives leeway, allowing for individual creativity, like a family who gives its teenagers the freedom to express themselves as they test their new powers. The hair on our heads tells us this, even as their number speaks of His knowledge and care for us (Luke 12:7).*

---

[66] Martin Luther, "Martin Luther," AZ Quotes, https://1ref.us/1ic (accessed January 19, 2021).

This thing, hair, allows us to profoundly alter our countenances; we are not wedded to a certain look for our entire lives, but can vary our appearance radically—a difference over which we have complete control. This ability is a freedom that God has given to us to exploit as we see fit.

God thus shows His desire to give us control over ourselves—even over our appearance. He did not make us so that we had to remain the same throughout our lives, like the robots that men make, or even the animals, but gives us the capability to vary our facial features. It also shows His desire for diversity and freedom of expression.

Some think of God as rigid and stern, but our hair tells us otherwise. He gives leeway, allowing for individual creativity, like a family who gives its teenagers the freedom to express themselves as they test their new powers. The hair on our heads tells us this, even as their number speaks of His knowledge and care for us (Luke 12:7).

HAIR PART 2

March 23

1 Peter 3:3–4, "Your beauty should not come from outward adornment, such as elaborate hairstyles and the wearing of gold jewelry or fine clothes. Rather, it should be that of your inner self."

If God gave women their beautiful head of hair, enabling them to change their appearance with ease, why does Peter say that their beauty should not be based on such a gift? Is God jealous? Does He give gifts and then advise us not to use them? Was Peter intimidated by beautiful women?

God loves giving gifts and a woman's hair is indeed a wonderful gift through which she can express her own personality and creativity. God is not stingy in His giving and in fact glories in the giving of such gifts.

But He knows that His gifts can become tools of Satan to lead us into sin and even destruction.

Beauty can be a curse. We all know handsome people who display haughty pride and cruelty. Their beauty has become to them a terrible stumbling block. And so, God warns us through Peter to be careful how we deal with His gracious gifts of beauty and charm.

God gave Satan wonderful gifts as well, installing him as a covering cherub. Pride in his beauty led to his downfall. "Your heart became proud on account of your beauty" (Ezek. 28:17).

We are in danger of the same fate if we become proud of our personal appearance rather than in humility thanking our Creator for His wonderful gifts.

Peter's wise words point to the solution to pride. Be humble in appearance with the emphasis on inner beauty rather than outward adornments. Such an attitude will keep us from temptation.

HAIR PART 3
March 24

Luke 12:7, "Indeed, the very hairs of your head are all numbered."

This statement seems almost ridiculous. Does God actually keep track of the number of hairs on our heads? Especially one such as mine that is losing them on a daily, perhaps hourly basis? This seems too trivial a thing for God to concern Himself with.

This statement is an example of hyperbole and Jesus used this type of speech on several occasions to show various aspects of His teaching.

In this instance, He is speaking of God's infinite care for us, even as if He were watching the hairs on our heads, keeping count on those that fall or grow back.

Hyperbole is a figure of speech. A hyperbole is an extreme exaggeration used to make a point. It is the opposite of an understatement. It is from a Greek word meaning "excess."[67]

Here is an example from S.E. Schlosser in *Babe, the Blue Ox*:[68]

"Well now, one winter it was so cold that all the geese flew backward and all the fish moved south and even the snow turned blue. Late at night, it got so frigid that all spoken words froze solid afore they could be heard. People had to wait until sunup to find out what folks were talking about the night before."[69]

This numbering of hairs is such a statement. The cutting off of the hand or plucking out of the eye rather than sinning (Matt. 5:29–30) and the eating of His body as stated in John 6:54 are examples as well.

We use this type of speech all the time (he is older than the hills) but it seems almost scandalous that Jesus would use it, after all, He is God and would not stoop to such low forms of speaking.

But in fact, He did. Why?

First, it is an effective form of speech that gets attention. Hyperbole adds color and even fun to speech. Jesus used it to pique the people's interest.

---

[67]"hyperbole," Merriam-Webster, https://1ref.us/1i6 (accessed January 19, 2021).
[68]S.E. Schlosser, "Babe the Blue Ox," American Folklore, https://1ref.us/1i7 (accessed January 19, 2021).
[69]Ibid.

Second and most importantly, Jesus came as a man and when He came among us, He used the techniques of the good speakers of His day and culture. He adapted Himself to His situation and took advantage of the styles and uses that were common at that time so that He might communicate with His audience. And the crowds He gathered testify to His skill.

God does not shrink from the human touch. He became a man and was all that a man is, even in the culture of His time. Instead of coming as One who required that we adapt to Him, He respected our culture and practices and adapted to them. He talked the talk of the speakers of His day, including the use of hyperbole. He really became one of us.

Jesus spoke as a man. And I am grateful He so identified with me that He even spoke as I do.

ALIENS AND MEN
March 25

Genesis 1:31, "God saw all that he had made, and it was very good. And there was evening, and there was morning—the sixth day."

My wife and I were discussing the entry about hair when she noted that when men created alien creatures in the movies, they did not have the ability to change their appearances with their hair as we do.

Something else was noted. Almost always, when men create aliens, creatures from other places or planets, they are uniformly unattractive, most often ugly. Their skin has sallow hues, their arms are grotesque appendages and they have all manner of what we would consider deformities. ET was actually ugly.

God, on the other hand, has made us beautiful and attractive. No, we are not all like Miss or Mr. America, but we are not anywhere near Jabba the Hutt.

God made man after His own image, a man of wonderful strength and power, a son of the Most High.

We, on the other hand, do not create creatures as God did, but envision ones after the twistedness of our sinful minds and create creatures that are inherently repulsive.

God had no insecurity within Himself that required making His creatures defective. He created wonderful beings, with all the ability to act independently. They had such beauty that one became so enamored with himself that he rebelled.

God had not stinted with Satan. He was beautiful. God was not afraid to make His creatures like that. We, on the other hand, are fearful of being removed from the top of the pile.

But God? He made us lovely in form and graceful, full of potential. And He celebrated His work with joy on the day of our creation.

THE ELEPHANT MAN
March 26

Luke 5:12–13, "While Jesus was in one of the towns, a man came along who was covered with leprosy. When he saw Jesus, he fell with his face to the ground and begged him, 'Lord, if you are willing, you can make me clean.' Jesus reached out his hand and touched the man. 'I am willing,' he said. 'Be clean!' And immediately the leprosy left him."

But what of those who we don't perceive as beautiful? What about those that seemingly have nothing that would make them attractive? The ones that God seems to have cursed?

The Elephant Man, Joseph Merrick, was just such an individual. During his childhood, he slowly developed terrible deformities of his head and face, right arm and leg. These worsened over time and to support himself, he became the member of a freak show that toured England and France. While in Europe, his savings were stolen by his agent, leaving him destitute. He managed to return to London where he was befriended by a physician, Dr. Treves, who arranged for him to be cared for at his hospital.[70]

What about him?

When Jesus was here, a man similar to Merrick approached Him. Luke says he was full of leprosy (Luke 5:12), a disease destroying the sense of pain, causing a person to injure and burn themselves unknowingly. They would gradually lose their nose, ears and fingers and develop non-healing wounds that covered their bodies.

But when Jesus met this man, He did not hesitate. He touched him, and health was restored. This cure was a token of God's will for the unlovely and deformed.

Merrick was a devoted Christian. He had met the Savior and fallen in love with Him. But he was not cured of his affliction. He took Jesus at His Word, though, and believed that renewed life awaited him on the redeemed earth. The promise enlivened his outlook, preventing hopeless nihilism.

---

[70]"Joseph Merrick," Wikipedia, https://1ref.us/1i8 (accessed January 19, 2021).

ADAM AND THE ANIMALS PART 1
March 27

Genesis 2:19, "Now the LORD God had formed out of the ground all the wild animals and all the birds in the sky. He brought them to the man to see what he would name them."

The story of the naming of the animals reveals much about God.

God makes Adam and then, according to Genesis 2, parades the animals before him "to see what he would name them" (Gen. 2:19). God uses His creative power to fill the earth with a vast array of creatures of astounding variety. Why not just name them Himself? Why not just call Adam from his leafy bower and give him a list? God wants Adam to have the excitement of discovery and the pleasure of putting his own mark on the Creation. Because God has truly made the earth for the man as his domain, these are his creatures, and he should have the right to name them, even though he has not done any of the creating. This shows the respect God has for His son, Adam. He endowed him with a mind, then challenges it and desires that he use it creatively.

Just think of the thrill of all this. Adam is introduced to each of the creatures over which he is to rule. He chooses a name for them, just as we name our children, and now can call them to him at his will. He has been set over them as the ruler, has gotten to know them in a significant way and has chosen some characteristic with which to identify them. Now they are his.

All is well. Adam has a kingdom to rule and creatures to rule over. What could be wrong? But there is something wrong. Quite wrong.

ADAM AND THE ANIMALS PART 2
March 28

Genesis 2:20, "But for Adam no suitable helper was found."

After Adam had been given the earth to rule and had named all the animals over which he was to rule, all was complete and Creation was finished.

But no, there comes a jarring announcement. God says, "It is not good" (Gen. 2:18).

In Genesis 1, after each day, everything was pronounced good and even very good. But now, something was wrong. Something was incomplete. Something was missing. Adam noticed that all the animals had companions. They had someone like themselves, someone with whom they could be particularly intimate. But he had none.

Strange though it may seem, God was the One who brought this to light. He wanted the man to see the need himself. Eve was not just brought to Adam out of nowhere. The desire for a companion gradually dawned on him as he observed the relationship of the animals with their mates. In the depths of his soul he realized a great need and he longed for one like himself.

See here the unselfishness and generosity of God! He could have left this whole discovery out of the mind of man. Who would have known? He could have had Adam all to Himself, so that He could be worshiped solely without competition. One could even criticize God for allowing this intruder into the life of Adam, especially when we read of the fall and Eve's part in it.

But God would not have it. Why not just let Adam know of God, and make Him the only object of his love? The answer is because God would fill the earth full of love, as the Trinity is full of love. So, He created a companion for the man, one like himself. Only then was Creation complete.

IT IS NOT GOOD FOR MAN TO LIVE ALONE
March 29

Genesis 2:18, "The Lord God said, 'It is not good for the man to be alone. I will make a helper suitable for him.'"

The story of Adam's desire for a companion and the creation of Eve tells how God met the need that Adam recognized when he named the animals. Eve was the helper that God made for Adam.

This simple interpretation of the story overlooks an even deeper answer God gave to Adam's need. God had an even greater answer that was not apparent for some time, even after the expulsion from the garden.

With Eve came an even greater gift. The pair were thus able to have children. They could help create little ones like themselves, thus filling the earth with people.

There could be sons and daughters, brothers and sisters, aunts and uncles, nephews and nieces, grandmas and grandpas and cousins of all varieties. And then all the in-laws that result from a simple marriage of members of two families. One can get a whole new family because of the one that their mate or their brother's or sister's mates bring with them. Even members of unrelated families could become involved with all kinds of friendly relationships.

God did not just answer the problem of aloneness with Eve, but with her He gave a multitude of answers to the problem of loneliness.

When God gives an answer, it is often a much bigger one than we anticipated. God surprises us with the answers He gives to our problems.

If we will but sit still instead of trying to solve all the problems on our own, God will set the stage for the answer we need.

THE TREES IN THE GARDEN
March 30

Genesis 2:9, "The LORD God made all kinds of trees grow out of the ground—trees that were pleasing to the eye and good for food. In the middle of the garden were the tree of life and the tree of the knowledge of good and evil."

When God created a garden home for Adam, He filled it full of trees. Now, for Near Eastern peoples living in arid surroundings, an orchard full of trees bearing all manner of fruit was almost unknown and of great blessing and value. But to make one's home there was unheard of.

And when God made the garden, He gave it all to Adam and Eve. They could eat of any tree—all of them save one.

Think of wandering through such a garden. Apples, oranges, pears of many varieties, guavas, mangos, bananas, loquats and the many odd and different fruits that we now know because companies have perfected shipping of perishables from all over the world. Even durian ("The Smelliest Fruit in the World") of which there are some 100+ varieties. All of this for the two of them to enjoy days of discovery and pleasure. And then think of all the development of varieties they could have conducted.

And God only forbade one tree. Out of all of them, He banned only one. He even planted one whose fruit bestowed eternal life!

Our sinful natures complain of the narrowness of God. But here He demonstrates His largesse. The trees of the garden show just how expansive God's desire for our lives is. Adam was allowed to eat of all but one. Hundreds of trees, and only one disallowed!

How silly to concentrate on the one forbidden tree when the whole forest beckoned for exploration! How narrow-minded indeed.

THE GIFT OF THE LAW
March 31

James 2:12, "Speak and act as those who are going to be judged by the law that gives freedom."

While thinking on the trees of the garden and the vast array open to Adam and Eve, with only one tree kept from them, the law of God also comes to mind. Many feel that the law is confining, that it is a negative thing, emphasizing only that which is forbidden.

But the law, as noted by James, is actually a law of freedom, not slavery. Yes, the forbidden is mentioned. This is true. But it is mentioned because in its category, it is the only forbidden thing.

Take the seventh commandment: "You shall not commit adultery" (Exod. 20:14). This commandment addresses the relationship between the sexes. How shall men and women relate to one another?

There is one relationship that is forbidden, that of adultery. All other relationships are allowed. I may relate to a woman as mother, sister, aunt, wife, niece, employer, employee, subordinate, grandmother, grandchild, friend, student, teacher, client, etc. All manner of relationships are allowed and may be explored. One only is disallowed, adultery. That is the only one forbidden and excluded.

By looking at the law in this manner, we see the liberty that we indeed possess when we follow the way of God. He does not confine us, but tells us only what is forbidden, allowing all the others to be freely available to us. Just like the trees in the garden, so much is available for our free use.

God does not restrict us, forbidding pleasure and freedom. He keeps us from that which would bring us into slavery to sin. All the good is given freely as is His habit and custom.

Thank God for His goodness and love.

THE LIE OF THE GARDEN
April 1

Genesis 2:8, "Now the LORD God had planted a garden in the east, in Eden."

Any scientist who had opportunity to visit the Garden of Eden would have thought it was very old. The trees had the look of maturity. The soil was rich and full of nutrients, certainly the result of years of plant growth. The birds and animals had the look of adulthood. Some may even have been pregnant! The stars shining down on the scene had light that appeared to be millions, and even billions of years old. And Adam himself was an adult.

Thus, the garden told a lie. It had just been created recently but had the look of age and maturity. Why would God deceive us with such a situation? Why could we not learn the truth by just looking at the processes going on in the garden and make a right assumption about its age? Was it God's purpose to lie to us? Was this an intentional manipulation?

No, of course not. But the evidence there was not the only evidence that God presented to any who would have wanted to examine His handiwork. He was there to speak to any visitor and inform them of what had just happened.

And He has done just the same by informing us in His book, the Bible. Natural evidence notwithstanding, the Bible tells the actual story of the Creation.

The prophecies give evidence of its veracity and trustworthiness, and Jesus satisfies our most deeply felt needs.

But examining the garden to find its actual age? It was not to be found there.

We can choose to believe the Bible or not. But God has warned us of the pitfalls of natural evidence. They may not be accurate.

THE SABBATH PART 1
April 2

Exodus 20:8–9, "Remember the Sabbath day by keeping it holy. Six days you shall labor and do all your work."

The Sabbath command to memorialize the Creation is surprising, especially when compared to the Creation myths of Babylon.

In the Epic of Gilgamesh, the gods create men. But the motive for this is to have slaves for their use. Men are to serve them and do their bidding, offering sacrifices and labor.[71]

But God, when He gives His commands, gives one that strikes at the very root of the myth. The command to honor the Creation is not one to serve and work, but rather to rest! We are not created to be the slaves of God as the great religion of Babylon says. Rather we are to be the friends of God and to have a day of rest and fellowship with Him. Instead of work, it's a party!

It is an alien idea in stark contrast to any in the Babylonian story and shows a profound difference envisioned for man.

Jesus further revealed the nature of the Sabbath and the thinking of God by saying frankly, "The Sabbath was made for man, not man for the Sabbath" (Mark 2:27).

The Sabbath was made for us, not so we can serve God on that day, but for Him, in a way, to serve us. He forbids work so that we may be refreshed. He comes to meet us on this special day for fellowship, a date of sorts, the high point of the week. The day is even a memorial of our salvation in which we had no part.

The Sabbath also shows the value God places on man. It is not what man can do that is important; it is what he is, a beloved creature. It is not work and slaving that God is looking for, but us, His creatures, the apple of His eye (Zech. 2:8).

The Sabbath thus shows the difference between pagan thinking on the Creator and the actual God of Creation.

---

[71] *"Epic of Gilgamesh,"* Wikipedia, https://1ref.us/1i9 (accessed January 19, 2021).

THE SABBATH PART 2
April 3

Genesis 2:2–3, "[O]n the seventh day he rested from all his work. Then God blessed the seventh day and made it holy, because on it he rested from all the work of creating that he had done."

When God set up a special place where He could meet with the beings He had created, He was careful to make it available to all of them. God is not a respecter of persons (Acts 10:34): He plays no favorites. So, His choice had to be a place where all would have access.

Thus, He made the Sabbath. A "Temple in Time"[72] from which none are excluded.

First, it could not be a physical place, like the Hebrew sanctuary. Any such place would limit accessibility, for there would always be some who would not have the wherewithal to reach it because of some limitation, physical weakness or lack of financial means. God would also not require toilsome pilgrimages allowing for only occasional communion.

Secondly, a feat of some type would also limit accessibility by preventing all but the strongest or most righteous from entering His presence.

So, instead, God set aside a special time where we could be in communion with Him. It is not that we could not have fellowship at other times, but that He would be there in a special way. It is similar to a date with your sweetheart. And God made the date Himself. That is, *He* set the time on *His* calendar. No one else had power to cancel or break it.

Time is a commodity that all possess. Like time, no one can take the Sabbath from us unless they take our lives. The Sabbath comes every seventh day and men can't stop it. Even if they cast us deep into the dankest dungeon, fastening the doors with the strongest locks, they cannot keep the Sabbath from entering there. It comes each week and their wills are powerless to prevent it, even as they are powerless to prevent the spinning of the earth.

The Sabbath is one of God's most gracious gifts, the gift of Himself, and is open to all regardless of station. Only our refusal to enter in keeps it from us—a terrible loss.

---

[72]Ismar Schorsch, "Shabbat: A Temple in Time," Jewish Theological Seminary, https://1ref.us/1ia (accessed January 19, 2021).

THE SABBATH PART 3
April 4

Mark 2:27, "The Sabbath was made for man, not man for the Sabbath."

How does one really keep the Sabbath?

From my youth, I have been a good Sabbath keeper. I have rested. I have not done what I felt was wrong on the Sabbath. I have been careful, even compulsive about the rules. I went so far as to oppose my father on a Sabbath issue; something that, as a compliant son, was a difficult thing for me. And God honored me for my devotion.

But I have realized that the Sabbath is not keeping a set of rules. That is, it is not merely refraining from doing certain things and doing other things. Yes, God has said, "Six days you shall labor" (Exod. 20:9), but that is just the beginning. In that regard, one could argue that sleeping twenty-four hours every seventh day was the proper way to keep the commandment!

God gave the command that we might be free to turn in a different direction—upward.

Sabbath keeping, at its heart, is a weekly meeting with the Creator. It is a coming into His presence with all the profundity that that entails. It's actually an invitation to visit the throne room of the universe, where the Deity dwells. To come into His presence with joy and singing and celebration. And it is commanded so that we might know that it is exactly what God wants. He desires our presence there, and longs for us to cease our busy and bustle that He might have us to Himself. It is a love relationship after all and such relationships require intimate time together.

The rules? It is not that they are bad, but that they are a means to an end, and not the end in itself. To focus there is to miss the whole point. The Sabbath is about the Creator, the God of love, who passionately desires us.

THE SABBATH PART 4
April 5

Daniel 7:25, "He will ... try to change the set times and the laws."

The change of the Sabbath to Sunday occurred early in the second century, during the reign of Hadrian, in the AD 130s, after the Bar Cocheba revolt (AD 132–135).[73] It was so early in the history of the church, that though the Bible does not mention such a change, Sunday observance was present very shortly after its writing. The impetus for the change was to distance the church from the Jewish religion which had become a stench in the nostrils of Rome.[74]

But changing the day changed everything.

Such an action assumes a God-like prerogative. To change the day of worship from one to another without a distinct command from Him? How dare we do such a thing?

If God has made a date with us, can we change it on our own, even when He has not given a signal that He approves of such a change?

There is a sense that the Christian world has stood Him up. He made an appointment to meet with us, and we have found it inconvenient, and so have made it a day that is better for us, regardless of what He has said.

And finally, if God blesses a day, how can any other day be blessed? We certainly, sinners that we are, cannot bless anything or make it holy. It is the privilege of Divinity to do such a thing.

We thus lose any blessing that we might have obtained.

And the very way Christians keep Sunday betrays this fact. It is not a Sabbath of rest in most cases, but a day to attend church and then do what one pleases: chores, football, work or whatever.

Can we forfeit what God really has for us because it is inconvenient? The Sabbath is a blessing given to man for his benefit. Ignoring it is a great loss.

---

[73] Samuele Bacchiocchi, *From Sabbath to Sunday: A Historical Investigation of the Rise of Sunday Observance in Early Christianity* (Rome: The Pontifical Gregorian University Press, 1977), pp. 165–212.
[74] "From Sabbath to Sunday," United Church of God, https://1ref.us/1ib (accessed January 19, 2021).

THE SABBATH PART 5
April 6

Matthew 11:28, "Come to me, all you who are weary and burdened, and I will give you rest."

I had had a troubled week. Things had gone awry, and the pressures of work and family had been heavy on me, destroying my peace. Satan had reminded me of my own sinful weaknesses and shortcomings, arraying these before me to harass and depress.

But it was Sabbath, and when I awoke in the early morning, I turned my mind to God. It was the Sabbath! And He was there to give me the rest He had promised, the blessing that has been in that day since the world began.

And I had peace.

God has bestowed on us this day each week, as a time for us to seek His presence, for He is in the day itself. When God blesses something, He is giving part of Himself. The Sabbath is a day where He has poured Himself into time in a way that He has not into the days of labor.

Jesus said that He would give us rest (Matt. 11:28). That rest has been available each Sabbath since the Creation of the world, available to any who would take advantage of the gift of it. We have rest each week if we will. As water is to thirst, so the Sabbath is to weariness. It was given even before our peace had been broken by sin. The Sabbath rest was necessary even in the perfection of Eden.

God has put into the very creation of time a remedy for the affliction He knew would come to us.

We can ignore the blessing, but then we suffer from the very thing we so need in this difficult place: rest for the weary. Let us then enter into that rest.

THE SABBATH PART 6
April 7

Exodus 20:9–10, "Six days you shall labor and do all your work, but the seventh day is a sabbath to the LORD your God."

The Sabbath is the very epitome of grace and was given even before sin to let us know of the grace God has bestowed on us.

How is that so?

The Sabbath comes every week, regardless of what we have done during that week.

What if I have been doing God's work, fulfilling His commands to me, being faithful in all that I do, looking to Him who is the Way of salvation? What if I have been serving His children with all my heart? At the end of such a week, the Sabbath comes to me and I may enter it with rejoicing.

But what if I have not done the work of the Lord and have been disobedient and unfaithful? What if I have utterly failed to follow His commands to me for the good of myself and my family?

Amazingly, the Sabbath comes as usual at sundown on Friday night and I too may enter it with rejoicing. God invites me into His presence again, regardless of my performance during the week.

The Sabbath does not depend on us. It is not present in the week when we do well and absent when we do ill. No, it comes every week regardless of us. It is, in fact, a gift of grace to us, coming each week as an invitation to enter the throne room of our Maker. We are His children when we are bad and when we are good. The Sabbath bids us to look up from our own soiled souls and look rather to the God of all grace, who has even commanded us to turn from the world and work to spend the day with Him.

Let us then enter into that rest.

CUISINES
April 8

Genesis 1:29, "Then God said, 'I give you every seed-bearing plant on the face of the whole earth and every tree .... for food.'"

When God made the heavens and the earth, He created a rich garden of flavorful herbs, plants and seeds to enliven our food. He scattered them over the face of the whole world, favoring some places with pungent varieties, while giving to others a more subtle array.

With these herbs and spices we have developed our national cuisines. I am astonished at the variety of them. There is Mexican, Italian, Greek, Thai, Indian, Jamaican, Chinese and all manner of central Asian palates—all so different! The Africans have a thick porridge they consider their staple, which they flavor with sauces of all types. Their spinach and tomato concoction with peanut meal is surprisingly delicious.

I like a rather bland set of tastes myself, but my daughter, who manages a restaurant, is a more adventurous sort, willing to experience all manner of strange "delicacies" from all continents. Give me a tomato with mayo on rye bread and I will be content.

But are any of these cuisines wrong? Or evil? No, God has not denied the use of the plant world in all its variety but gave it all to us for our pleasure. In fact, "home cooking" is a matter of country of origin and personal taste. God did not forbid these cuisines but has allowed us to experiment and test to develop our own preferences. He gives us a wide latitude in this regard.

And that is who He is. He is not a stern Deity forcing His view on us, but He allows for freedom of taste in our daily nourishment. He has made the vegetable world capable of supporting us with proper nutrition even with all its variety. The variety may possibly be essential.

So, sit down and enjoy some durian! (An absolutely disgusting or beloved fruit from Malaysia and Indonesia. The reaction to this fruit is one of either total delight or disgust with no in between.) God gave it to ... well, some of us. It is just another token of the freedom that is His will.

THE BODY AND THE NERVOUS SYSTEM
April 9

Psalm 139:13, "For you created my inmost being; you knit me together in my mother's womb."

During development in our mother's womb, our bodies undergo a strange and wonderful transformation.

The body starts as a group of undifferentiated cells in a hollow ball called the blastocyst. The ball flattens out to form an embryo with three separate layers: the endoderm, the mesoderm and the ectoderm. Endo—means inner, meso—middle and ecto—outer. The endoderm becomes the digestive and respiratory tract, the mesodermal the muscles, blood vessels and heart, and the ectoderm the skin and brain.[75]

The different parts of the body develop over the next several days as the embryo starts to look more and more like a human being. The limbs develop muscles and tendons, the endoderm becomes the esophagus, teeth, stomach and intestines. And while the brain develops in the cranium, the skin develops to cover the body.[76]

But then an amazing process begins, a process developed by God for us. The nervous system begins to send out tentacles to the whole body, even in a sense invading each organ and starting to take control. The heart has been beating at a slow rate, but as the nervous system takes over, it begins to beat faster. The muscles are each brought under the control of the brain so that they can be coordinated in a smooth and efficient way. This is not complete until a couple of years after birth; we all see how uncoordinated a baby's movements are. But after several months, they can walk and even run. At about age four or five, all the connections are complete and a child can start to learn to do complex tasks.

God has given us this wonderful gift—bodies that are under our command. It is a gift valuable beyond computation. But that is His generosity, to give gifts that can never be measured. Grace beyond grace.

---

[75] "13.2 DEVELOPMENT AND ORGANOGENESIS," BC campus, https://1ref.us/1id (accessed January 19, 2021).
[76] Ibid.

MY DAUGHTER'S HONEY
April 10

Psalm 119:103, "How sweet are your words to my taste, sweeter than honey to my mouth!"

The other day, my daughter brought home some honey she had just taken from her hives—her first crop. She lives in the dry semi-desert of the Texas panhandle and the only plants the bees can gather from are the wildflowers growing along the roadside. But I had never tasted anything like it. The flavor was strong and full, with a hint of cinnamon and not at all like the bland stuff we have purchased from the store in those little plastic bears.

Why such a difference? The honey that we buy commercially has been homogenized and blended to make it all uniform in flavor and color. Raw honey, on the other hand, coming straight from the hive, has the taste and freshness of the flowers from that particular countryside.

God made these little creatures capable of making a product of amazing diversity. The nectar and pollen of the plants they visit determine the character of the honey they make, and the mixture of flowers from each hive's honey is slightly different.

Our commercial companies want uniformity, a sweet sameness that can be reproduced in large quantities without variation. But God created the bees to make something with delightful diversity. He apparently desired that each honey be different, as distinct as the landscape from which the bees gather their nectar.

So, He values the differences in us. He is not looking for a cookie-cutter Christian, but one who has a unique experience with Him, and a unique contribution to make to his or her fellow travelers on this dark planet.

"[L]et your light shine before others, that they may see your good deeds and glorify your Father in heaven" (Matt. 5:16).

THE OIL SET
April 11

Jeremiah 31:3, "I have loved you with an everlasting love."

I bought a small set of oil paints a few days ago. I have been wanting to paint for some time but have lacked opportunity.

When I took my set home, I thought about the gifts God has given so that we can do such things as put oil on canvas.

Firstly, I have eyes so that I might detect electromagnetic waves. It is a limited spectrum, but very useful. If I could detect the whole spectrum, it would be overwhelming, but the small part I can see allows me to enjoy the millions of tints and shades that make seeing so pleasurable. God did not give too much, nor too little.

Then, I have hands and arms that can be used to maneuver the tools I need to paint. I can make all manner of movements both large and small so that I might get just the touch I want on the canvas. Delicate or bold, small or large, subtle or flamboyant. These appendages are the most creative "tools" we have to work our will on the planet. I can learn to use them to create beauty, something that can be very satisfying.

Then God has given us the material resources so that I might paint. These include the pigments and oils, the plants and fibers that can be worked into canvas and the paints that I can choose to use for my painting. And there are the various bristles and brushes, knives and other devices that I will use to put the oil on the painting. I could not do it without these and the easel and stand, chairs and all that are necessary.

It was a simple oil set, but it revealed the love God has bestowed on us, allowing such freedom of expression. Even in such a simple thing, He showers love on us every day, even every hour.

THE DAWN
April 12

Isaiah 26:9, "My soul yearns for you in the night; in the morning my spirit longs for you."

A few days ago, while taking a vacation on the Alabama coast, I arose just at dawn. It was a humid day, as is often the case on the Gulf, and there were billowing cumulous clouds towering in the western sky. Their hues were the subtle shades of the morning: pinks, yellows and grays that blended to make a riot of color, covering the sky like one vast canvas of impressionistic art. But unlike a painting, the clouds were ever changing as the light played on them in different ways and from different angles. Oh, it was a silent color show of awesome beauty and wonder.

But it was not just there for me. Yes, God gives me tokens of His love each day and is generous beyond my capacity to receive. But that sunrise was for all along the coast, and even for those flying overhead. God gave a gift to tens of thousands of people that morning—sinner and saint alike. His display was for the just and the unjust, just like the rain and dew of heaven. And that time of year the gift comes nearly every morning and evening. And even during the day, God uses the clouds to decorate the azure sky in delightful shades of white and gray.

We often fail to appreciate the generosity of God. All of nature, the earth, the sky, the weather, the stars, all the minutiae of Creation and life itself are ours to enjoy. And for free! There is no stingy grasping on His part. None are excluded, and the rankest atheist may make a life of studying them, writing academic tomes describing their wonders, becoming an expert in their intricacies. His rebellion does not prohibit his pleasure.

Now that is gracious largess even offered to those who refuse to acknowledge Him.

THE TEMPERED SCALE
April 13

Psalm 98:4-6, "Shout for joy to the LORD, all the earth, burst into jubilant song with music; make music to the LORD with the harp, with the harp and the sound of singing, with trumpets and the blast of the ram's horn—shout for joy before the LORD, the King."

God has blessed us with the ability to make music and to enjoy it, and our lives are filled with it. Some listen to it constantly on their electronic devices or in concerts, etc.

But the foundation for that blessing is rather complicated and was not thoroughly worked out before a few hundred years ago, when the tempered scale came into wide use in the West. In this scale, each note is equidistant from the surrounding notes. The "Just Scale," on the other hand, is based on ratios that are most pleasant to the ear. They are different. The development of the tempered scale made it possible to play an instrument (especially a keyboard instrument) in any key and to modulate to any key without having to retune.[77]

This advantage has allowed for the great music that we enjoy, compositions that can be played with large orchestras, hillbilly ensembles or soloists of any kind. Classical, country, jazz, all depend on this scale.

God gave us this gift that we might enjoy the pleasure of music and the joy of experiencing the emotions that such music creates in our hearts. The birds and the "music" of nature is beautiful and soothing. To listen to the waves as they break on the beach, a kind of white noise, is restful.

But it does not compare to the music we can create with our voices or the contrived instruments available to us. And the beauty there is built into the very physics of sound by our wonderful God. Praise to His name!

---

[77]"Physics of Music-Notes," Michigan Technological University, https://1ref.us/1ie (accessed January 19, 2021).

WATER

April 14

John 4:10, *"Jesus answered her, "If you knew the gift of God and who it is that asks you for a drink, you would have asked him and he would have given you living water."*

Water is indeed a gift of God.

It may surprise you to know that water is the most amazing chemical in the universe.

It is a combination of the gases hydrogen and oxygen. When hydrogen combines with the elements near oxygen on the periodic table, the compounds are poisonous or corrosive. Ammonia, NH3, hydrogen sulfide, H2S and hydrofluoric acid—HF—are nasty actors. But water? It is life-giving. Scientists call life carbon-based because of the importance of that element in our chemistry.[78] But without water, there would be no life at all. Life might even be more accurately called "water based."

Water has a high specific heat, that is, it absorbs a lot of heat as it increases in temperature. This characteristic means that it takes time to cool or heat, tempering the climate and making our body's temperature stable.

Water is a polar compound, meaning that one side of the molecule is slightly positively charged and the other negative. This allows for the chemistry of life. But oxygen, a non-polar molecule, can dissolve in it, allowing for life in the sea.

It has a wonderful refractive index so that light reflects from its surface: the delightful mirror-like images of the surroundings of a lake are the result.

And what of the clouds that beautify the atmosphere? Or the snow spread on mountain peaks that make the dark crags striking with white contrast?

God is the master Craftsman who can do so much with so little. And He can do much with our little as well. We may give it to Him in peace.

---

[78] "Fun Fact – Nonmetal Hydrides," Karl's Personal Web Site, https://1ref.us/1if (accessed January 19, 2021).

MARRIAGE

April 15

Genesis 2:24, "That is why a man leaves his father and mother and is united to his wife and they become one flesh."

God's plan for all humans is that they are born into a family with a father and a mother to nurture and protect them. But God does not make individuals form families or force any to enter into a relationship with another.

We cannot choose our families, that is, we are born into them. But when we become a certain age, we can choose to form a family of our own. God does not introduce us to an individual that we must form a relationship with. There is a certain sense that we may choose freely.

When we come into the world, we have no choice about which family will be our place of nurture. Someone else decides on this most important fact of our lives, and even that we will be born at all! The power of our parents over us is truly amazing. They are the ones that made a decision and we had not a whit to do with it whatsoever.

But even those that have had a disadvantaged childhood have been given an amazing gift by God. They can choose to form a family of their own, one that they have the power to influence and make successful in spite of any failure they have experienced.

God does not force us to enter into a relationship with anyone. We are the ones who choose who we will marry or set up house with. Falling in love is a personal matter. Each family formed is based on a choice we make and we are the ones who can make such families a success or failure.

There is something liberating about going out on your own and leading your life as you would lead it. It is a natural instinct that God has put within each of us. We could not choose our family, the ones that brought us into the world, but God allows each of us to start afresh, anew with the ability to do it "our way." We are not bound by what our parents have done but may choose a way of our own. That is a precious gift of freedom.

MY FATHER'S CHOICE
April 16

Genesis 29:18, "Jacob was in love with Rachel and said, 'I'll work for you seven years in return for your younger daughter Rachel.'"

My father grew up in Cleveland, OH, and New York in the 1920s and 1930s, living on Staten Island when it was considered country (no bridges connected it to New York City). His parents did not get along. Often, as he lay awake in an upstairs bedroom, he could hear them fighting in the living room below.

As he lay there listening, he made a promise to himself to never let his home experience that sort of thing. He made a conscious choice to prevent it.

And so, as I grew up, I never saw my parents argue in front of us except once. It was a shock to us when it happened. But it happened only once.

> *God has given us just such freedom to make our homes as we would have them. Let us take advantage of such freedom to make them the best.*

Oh, they had their differences. One time when my dad came home with a small Honda motorcycle, my mother did not talk to him for a month. She did not want her babies riding on such a dangerous machine. But our home was never filled with loud arguments or disagreements.

Who were the beneficiaries of my father's decision? His family. It was me and my siblings.

He had decided to have a home that would be peaceful. And he would not let little annoyances disturb it. And so, my childhood was one of peace and happiness, with a stable and loving marriage as its foundation. Not until later did I realize what a gift it truly was.

God has given us just such freedom to make our homes as we would have them. Let us take advantage of such freedom to make them the best.

WHAT GOD HAS JOINED …
April 17

Matthew 19:6, KJV, "What therefore God hath joined together, let not man put asunder."

As noted, we are free to choose whom we will marry. God does not dictate to us the one we marry or set up house with. We are given more or less free rein in the matter.

But although we are the ones doing the choosing, it is God that forms the union. The thing that binds a man and a woman together is not of their making. It is something that God Himself has devised and planned for each of us. The bond between the sexes is an amazing one, and one that God Himself created, and cannot be dealt with lightly. It changes us.

Paul tells us that even if that bond is formed casually, it is still something that is profound, and makes an indelible impression on us (1 Cor. 6:15–17). No man is to break it, no man is to put it asunder.

When taken as God would have us take it, the sexual union is a holy and wonderful thing. It is the most intimate of relationships and is meant to be the foundation for a lifelong union between a man and a woman, bringing them into a union deeper than any other that humans can experience. Although we choose with whom to enter this union, it is one of God's making and so has His blessing and creative power. When Adam "knew" his wife it was much more than just the physical touch, but an experience that had an effect on his mind and even his soul (Gen. 4:1, KJV).

God would have us enjoy this wonderful union in the most profound and enduring way possible. Following His plan will result in the most blessing.

Section 5

The Fall and The Flood

The fall and what the results of that tragedy were for the world.

> "Since by man came death,
> By man came also the resurrection of the dead.
> For as in Adam all die,
> So in Christ shall all be made alive."[79]

---

[79] Charles Jennens, Messiah libretto: Part 3, 46 chorus: "Since by man came death," 1741.

ADAM AND EVE AT THE TREE PART 1
April 18

Genesis 3:1, "[T]he serpent .... said to the woman, 'Did God really say, "You must not eat from any tree in the garden?"'"

After God had made all things, and the two new humans had been joined together in marriage, the first thing recorded is the discussion at the tree of knowledge. The two of them must have been loitering near enough for Satan to speak to them. How soon the pair were in danger!

God spoke to Adam about the tree in Genesis 2:17, but the serpent did not address him. Why was Adam silent here?

Eve knew of the prohibition, even though God had not spoken to her directly about it. But the snake initiated the conversation.

"Did God really say ...?" (Gen. 3:1).

And the discussion was about theology! An argument over God's words and motives! The serpent was cunning and instead of a direct confrontation, he asked a question of clarification.

This is often the way we are led into temptation. A discussion of clarification. Did He really mean this? Is there really a restriction to our actions? Does God not care for my wellbeing such that He would deny me this very useful and beneficial experience?

"What's wrong with it, anyway?"

This is the way of sin, and Satan often traps us with his wiles in this manner. It all seems so innocent, but it really belies a lack of faith in the Word of God.

In such circumstances, it is better to leave the discussion and attend to the known will of God that He has revealed. Concentrating on His will in our lives rather than debating the fine points of His thinking is a much safer plan of action. The path to heaven is paved by the determination to do His will.

ADAM AND EVE AT THE TREE PART 2
April 19

Genesis 3:4–6:

> *"You will not certainly die," the serpent said to the woman. "For God knows that when you eat from it your eyes will be opened, and you will be like God, knowing good and evil." When the woman saw that the fruit of the tree was good for food and pleasing to the eye, and also desirable for gaining wisdom, she took some and ate it. She also gave some to her husband, who was with her, and he ate it.*

The thing the serpent did first was to cast doubt on the character of God. As he implied, God had been careful to withhold something from them. Something that was a positive good: the knowledge of evil. Why would God do that? It must be that He was selfish.

The argument of the serpent is silly on the surface when you consider it carefully. Adam and Eve were made in God's image. They were like Him already! How would they gain anything more when they already had what the fruit had to offer?

But Satan would not have them make those considerations. He has nothing to offer, but would make God look deceptive and selfish. So, he suggested an advantage to eating the fruit, an advantage that implied that God did not have their best interest at heart.

That is why the most basic sin is disbelief. God has given us all things. He gave them a wonderful home, food of all kinds and the companionship of one another. To believe other than that He was a God of love was the first error, an error against all the facts before them.

Yet they believed the serpent in spite of all the evidence against it. It was an active disbelief. And it was sin.

THE GIFT AND THE TEMPTATION
April 20

Genesis 2:21–22, "So the LORD God caused the man to fall into a deep sleep; and while he was sleeping, he took one of the man's ribs and then closed up the place with flesh. Then the LORD God made a woman from the rib he had taken out of the man, and he brought her to the man."

Sin is an amazingly destructive force. Even God's best gifts can become the basis for the strongest temptations.

An example is Eve.

God saw that man was lonely in the garden. He had named the animals and realized that there was no companion for him. God put Adam into a deep sleep, the first anesthesia, and performed the first operation—removing a rib. From it, He shaped the first woman and brought her to Adam.

Adam was astounded by the gift and broke into song, "[B]one of my bones and flesh of my flesh" (Gen. 2:23). He sees in her the completion of himself and is immediately in love.

But then they visit the tree of knowledge and Eve reaches out and takes the forbidden fruit. She turns to Adam and offers it to him. She was deceived, but he is in full command of his faculties.

What is he to do? She is the most beloved and beautiful of all the Creation and could be considered its acme! She is God's greatest gift and now is the strongest temptation! How can he turn his back on her? On *her*?

It is the same with us. Wealth, property, talent, our own children, even our purest motives can all be used by the devil to tempt and destroy us. Abraham's love for his son Isaac, the child of promise, had begun to border on the idolatrous, and God had to step in to remedy this false worship.[80]

We are so weak that the only solution is to give ourselves daily to Him that He might save us from ourselves. Even the best gifts can become idols and undo us.

---

[80] A.W. Tozer, *The Pursuit of God* (Camp Hill, PA: Christian Publications, 1993) p. 24.

NAKEDNESS PART 1
April 21

Genesis 3:7, "Then the eyes of both of them were opened, and they realized they were naked; so they sewed fig leaves together and made coverings for themselves."

The first result of sin was a realization of nakedness. Their eyes were indeed opened as the serpent had said. But it was not what they had expected at all.

This nakedness signaled the entrance of sin. They were no longer under the care of God and His covering wings but had stepped out of the protection of His will. They were on their own.

The contrast is a stark one. When they were first created, they *were* naked as the Bible says: "naked, and they felt no shame" (Gen. 2:25). But now they are naked *and* afraid, afraid of the very God who had created them, and would come to fellowship with them in the cool of that day, the preexistent Christ.

The nakedness revealed their new relationship with the universe. Utter aloneness, without protection, the prey of any who might wish to take advantage. Like slave girls, without family or relatives, free to be exploited at the whim of any who might take them. Especially were they now accessible to the wiles of the devil. And they were defenseless.

All evil, debauchery, disillusion, intemperance, death, disease and pain, all that God had excluded from paradise became their inheritance. Yes, they were naked indeed.

Despair would seem the only logical response. As Albert Camus once said, "There is but one truly serious philosophical problem and that is suicide."[81]

But God would not leave them alone in their nakedness. He stepped between them and death, the consequence of their act.

---

[81]"Quotable Quote," goodreads, https://1ref.us/1ig (accessed January 19, 2021).

THE SEED OF THE WOMAN
April 22

Genesis 3:15, KJV, "And I will put enmity between thee and the woman, and between thy seed and her seed; it shall bruise thy head, and thou shalt bruise his heel."

In many more primitive cultures, there was an agricultural metaphor for reproduction. Men were said to "plant" their seed in a woman's body, and a child would result from that planting. But in this way of thinking, women did not have seed, only men did.

Commentators have interpreted this verse to mean that Eve's children would hate snakes and crush them when they could.

Others have seen a reference to Christ in the seed, as the seed is referred to as a singular individual in the next phrase: "[H]e will crush" (Gen. 3:15).

It certainly seems to indicate Jesus in some way, for He is the One who did crush Satan at the cross, and who brought an end to sin by His death.

But the statement also gives a hint to us about the birth of Jesus. There was no "man's seed" in the virgin birth. God overshadowed Mary, and He that was born of her was divine in origin. As the angel said, "the holy one to be born will be called the Son of God" (Luke 1:35).

Thus, at the very beginning God gave a clue as to the nature of His Son. Even at the dawn of sin, there was evidence of His divine origin and miraculous birth.

It was not from man's seed that He would arise, but from this seed of the woman (Gen. 3:15).

God's ideas are far above ours. He graciously prepared us for the work He would do so that we would not reject it. Such is this statement about the seed of the woman.

THE CURSES PART 1
April 23

Genesis 3:14, "So the LORD God said to the serpent, 'Because you have done this, Cursed are you above all livestock.'"

Their shame prompted them to make garments of leaves and to hide among the trees of the garden. That evening God came at His usual time. Instead of running to meet Him they answered His call from among the trees.

"I heard you in the garden, and I was afraid because I was naked; so I hid" said Adam (Gen. 3:10).

"Who told you that you were naked? Have you eaten from the tree that I commanded you not to eat from?" God asked (Gen. 3:11).

Adam replied, "The woman you put here with me—she gave me some fruit from the tree, and I ate it" (Gen. 3:12).

God asked Eve, "What is this you have done?" (Gen. 3:13).

She answered, "The serpent deceived me, and I ate" (Gen. 3:13).

God then pronounced curses.

But He did not curse the human pair.

It may seem strange that He did not do such a thing, for they had just brought sin into a place He had created perfect. He knew what the future held for them and for His Son, but in this crisis, He would not curse them.

He first addressed the serpent. The snake was to eat of the dust of the ground, crawling on his belly (Gen. 3:14).

But most importantly, there would be enmity, antagonism and hostility between the serpent and the offspring of the woman (Gen. 3:15). And this is generally true even to the present day.

In reality, God was speaking to Satan, the metaphorical serpent. God said that a child of humanity, the weakest of all, one of the fallen race would crush his head (Gen. 3:15).

It is a stunning pronouncement. Satan appears to have gotten the upper hand. The humans would face pain and death, and become citizens of his kingdom, but One would arise from among them to defeat him so soundly it would be described as a crushing blow.

Amidst the curses was a ray of hope.

THE CURSES PART 2
April 24

Genesis 3:16, "To the woman he said, 'I will make your pains in childbearing very severe; with painful labor you will give birth to children. Your desire will be for your husband, and he will rule over you.'"

In reverse order, God addressed the woman after the serpent.

The serpent was cursed as was the ground, but the speech to the woman is not said to be a curse.

Apparently, God had not intended that childbirth be a painful process. But now it was to be so. Labor we call it.

Why did God make this pronouncement? It is really an extension of the warning that eating of the tree would bring death.

Women bring life into the world by bearing children. Without them there would be no life for the next generation. Before their disobedience, bringing life would have been easy. But now, like the man, living life would be hard and painful. By the sweat of her brow would she bear the fruit of her womb.

Secondly, her relationship with her husband would change. Instead of a relationship between equals, she would become subordinate.

Modern Eves bristle at such talk. They are independent and can take care of themselves. Why need they be subordinate to any man?

But modern western culture is an anomaly in this regard. In almost all other cultures and ages, women have had a subordinate role. Men are stronger and many cultures require that a woman be under a man's protection and that she submit to his will in most things.

And although modern Millies may resent this fact, it has been and remains one for most of the world. This was not God's will, but a result of the choice they made in taking the fruit. A sad result indeed.

THE CURSES PART 3
April 25

Genesis 3:17–19, "Cursed is the ground because of you; through painful toil you will eat food from it all the days of your life. It will produce thorns and thistles for you, and you will eat the plants of the field. By the sweat of your brow you will eat your food until you return to the ground, since from it you were taken; for dust you are and to dust you will return."

The last curse involved the ground, the domain where Adam spent his days in labor, having previously been given the responsibility to tend the Garden of Eden.

As with Eve, the curse involved the character of the labor of his life. That labor would now become grinding toil requiring sweat and strain to persuade a reluctant earth to yield its bounty. And even that bounty would be cursed, for instead of useful crops, the ground would produce a wounding tangle of useless growth requiring even more toil to control. Thus began the everlasting battle to wrest life from the soil.

Then, God spoke His final word to both of them.

"[F]or dust you are and to dust you will return" (Gen. 3:19).

God had animated the dust at the beginning, showing His great creative power. There was no hint then that a reversal of that act would occur, but with the entrance of sin, the miracle could not be maintained and the humans returned to their humble beginning: the dust of the ground. A humiliating and saddening prospect.

God had given them a beautiful home and wonderful tasks: gardening and the nurturing of life itself in birth and child rearing. But now these tasks would be difficult and wearying.

But even here, there was unforeseen blessing. As we say, "No pain, no gain." The curses even brought blessing because they came from the hand of God.

NAKEDNESS PART 2
April 26

Genesis 3:21, "The LORD God made garments of skin for Adam and his wife and clothed them."

With the conversation finished, one more thing remained. God called two of the animals of the garden to Him. We do not know which animals these were, but no doubt they were some of those Adam had named at the beginning. Most likely sheep or goats.

God took them and killed them. Then He removed their skins and fashioned clothing for the pair. Their crumpled bodies lay sprawled at the foot of the tree of knowledge, a grotesque testimony to the results of sin.

Their deaths were the first recorded deaths in earth's history, even the history of the universe. Two animals sacrificed so that the naked pair might be saved from their shame. What a shock it must have been to see them there, a memorial in flesh of their choice to disobey.

Did Adam and Eve watch as the drama played out? Did they see their companions' last breath as they gave their lives?

God demonstrated to the fallen couple that He was the answer to their nakedness of body and soul. Yes, they had rebelled, but He cared for them still.

And the clothing represented the righteousness that the Son was to give them with His life. He, too, died that we might be clothed. We exchange our nakedness for His clothing of righteousness. But His death was necessary to effect such a change.

Praise God for His unspeakable gift! He did not spare Himself that we might live. It is a wonderful God we have.

LIKE ONE OF US, KNOWING GOOD AND EVIL
PART 1
April 27

Genesis 3:22–23, "And the LORD God said, 'The man has now become like one of us, knowing good and evil. He must not be allowed to reach out his hand and take also from the tree of life and eat, and live forever.' So the LORD God banished him from the Garden of Eden."

This surprising comment by God would seem to confirm what Satan had said at the tree: they would become like God.

Was Satan right?

It was never God's intention that any of His creatures should know evil. He had withheld such knowing from humans but had allowed access to it through the tree of knowledge; but He warned them of the consequences of such knowledge.

But here God says that He Himself knew evil. God knew evil?

What could that mean?

God had set up the universe without evil, He had intentionally kept it to Himself. There was no tree of knowledge in heaven.

But Satan with his massive intellect had detected its possibility and decided that he would make it the basis of his kingdom. God had clearly kept it from the angels, so He could rule that realm Himself.

As Ellen White notes, when Satan began to speak of the law of God, it was a surprise to the angelic hosts. Their obedience had always been an act of love, not duty. So, it came as a new revelation that there was a law.[82]

Satan painted God's government with the darkest of hues and one-third of the angels—either from a desire for independence or for love of Satan—rebelled against God and came to know evil. Thus, evil entered the universe.

And man, by taking the fruit of the tree, came to know it as well. The history of the earth has demonstrated its baleful influence.

---

[82]Ellen G. White, *Thoughts from the Mount of Blessing* (Mountain View, CA: Pacific Press Publishing Association, 1896), p. 109.

LIKE ONE OF US, KNOWING GOOD AND EVIL
PART 2
April 28

Genesis 3:22-23, "And the LORD God said, 'The man has now become like one of us, knowing good and evil. He must not be allowed to reach out his hand and take also from the tree of life and eat, and live forever.' So the LORD God banished him from the Garden of Eden to work the ground from which he had been taken."

God had said that if the couple ate of the tree of knowledge, that they would die. But now God says that if He allowed them to eat of the tree of life, they would live forever. He thus is going to refuse them access to it.

What is going on here?

Was it eating of the tree that caused death or not being able to eat of the tree of life that caused death? Was it possible to sin and yet be immortal?

It must be so, for God worked to prevent it. An immortal sinner would have been a disaster for the universe. Think of a mafia don who could live forever and become more and more skillful at his craft. An immortal sinner would certainly have been a catastrophe.

It seems that man could have been such a creature if he had been able to eat of the tree forever. So, to protect the universe, God forbade it.

But what about Satan? Is he not an immortal sinner? He does not have access to the tree, but he has been alive for millennia.

He is not an immortal sinner. He can die and does not have a right to the tree of life as redeemed sinners will.

The taking of the forbidden fruit meant Adam and Eve would be denied the fruit from the tree of life. The eating of the tree of knowledge did not cause death but meant they would lose access to the tree of life.

Although it might seem cruel to deny them, life as immortal sinners would have been a worse curse. Eternal woe and pain. This is certainly not a gift at all.

LIKE ONE OF US, KNOWING GOOD AND EVIL
PART 3
April 29

Genesis 3:22, "And the LORD God said, 'The man has now become like one of us, knowing good and evil. He must not be allowed to reach out his hand and take also from the tree of life and eat, and live forever.'"

At the very beginning, God gives a hint, a revelation about the nature of man.

Man does not have an immortal soul. In order to live forever, he must have access to something that will give him that ability.

This revelation strikes at the foundation of spiritualism. This system proposes that men are immortal and that they live in a conscious spiritual state after death, and that they can be contacted by one who has the skill to do so—a medium.

But here, God prevents Adam and Eve from eating of the tree of life. He states that if they should eat, they would live forever as sinners. And He will prevent that tragedy.

So, God put a sword at the entrance to the garden to prevent any human from becoming an immortal sinner. Immortality was clearly shown to be a gift from God through the life-giving properties of the tree of life. Man does not have it naturally without access to the tree.

But men are charmed by the words of Satan, "You will not surely die" (Gen. 3:4, NKJV), and they believe them even to the sacrifice of their souls (see 1 Sam. 28).

God knows that we want eternal life. It is a desire buried in the depths of our souls. And it is longed for, especially when we face death.

But God would not have us deceived. We do not have immortality but may obtain it from Him.

Praise Him for His wonderful gift.

GOD'S RESPECT FOR OUR CHOICES
April 30

Genesis 3:6, "When the woman saw that the fruit ... was good for food and pleasing ... she took some and ate it."

Mark 10:21–22, "Jesus looked at him and loved him .... [and] said, ... '[C]ome, follow me.' At this the man's face fell. He went away sad, because he had great wealth."

> *He did not intervene at the tree, but allowed Eve to choose freely, though it meant that sin entered the world. The respect for her choice and personality, the integrity of her soul in its entirety was more important than sin entering the world. That is the length to which God will go to respect our personhood.*

The all-powerful God does not force His creatures. He has limited His Almightyness. It ends where our own souls begin. We are the work of His hands, but instead of forcing us to choose Him, He longs for the love that our free choice of Him gives.

Therefore, He respects our choices. He did not intervene at the tree, but allowed Eve to choose freely, though it meant that sin entered the world. The respect for her choice and personality, the integrity of her soul in its entirety was more important than sin entering the world. That is the length to which God will go to respect our personhood.

Jesus did not pursue the rich young man, trying to convince him of the value of obedience. He allowed the young man to choose freely. He did not nag him or pressure him until he relented. That is not how God deals with us.

This fact of His limiting Himself so that we might be free is a great gift and allows us to be like Him. We can think and do, and it will affect the world and eternity itself. We have an influence like He does.

With this influence comes responsibility. What we do makes a difference. We are not robots, but free agents with power over our destiny and even the destinies of others.

This is impetus to submit to Him that our words and deeds might be only an influence for good.

MY WAY OR THE HIGHWAY
May 1

Genesis 3:23, "So the LORD God banished him from the Garden of Eden to work the ground from which he had been taken."

Some say that God's attitude towards us is "My way or the highway." After all, isn't hell the place for the disobedient? Isn't death our lot unless we submit to His mighty hand?

But that is not God's attitude at all.

When Adam sinned, he was cast from the home God had made for him, but he was not destroyed. If God's attitude was "My way or the highway," there would have been no place for Adam in the universe. He would have simply vanished.

But instead, although he had rebelled, a *place* was made for him. The rest of the world became his home. He might live anywhere he wished except the garden; the whole creation was open to him and his offspring. And so, the world became populated by a race of sinners, just as it is today.

When Adam sinned, God withdrew, but He did not destroy him. God's command had been disobeyed and death became the lot of humanity. But he was provided a place to live and thrive.

It is like this: if a young person who has been supported by his parents rebels against them, he may be asked to leave the home. He has to make it on his own on the outside.

But what parent would build a house and provide for such a one? What parent would set up a place for them to live that they might survive doing not what the parent wanted but what the rebellious child wanted?

That is exactly what God did. He made a place for the rebellious pair to live and make it on their own. He gave it to them, withdrawing so that they might be free from His presence.

It was not "My way or the highway," but rather, "If you want to be free from Me, I will make that arrangement, but it will mean suffering and death. I did not wish that for you, but since you have so chosen, I cannot do other than this. I love you."

The attitude of God is love, not hate.

CHILDREN

May 2

Genesis 4:1, "Adam lay with his wife Eve, and she became pregnant and gave birth to Cain."

When Adam and Eve sinned, they were sent from the garden they had grown to love. Their garments of light were stripped from them by sin, and they were now clothed with the skins of animals God had slain so that they might be covered. The trees of the garden were no longer available, and now they had to scrap and scrape the ground for food instead of just picking it from the boughs of the trees.

They had arguments about the fall, each blaming the other for the tragedy, each retreating into his/her own miserable existence. We know this from the conversation they had with God in Genesis 3. What despair must have gripped their souls as they looked at the angel guarding the garden and the tree of life! Ellen White says that as they viewed the falling leaves of autumn that they wept as deeply as we now weep at the death of our loved ones.[83] All seemed darkness and desolation.

But God had reserved something to lighten the burden of His benighted people. There was another gift.

Some have said that two gifts were taken from the garden when they were cast out: the marriage relationship and the Sabbath. But God had another gift for them in the time of terrible anguish: the gift of children.

God had provided every gift in the garden: food, companionship and a delightful place to live. But these had been lost! They had to work for food, God no longer met with them and they were outside the garden.

But in their darkness, God sent another gift: the prattle, play, and laughter of little children that brighten our days when they come to dwell with us. This gift came after the fall as a precious token of God's love to the grief-stricken couple and to us as well. God was not done giving when He completed the Creation, but reserved one gift to be given in a terrible time of need. That is the God He is, sending blessing in times of cursing.

---

[83]Ellen G. White, *Patriarchs and Prophets* (Mountain View, CA: Pacific Press, 1890), p. 62.

THE DISCIPLINE OF CHILDREN
May 3

Proverbs 7:1–2, "My son, keep my words and store up my commands within you. Keep my commands and you will live; guard my teachings as the apple of your eye."

God created the family that children might learn the ways of life from their parents. Happiness in this life and our life in heaven depends to a large extent on the discipline of the home. Ellen White says this:

> In childhood and youth the character is most impressible. The power of self-control should then be acquired. By the fireside and at the family board influences are exerted whose results are as enduring as eternity. More than any natural endowment, the habits established in early years decide whether a man will be victorious or vanquished in the battle of life. Youth is the sowing time. It determines the character of the harvest, for this life and for the life to come.[84]

"Parents and teachers should aim so to cultivate the tendencies of the youth that at each stage of life they may represent the beauty appropriate to that period, unfolding naturally, as do the plants in the garden."[85]

The world offers the children much to distract them from the path of righteousness. Encouragement to study the Word of God daily, to search their characters for the weaknesses that we each have and to grip the hand of God that they might be victorious is a vision that a parent can give to a child. Watching and prayer are necessary to keep the vision clearly before them.

God is at the side of each parent to give power and insight into the characters of their beloved flock. Let us remember to ask His help in all we do.

God is at the side of each parent to give power and insight into the characters of their beloved flock. Let us remember to ask His help in all we do.

---
[84] Ellen G. White, *The Desire of Ages* (Mountain View, CA: Pacific Press, 1898), p. 101.
[85] Ellen G. White, *Education* (Mountain View, CA: Pacific Press, 1903), p. 107.

AN INVESTIGATIVE JUDGEMENT
May 4

Genesis 4:10, "The LORD said, 'What have you done? Listen! Your brother's blood cries out to me from the ground.'"

There are several instances of investigative judgements mentioned in the Scripture. The first was actually when God visited Adam and Eve in the garden where they hid (Gen. 3:11). He came down to meet with them, but it became an investigation when it was discovered they had sinned.

This instance mentioned in Genesis 4:10 is the second one. God comes down to see what has happened between the two brothers. Other investigations came at the flood, the cities of Sodom and Gomorrah and when Jesus Himself came to investigate the Jewish people at the time when He walked the earth.

God does investigations to see what is happening. He takes a personal interest in the goings on here. He does not rule from above on the situation, but comes Himself or sends an angel representative to take a careful look at the actions of the people.

Here God appears to Cain. "What have you done?" He answered to Cain's curt, "Am I my brother's keeper?" (Gen. 4:9–10).

God then notes the obvious, there is a blood stain on the soil. Cain is called to accounting and is sentenced.

It is just as we have here in our own courts. One is accused, then all the evidence is brought forward to see if the accusation is correct. It is all done in the open so that all may see.

The present investigative judgment in heaven is of the same nature. All the evidence in the books is brought forward. The myriad angel witnesses are there. They have seen it all and can attest to its veracity. Judgement is then pronounced as all the evidence is brought forward.

God is open about these things. He is not trying to hide anything but does it all transparently. It is the best way.

THE OFFERING OF CAIN
May 5

Genesis 4:5, "[B]ut on Cain and his offering he did not look with favor. So Cain was very angry, and his face was downcast."

When Cain came before God, he brought an offering of the best of the fruits of his labor. And he was offended that God did not accept them. Modern Cains do the same thing, and it is not infrequent.

I have seen children, when asked to do a certain task, do another, one they think the parent will appreciate, but not the task that was requested.

They may even act offended when the "gift of their obedience" is not acceptable to the parent.

In fact, the acts of such children are utter disobedience and rebellion.

Saul demonstrated the same attitude when God told him to destroy the Amalekites (1 Sam. 15:1–10). Saul said when Samuel approached, "The LORD bless you! I have carried out the LORD's instructions" (1 Sam. 15:13). But he had been utterly disobedient. Samuel answered, "Does the LORD delight in burnt offerings and sacrifices as much as in obeying the LORD? To obey is better than sacrifice" (1 Sam. 15:22).

This sin is of such a serious nature that the children must be taught to avoid it. It is the sin of presumption, that God does not mean what He says, and they can trifle with Him in obedience. God rewards the obedient. He will not reward presumption.

David prayed, "Keep back thy servant also from presumptuous sins; let them not have dominion over me: then shall I be upright, and I shall be innocent from the great transgression" (Ps. 19:13, KJV).

The problem with presumption is that one feels they have obeyed when they have not. It is a deep self-deception and very difficult for the individual to discern. Prayerful appeal to the Spirit is essential.

DOES GOD CHANGE HIS MIND?
May 6

Malachi 3:6, ESV, "For I the LORD do not change."

Genesis 6:6, "The Lord regretted that he had made human beings on the earth, and his heart was deeply troubled."

Does God ever change His mind?

The two verses above seem at first to contradict each other. Malachi's verse says He does not change, but Moses says God repented (as the KJV says) of what He had done in creating man.

It is God's purposes that never change. He is true to Himself and to His holy character, making no compromise with sin or evil.

However, His methods may change. He may fulfill His will by a different strategy than He originally set out to do.

The world had become so full of sin and suffering that God became sad that He had created it. His heart was wounded and pained. He could not let the suffering continue, so He called Noah to build an escape for those that would believe so that He could destroy the rest.

How can we explain the flood? It seems that God failed and wiped out the mistake. A sort of divine initiated holocaust.

But in reality, it was only destruction that was able to end the suffering. The people were like those in Germany who killed the Jews. They had no compunction to stop their wickedness. Only death would do it. So, in this example, God changed His method of dealing with humankind. But His purpose always remained the same.

Let us not stand in judgement of God because of our small minds, but allow Him to do His will as He sees fit, without concerning ourselves with His integrity. He will always be true to that.

THE FLOOD
May 7

Genesis 6:5, 11, "The LORD saw how great the wickedness of the human race had become on the earth, and that every inclination of the thoughts of the human heart was only evil all the time .... Now the earth was corrupt in God's sight and was full of violence."

The flood seems to show the failure of God to control the wickedness of men, even a millennium after the Creation. The Bible says the thoughts of men's hearts were evil continually and that the earth was full of violence (Gen. 6:5, 11).

One could argue that this is proved by the fossil record: the dinosaurs include some of the most violent creatures that the earth has seen. The sea also contained huge, shark-like creatures whose teeth reveal that they grew upwards of seventy feet—three times the largest great white shark. This animal had the strongest bite of any animal that has ever existed.

The earth was indeed full of violence and so God swept it away with a flood.

Some feel that God will not intervene to kill or punish mankind, that He will not personally destroy, but only allows men to suffer consequences. But the flood seems to indicate that He will do so if He sees that there is no other way to stem an overwhelming tide of wickedness. It seems that the world would have destroyed itself if God had not done something to stop the violence.

True, He resorted to violence to do that, but to allow complete self-destruction would not have allowed for salvation. He had to bring the antediluvian world to an end, in mercy to mankind. It was humanity's only hope for future survival.

THE TOWER OF BABEL
May 8

Genesis 11:7, "Come, let us go down and confuse their language so they will not understand each other."

The Tower of Babel shows two things about the ways of God: His willingness to intervene to keep men from joining in a grand conspiracy to rule the earth and His creativity in dealing with the problem. It also shows how vulnerable we are, and how easily He could thwart any conspiratorial moves by men to unite all into one world government.

Men had joined together to build a tower that would reach heaven. Instead of scattering to the far corners of the earth, men decided to stay on the plain of Shinar and form a single government to rule all men. The danger here was that men would revert to the same wickedness that had characterized the days before the flood.

So, God came down to visit. Another investigative judgement. He saw the pride of their hearts and did a simple maneuver. He caused them to be unable to understand one another. That is, He confused their tongues.

It is a stroke of genius to meet the problem thus. The men would gather together in language groups that could understand one another. It was a simple process.

And since then, men have been striving to join in alliances that would be detrimental to godliness. Men desire control over their fellow creatures that they might concentrate power. But God has checked them for the most part by the simple confusing of their tongues.

Section 6

Abraham, Isaac and Jacob

How did God deal with the patriarchs?
What can we learn from His interactions with them?

"The God of Abraham praise, Who reigns enthroned above;
Ancient of everlasting days, And God of love;
Jehovah! Great I AM! By earth and heaven confessed;
I bow and bless the sacred name, Forever blest."[86]

---

[86]Thomas Olivers, "The God of Abraham Praise," *The Seventh-day Adventist Hymnal* (Hagerstown, MD: Review and Herald, 1985).

THE CALL OF ABRAHAM
May 9

Genesis 12:1–3, "The LORD God said to Abram .... 'I will make you into a great nation, and I will bless you; I will make your name great, and you will be a blessing .... [A]nd all peoples on earth will be blessed through you.'"

Why did God choose Abraham's descendants to be His special people?

This "choosing" of a people to be His was fraught with difficulties. Could they not become proud of this choice, thinking they were better than the rest of humankind? Envy by others could lead to persecution and even destruction. And if a certain group is known as God's favorite, what of the rest of us?

But it seems God felt the risks were worth taking, so He chose Abraham to be the father of the faithful, and his people would be a certain treasure to Him.

The choice seems a pragmatic one. After the people at Babel were scattered, corruption again became the norm. And so, God chose to concentrate His love on this one people so they could be a blessing to the world and give evidence of His love for all mankind. His love would be poured out on them so that the whole world could see that choosing to follow Him was a blessing.

God states the goals of this choice in the promise to Abraham in Genesis 12:

1. Abraham's descendants would become a great nation (verse 2).
2. His name would be great, and he would be blessed (Ibid.).
3. All the world would be blessed through him (verse 3).

And 3,000 years later, these things have come to pass, a testimony to God's faithfulness.

ABRAHAM'S WEAK FAITH
May 10

Genesis 20:2, 13:

> *[A]nd there Abraham said of his wife Sarah, "She is my sister." Then Abimelek king of Gerar sent for Sarah and took her .... [Abraham replied,] "And when God had me wander from my father's household, I said to her, 'This is how you can show your love to me: Everywhere we go, say of me, "He is my brother."'"*

Chapter 20 of Genesis tells of Abraham's dealing with Abimelek and the lie he had been telling for years so that the surrounding people would not kill him for his beautiful wife.

Usually they avoided trouble, but this time a local king called Abraham's bluff, and because he did not object, Sarah became a member of his harem.

Now this occurred just after God had promised the couple a son. Sarah might even then have been pregnant! So, by taking her, Abimelek put into question the patrimony of Isaac and the whole plan of God. Abraham's habitual dissembling about his wife jeopardized the promise. Isaac would have been considered the son of Abimelek.

But God intervened by sending a dream to the pagan king, preventing him from sin. He returned Sarah to Abraham with a rebuke about his own innocence. And Abraham told him of his habitual practice of telling strangers that Sarah was his sister.

And the amazing thing is that this episode is never mentioned again. Not in Romans or Galatians or Hebrews. Abraham is portrayed as the father of the faithful, when in fact, there were some incidents of faithlessness—even habitual ones.

God is gracious with us, overlooking the foibles and failings of His beloved ones, and even preventing sin in pagans. It is a grace we can depend upon.

ABRAHAM AND ABIMELEK
May 11

Genesis 20:6, "Then God said to him in the dream, 'Yes, I know you did this with a clear conscience, and so I have kept you from sinning against me.'"

Abraham had been traveling through Canaan when he came to a place called Gerar, and there told the local king, Abimelek, that Sarah was his sister. Abimelek took her to be one of his concubines, apparently without much protest from Abraham.

But God visited Abimelek in a dream, telling him to return her to her husband. Abimelek proclaimed his innocence, which God recognized. Sarah was given back to Abraham unharmed and unviolated.

The amazing part of this story is not so much the weakness of Abraham, though that is clear enough by his habit of saying she was his sister when there was any threat to his safety because of her. But what is a cause of wonder is how close God was to even the heathen king.

In the dream, Abimelek argued his innocence, and God told him that He had prevented him from sin by somehow keeping Sarah from him.

God had kept him from sin. He kept a heathen from sin! Now Sarah was to be the mother of the faithful and was protected in spite of Abraham's weakness. But God was with Abimelek as well, preventing him from sinning.

We must abandon the idea that God is not near us in all circumstances. Even this heathen chieftain had God near. We have difficulty believing what Paul said on Mars Hill, when he noted that God was not far from each one of us (Acts 17:27).

If God was near Abimelek, He is certainly near us in all situations. If only we would turn our minds to heaven, we could avoid much sin and suffering.

SODOM AND GOMORRAH PART 1
May 12

Genesis 18:32, "Then he said, 'May the Lord not be angry, but let me speak just once more. What if only ten [righteous people] can be found there?' He answered, 'For the sake of ten, I will not destroy it.'"

The story of Sodom and Gomorrah is full of insight into the ways of God.

God heard they were wicked but decided to come and see for Himself, not because He didn't know, but because He is a God who is intimately involved in earthly matters.

After speaking with Abraham about Isaac, God, noting that Abraham would become a great nation, decides to reveal His plan. The cry of abuse from them has reached heaven itself, and God will see if destruction is indicated.

Abraham contends with God. "You are judge of the earth! You would not destroy the righteous with the wicked, would you?" (Gen. 18:25, paraphrase).

Then Abraham starts asking if God would spare the city for fifty people and then bargains down to ten. God allows for each amount, showing His willingness to save the wicked and the just. It is as if He mentioned His plan just so Abraham could plead for the people there.

But ten righteous people could not be found. The angels take the hands of Lot's lingering family and deliver them from the city. Lot's wife, turning back to look at her beloved home, becomes a pillar of salt (Gen. 19:26).

How often are we interceding for the wicked as Abraham did? How often do we pray for mercy for the utterly wicked? God would have spared the city for ten. Our cities are full of wickedness. Do we bring them to God and then act with Christ to save them? Abraham did.

God longed to answer the prayer of Abraham but could not. He saved who He could. It is a wonder of grace that He did.

SODOM AND GOMORRAH PART 2
May 13

Luke 17:26, 28, "Just as it was in the days of Noah …. It was the same in the days of Lot. People were eating and drinking, buying and selling, planting and building. But the day Lot left Sodom, fire and sulfur rained down from heaven and destroyed them all."

These two men, Noah and Lot, represent two classes of Christians who live at the end of time. Each one saved himself, but Noah saved his family while Lot saved himself alone.

The message of mercy to the antediluvians was given for 120 years, the one for Sodom was given for twelve hours. Noah invested all in the ark and took his goods with him. Lot lost all he had invested in Sodom, leaving destitute and taking up abode in a cave.

Why the strange difference?

The answer is clear by the acts of each at the critical time at the end of their ministry. When the ark was done, Noah entered immediately, having put all he had into it. Lot on the other hand, lingered in Sodom. He was loath to leave, and the angels had to take him and his family out by the hand. However, his wife's heart remained in the city; she could not resist looking back at the place she loved, and she was lost to him. And his daughters acted the part of Sodomites, their offspring being wicked people who persecuted Israel and worshiped their gods with child sacrifices.

What a warning! Lot pitched his tent toward Sodom, then moved into the city, investing all his means there. Then when the messengers came, no one wanted to leave, dawdling at the place destined for destruction. We may do the same if we are not careful.[87]

---
[87]Ovid Redulescu, Sermon, April 2020.

THE SACRIFICE OF ISAAC PART 1
May 14

Genesis 22:1–2, "Some time later God tested Abraham. He said to him, 'Abraham!' 'Here I am,' he replied. Then God said, 'Take your son, your only son, whom you love—Isaac—and go to the region of Moriah. Sacrifice him there as a burnt offering on a mountain I will show you.'"

This shocking command out of nowhere, after a long fruitful life, comes as a startling coda to the life of Abraham. Yet it is one of the most precious gifts he has given to us.

"[Sacrifice] your son, your only son, whom you love." How each word must have pierced his heart! Was all the anxiety, the pain, the hope, the satisfaction and love to be spilled on the soil of a barren slope far away? How could he?

The record is spare and sparse. Abraham packs his mule, speaks to the boy and sets out for Moriah. Nothing is said until the walk up the mountain when Isaac asked about the sacrifice. "God himself will provide" (Gen. 22:8), is the profound answer.

And at the summit, Abraham raises the knife, about to carry out the command of God, when, indeed the Lord does provide.

Abraham's act gives us insight into the soul of God when, on another mountain, no one could stop the sacrifice of His Son for us. Such was real provision.

Pagans sacrificed their children to their gods to appease their wrath. And it seems God's command expresses His desire to be the sole recipient of Abraham's devotion. But the lamb shows the real desire of God. He Himself will provide the Sacrifice for sin, making a way of escape for our children and ourselves.

On that mountain long ago, we got a glimpse of the sacrifice of heaven. And it was all for us.

THE SACRIFICE OF ISAAC PART 2
May 15

Genesis 22:2, "Then God said, 'Take your son, your only son, whom you love—Isaac— and go to the region of Moriah. Sacrifice him there as a burnt offering.'"

There are times when God does something that seems to violate the laws He has given us, and even His character as revealed in Scripture. The sacrifice of Isaac is such an instance.

In Leviticus 18:21 God forbade the Israelites to sacrifice their children to Molech, the god of the Ammonites. Yet here, Abraham is commanded to sacrifice his son on an altar of stone.

Other instances where God seems to disregard His laws are His command to Hosea to marry a prostitute and the story of Job, who though righteous, was punished as if a great sinner.

We must pay special attention to these episodes in God's Word, for He is attempting to get our attention as He could in no other way.

With Abraham, God had a man who would obey faithfully. And so, God gave an object lesson that would reveal the sacrifice He would make, where there would be no lamb to prevent the death of His Son.

Hosea's home was shattered by Gomer's perfidy. And so, Hosea could write firsthand about the pain of betrayal and the piercing of the heart of God by His people. Job's experience revealed the truth about righteous living. It would not always bring blessing on this earth but would be honored in heaven.

These events should be our special study. God has gone to great lengths to give us these lessons, even to the apparent violation of His own laws. He has done that to get our attention, as we are so often dull of hearing.

He will reward our study with keen insights.

THE MARRIAGE OF ISAAC
May 16

Read Genesis 24:67 to Genesis 27:13.

The marriage of the patriarch Isaac finds its ending in a sad story of alienation.

Abraham prayed for a wife for his beloved son, and by a providential chain of events, Rebekah agreed to leave her home in Mesopotamia, and return to wed the son of this tribal chief far far away from her native land.

And Isaac loved her and she became his wife (Gen. 24:67).

But over the years, something happened to that love. The two of them began to work at cross purposes, one favoring Esau, the other Jacob. Now they were so far from one another that they no longer shared their inner thoughts but worked independently in a struggle of wills.

How long had Rebekah been listening secretly at the tent door to frustrate her husband's wishes? And how long had Isaac known of the secret conniving of his beloved wife? Such scheming does not come between two people in a trice, but over a period of at least months. But I suspect it had gone on for years.

Each of us, if we are married, can fall to the temptation to keep secrets from our beloved, plan for things that we know they would not agree with, work to do what we want to do without the input from our partner. It is a huge mistake and the results are shown to us in this marriage from so long ago.

The alienation even extended to the time of Christ when Herod, a descendant of Esau, ruled over Israel, and sought to kill the promised Seed of the woman, the Anointed One. How our little peccadilloes turn back and bite even our loved ones who outlive us!

Can we so love that we will be open with one another, vulnerable to love? May God help us to do so.

A DYSFUNCTIONAL FAMILY
May 17

Genesis 27:46; 28:8, "Then Rebekah said to Isaac, 'I'm disgusted with living because of these Hittite women. If Jacob takes a wife from among the women of this land, from Hittite women like these, my life will not be worth living.' Esau then realized how displeasing the Canaanite women were to his father Isaac."

Rebekah entered Isaac's life through an answer to prayer. She was sent as a comfort to him upon his mother's death. And he loved her.

But over the years something changed. The two, instead of supporting one another, became silent competitors, each choosing a son as their cause.

Then, when Jacob obtained the birthright by cunning, the break became public. The rift between the boys became permanent. Esau would kill Jacob when an opportunity presented itself. Jacob had to flee to save his life (Gen. 27:41).

Then Esau brought heathen women into the home to be his wives. They brought with them the basis for constant friction. God is worshiped in one part of the camp, while in the other, heathen rites were performed. It is a hard thing for parents when a child goes astray, but when he stays in the home and daily reminds them of his rebellion and their mistakes, joy is well-nigh impossible.

So it was in Isaac's home after Jacob fled. The warring parents were left with the wicked son, who had no interest in godly things. Their lives became a drudgery. A chasm of distrust separated them, leaving each lonely and bereft.

God will not prevent such situations even after answering our prayers, if we will not come to Him daily, surrendering our wills to His and letting Him have His way.

He would save us from ourselves.

JACOB AND RACHEL
May 18

Genesis 29:20, "So Jacob served seven years to get Rachel, but they seemed like only a few days to him because of his love for her."

The contrast between Isaac's marriage and Jacob's is striking. The reason Jacob is sent off to find a wife is that Rebekah is so disturbed by Esau's heathen wives, and Isaac and Rebekah do not want to have to endure another such problem. And Esau is so enraged by Jacob's deception that Jacob must flee for his life. There is no prayer mentioned and Jacob leaves home with no resources. He has to work for Rachel, as he has no wealth whatsoever.

And yet, he falls madly in love with her. It seems his love is based on sexual attraction as the NIV says, "[she] had a lovely figure and was beautiful" (Gen. 29:17). Is that the most appropriate way to choose a life mate?

I have not recommended such a strategy to anyone: most men do not need to be advised regarding such things, as it comes more or less naturally, but it was not like Abraham's way with Isaac at all!

But the bond formed was deep and enduring, unlike that of Isaac and Rebekah. As Jacob's long and eventful life was coming to an end, so great was his love for her, that the one thing he remembered was burying Rachel near Ephrath (Gen. 48:7).

Their secret of success is not revealed to us. But apparently they kept an open communion that allowed them to speak truly and frankly with one another, keeping nothing secret as Isaac and Rebekah did. The Bible does not show them as perfect by any means, but they had a wonderful marriage, a great blessing to anyone who has experienced such a boon.

Jacob was attracted to her for her figure and beauty—not character! But on this rather weak foundation, they built a wonderful edifice. We need not be discouraged if our endeavors are not always perfect, they still may be successful.

THE NIGHT OF WRESTLING
May 19

Genesis 32:24–28:

> *So Jacob was left alone, and a man wrestled with him till daybreak. When the man saw that he could not overpower him, he touched the socket of Jacob's hip so that his hip was wrenched as he wrestled with the man. Then the man said, "Let me go, for it is daybreak." But Jacob replied, "I will not let you go unless you bless me." The man asked him, "What is your name?" "Jacob," he answered. Then the man said, "Your name will ... be ... Israel, because you have struggled with God and with humans and have overcome."*

What can we learn of God through this incident in the life of Jacob?

First, God was not actually against Jacob here. If He had been, Jacob would not have survived (think of Ananias and Sapphira in Acts 5:5, 10). God came to meet Jacob here and bless him—and bless him He did.

Second, this episode shows how God stoops to meet us. Jacob did not meet God like Abraham did, at a meal, but rather at a crisis in his life when he was ready to fight. God and Jacob had a struggle, Jacob thought it was an enemy, but it was really a Friend all along. On occasion, we too must wrestle with our God. Not because He is such a hard God, but because we have such misconceptions that God must deal with.

God comes so unexpectedly! He came to Abraham as a travel-weary stranger, tarrying at his tent. Here He comes as an enemy to kill in the night (at least that is what Jacob thought). Both Abraham and Jacob were visited when they were not expecting Jehovah to appear. The same could happen to us.

God is free to come to us in any way He may choose. It is our privilege to be ready for Him.

JOSEPH
May 20

Genesis 40:15, "I was forcibly carried off from the land of the Hebrews, and even here I have done nothing to deserve being put in a dungeon."

Genesis 50:20, "You intended to harm me, but God intended it for good to accomplish what is now being done, the saving of many lives."

The life of Joseph is the Old Testament demonstration of Paul's encouraging words in Romans 8:28, "And we know that in all things God works for the good of those who love him, who have been called according to his purpose."

It is near impossible to believe that being sold into slavery by your own family could be used to work good, but that is what Paul and Joseph agreed was the result of that wicked act.

God does not promise that there will be no pain and even despair. At times, circumstances may look most unpromising and there may seem to be no way of escape.

After Joseph had interpreted the dream of the cupbearer, he pleaded with him to say a word to pharaoh, but in the joy of his restoration, the man forgot all about Joseph. Days turned to weeks which turned to months and years. Ellen White says, "For two years longer Joseph remained a prisoner. The hope that had been kindled in his heart gradually died out, and to all other trials was added the bitter sting of ingratitude."[88]

Betrayal, imprisonment, financial disaster, the rupture of the family and all manner of loss may come upon us. Discouragement and doubt may dog our steps. Hope may present no path forward, yet Joseph's words must not be forgotten: "You [his brothers] intended to harm me, but God intended it for good" (Gen. 50:20).

God's good intentions may masquerade as the works of evil men. But we must recognize their true character: His workers for good.

---

[88] Ellen G. White, *Patriarchs and Prophets* (Mountain View, CA: Pacific Press, 1890), p. 219.

Section 7

The Way of Grace

How might we come into fellowship with the holy God of the universe?

"Amazing grace! how sweet the sound,
That saved a wretch like me!
I once was lost, but now am found,
Was blind, but now I see."[89]

---

[89]John Newton, "Amazing Grace," *The Seventh-day Adventist Hymnal* (Hagerstown, MD: Review and Herald, 1985).

THE WAY OF SALVATION
May 21

Isaiah 45:22, "Turn to me and be saved, all you ends of the earth; for I am God, and there is no other."

God has made a way of salvation for us. He has made every provision so that we might be in heaven. He has called the whole earth to turn to Him so that they may not die but have life. But sometimes there is confusion and uncertainty about just how to go about obtaining this blessing from God. How can we know what we must do?

The Jews came to Jesus one day, asking Him, "What must we do to do the works God requires?" Jesus answered, "The work of God is this: to believe in the one he has sent" (John 6:28–29).

Paul and Jesus both agree that it is faith that saves us, that is believing in and trusting the One God has sent—Jesus. If we do that, we will be in heaven. It was all that was required of the thief on the cross whom Jesus saved at the ninth hour.

So all that is involved in this process might be understood more clearly, the following seventeen entries go over the way God has set up His plan of redemption, and some details that are often misunderstood.

God has not made the way complicated, but so simple that children can understand and sometimes accept intuitively because they have the ability to have faith in ones they trust. They then transfer that faith to God, who is ready to make them members of the heavenly family. Adults often have a harder time because they no longer trust intuitively. But all can be saved: God has made provision for everyone.

THE NATURE OF SIN
May 22

Genesis 3:22, "And the LORD God said, 'The man has now become like one of us, knowing good and evil. He must not be allowed to reach out his hand and take also from the tree of life and eat, and live forever.'"

When God made the Garden of Eden, sin was not there. But through the tree of knowledge, Adam could experience sin.

God had excluded it by His choice during His creating. And by excluding it, He excluded death as well: death is a part of the thing called sin. When He made the world, His proclamation was that it was good, even very good (Gen. 1:31). There was nothing bad about it.

And yet, when Adam and Eve fell, God states that they had become like Him in some way, knowing good and evil. What is the nature of this thing called sin?

> *God has put before us life and death, belief and unbelief. Let us choose to believe Him and save ourselves and by example, some who see our lives of faith.*

The most basic definition is that whatever is not of faith is sin (Rom. 14:23).

Thus, the sin of Adam and Eve was unbelief. They did not believe God. They did not accept that He had only their good at heart and instead believed Satan's accusation that God was withholding something good from them: the knowledge of evil. This called into doubt the reason for the command of God to not eat of the tree. After all God had done, creating a beautiful home for them, giving them every gift, even companionship with Him, they doubted His love! And that doubt brought sin because they acted on their disbelief.

Jesus in His life demonstrated just the opposite. Though called on to endure the cross, He believed God's will was the best and would lead to only good. Adam's temptation, by contrast, was utterly easy.

God has put before us life and death, belief and unbelief. Let us choose to believe Him and save ourselves and by example, some who see our lives of faith.

GRACE PART 1
May 23

2 Corinthians 5:19, "God was reconciling the world to himself in Christ, not counting people's sins against them. And He has committed to us the message of reconciliation."

We are saved by grace through faith (Eph. 2:8).

Grace is the attitude of God toward us. He does not intend evil toward us, but rather desires our good. His grace made Him provide a way for us, by the sacrifice of Himself, that He might be reconciled to us.

If we would realize this attitude and how all-encompassing it is toward us, we would not hesitate to come to Him and enter His presence. He has won for us this right and will not deny any that wish to take advantage of it.

A wonderful example of this grace is the thief on the cross. Mark tells us that both thieves were mocking Jesus when they were first crucified (Mark 15:32). But at some point, one began to realize Jesus' divine and gracious nature.

Convinced of this, he made an utterly audacious request for one being punished by death for admitted evil: "[R]emember me when you come into your kingdom" (Luke 23:42). How dare anyone in a position of such guilt ask such a thing? He was a thief who had just confessed the righteousness of his punishment (Luke 23:41).

But Jesus did not hesitate, "Truly I tell you, today [while I am dying here] you will be with me in paradise" (Luke 23:43).

The thief recognized a grace Jesus could not hide and cast himself on it. He was not disappointed. He is the only individual in the New Testament that we know for certain will be in heaven.

We may take advantage of this grace as well. Our guilt often keeps us from coming, but the thief was wiser than we are in this regard. No sin can bar us unless we allow it.

Let us come and be satisfied.

GRACE PART 2
May 24

Matthew 22:8–12:

> Then he said to his servants, "The wedding banquet is ready, but those I invited did not deserve to come. So go to the street corners and invite to the banquet anyone you find." So the servants went out into the streets and gathered all the people they could find, the bad as well as the good, and the wedding hall was filled with guests. But when the king came in to see the guests, he noticed a man there who was not wearing wedding clothes. He asked, "How did you get in here without wedding clothes, friend?" The man was speechless.

This parable (Matt. 22:1–14, the parable of the wedding banquet) tells of God's grace. The first guests refused the invitation, so the good and bad were called and the banquet hall was filled. So, God's invitation to all, bad or good, is spread to the world.

But then at the entrance, a wedding garment was supplied to each guest. This is the robe of Christ's righteousness, a righteousness that we do not have, but that is given to us, imputed.

This is real grace. I receive a robe of righteousness, not of my own making, but of His doing. It is not my performance that matters, but His. There is a sense that I must stop looking at my own actions and look to His ability to act in my behalf. I can stop worrying about my goodness and accept His.

He will then work in me to do His good pleasure (Phil. 2:13). My only need is to give myself to Him and let Him do the work.

Then in heaven, I am clothed with a garment of righteousness as bright and pure as the sun, given to me by my Savior at great cost (Rev. 19:8). Oh, what love I am shown!

THE IMPORTANCE OF THE WILL PART 1
May 25

Revelation 22:17, "The Spirit and the bride say, 'Come!' And let the one who hears say, 'Come!' Let the one who is thirsty come; and let the one who wishes take the free gift of the water of life."

Many are inquiring, "*How* am I to make the surrender of myself to God?" You desire to give yourself to Him, but you are weak in moral power, in slavery to doubt, and controlled by the habits of your life of sin. Your promises and resolutions are like ropes of sand. You cannot control your thoughts, your impulses, your affections. The knowledge of your broken promises and forfeited pledges weakens your confidence in your own sincerity, and causes you to feel that God cannot accept you; but you need not despair. What you need to understand is the true force of the will. This is the governing power in the nature of man, the power of decision, or of choice. Everything depends on the right action of the will. The power of choice God has given to men; it is theirs to exercise. You cannot change your heart, you cannot of yourself give to God its affections; but you can *choose* to serve Him. You can give Him your will; He will then work in you to will and to do according to His good pleasure. Thus your whole nature will be brought under the control of the Spirit of Christ; your affections will be centered upon Him, your thoughts will be in harmony with Him.

Desires for goodness and holiness are right as far as they go; but if you stop here, they will avail nothing. Many will be lost while hoping and desiring to be Christians. They do not come to the point of yielding the will to God. They do not now *choose* to be Christians.[90]

---
[90] Ellen G. White, *Steps to Christ* (Mountain View, CA: Pacific Press, 1892), pp. 47–48.

THE IMPORTANCE OF THE WILL PART 2
May 26

Ezekiel 36:26, "I will give you a new heart and put a new spirit in you; I will remove from you your heart of stone and give you a heart of flesh."

Many of us expect, when we give our hearts to God, that we will feel different. But it is not necessarily so. There may be no ecstasy of feeling. There may be no feeling at all.

When I walked down the aisle after I was married, there was no feeling of change. I felt the same as before. But there was actually a huge change. I was married! Now on that day, with the stress and strain of the ceremony, the "feeling" was not there. But that did not change the fact of my marriage.

Ellen White says this about the giving of our wills to God: "You have confessed your sins, and in heart put them away. You have resolved to give yourself to God. Now go to Him, and ask that He will wash away your sins and give you a new heart. Then believe that He does this *because He has promised* .... *Do not wait to feel that you are made whole,* but say, 'I believe it; it *is* so, not because I feel it, but because God has promised.'"[91]

God's promises are true, whether we feel them or not. When Samaria was surrounded by the forces of Aram, Elisha's servant feared for the worst. He felt afraid, but in fact when his eyes were opened, he realized the fear was baseless, for the chariots of God surrounded the army of the enemy (2 Kings 6:17).

It is not the feeling that counts, it is the reality. If we move out onto the promises, they will support us. He has promised after all.

---

[91] Ibid., pp. 49–51, emphasis added.

REPENTANCE

May 27

Mark 1:15, "Repent and believe the good news!"

There is a misconception about repentance that has kept many from coming to the Savior where they might receive grace to help in their time of need (Heb. 4:16).

That idea is that we must first repent before we come into God's presence. If we are repentant then He will hear our prayers and allow us to come to Him. This is a serious error.

Jesus said in Matthew 11:28–29, "Come to me, all you who are weary and burdened, and I will give you rest. Take my yoke upon you and learn from me ... and you will find rest for your souls." He did not say, "Repent and you will find rest."

We cannot generate repentance on our own. But we can come to Him when weary and burdened. And He will receive us.

Peter said in Acts 5:31, "God exalted him [Jesus]... that he might bring Israel to repentance and forgive their sins."

Here is what Ellen White says: "I ask, How can I present this matter as it is? The Lord Jesus imparts all the powers, all the grace, all the penitence, all the inclination, all the pardon of sins, in presenting His righteousness for man to grasp by living faith—which is also the gift of God."[92]

> *God's grace is wonderful in its scope. Even repentance is given to unrepentant sinners if they will come to Him.*

Is repentance needed for salvation from sin? Yes, absolutely necessary. If we cling to sin, and do not wish to turn from it, then we will not be able to enter the kingdom.

But we cannot become repentant on our own. God, however, will give it as a gift and is very willing to give it if we will receive it. It only remains for us to accept.

God's grace is wonderful in its scope. Even repentance is given to unrepentant sinners if they will come to Him.

What is keeping you from taking that step? You are weary, burdened and sad. He will give all that is needed. Even repentance.

---
[92]Ellen G. White, *Faith and Works* (Nashville, TN: Southern Publishing Association, 1979), p. 24.

YE MUST BE BORN AGAIN
May 28

John 3:3, "Very truly I tell you, no one can see the kingdom of God unless they are born again."

When I was young, this statement troubled me. What could it possibly mean? Fortunately, Ellen White has given a description of her experience to help us.

She grew up in a devout Methodist family. At the age of twelve or so, she began to feel anxious of her own salvation. She did not feel accepted by God and spent days in anguish about salvation.

At about this time she attended a meeting where the speaker told those torn between hope and fear to turn to Jesus for relief. That day she put her trust in Him.

She says: "[S]uddenly, my burden left me, and my heart was light. At first a feeling of alarm came over me, and I tried to resume my load of distress. It seemed to me that I had no right to feel joyous and happy. But Jesus seemed very near to me; I felt able to come to Him with all my griefs, misfortunes, and trials, even as the needy ones came to Him for relief when He was upon earth."[93]

The sun shone with brighter rays and nature seemed to rejoice with her, but a bit later she fell into despondency when she dwelt on the holiness of God. She says, "Could the truth have been presented to me as I now understand it, much perplexity and sorrow would have been spared me. If the love of God had been dwelt upon more, and His stern justice less, the beauty and glory of His character would have inspired me with a deep and earnest love for my Creator."[94]

Thinking on these things will do the same for us. We will change by beholding. We may start today.

---

[93] Ellen G. White, *Life Sketches of Ellen G. White* (Mountain View, CA: Pacific Press, 1915), p. 23.
[94] Ibid., p. 31.

LOOKING TO JESUS
May 29

Hebrews 12:2, "[F]ixing our eyes on Jesus, the pioneer and perfector of faith."

There is a secret to the Christian life that so many miss. This secret is God's way of changing us to the faithful Christians He would have us to be. And it is so simple, but so often overlooked.

The secret is to fix our eyes on Jesus and nowhere else.

We are often tempted to look at ourselves and the lives we live. When we do this, two errors are possible.

First, we may think our performance is quite exemplary. We do the right things, pay our tithe, act properly, even take care of the less fortunate and downtrodden. This leads to pride in what we are or do. So, instead of looking to Jesus, we look to ourselves and become proud, feeling we need nothing.

> *There is a secret to the Christian life that so many miss. This secret is God's way of changing us to the faithful Christians He would have us to be. And it is so simple, but so often overlooked. The secret is to fix our eyes on Jesus and nowhere else.*

More commonly, we look at ourselves and see that we have been unable to do what God has commanded. We have so utterly failed that we feel that there is no way that we could possibly enter heaven. We are just too evil.

Both of these mistakes result from ignoring the verse above.

The Bible says our righteousness is as filthy rags (Isa. 64:6). Why would we look to rags for cleanliness?

No, it is to Jesus that we can look for righteousness. He said in the Beatitudes that those who hunger and thirst after it will be filled (Matt. 5:6). Again, if we come to Him, He will take care of this deficiency as well!

There is no use looking to ourselves for this, but looking to Jesus turns us from our weaknesses to One who is an adequate Savior, who has dealt with sinners for centuries and can succor us in His love.

Let us then turn from ourselves and to Him who can save.

FAITH PART 1
May 30

Matthew 17:20–21, "Truly I tell you, if you have faith as small as a mustard seed, you can say to this mountain, 'Move from here to there,' and it will move. Nothing will be impossible for you."

These and other verses similar to it have always troubled me. Of course, Jesus is using hyperbole to make a point, the landscape remains undisturbed. But, "Nothing will be impossible for you"?

Jesus here reveals the unlimited possibilities of the unseen world where He dwelt with the Father. There, God is in control and all His creative power is available for whatever He desires. And His desire is to save us, as many as are willing.

But we focus on our own weaknesses and infirmities. His words seem foolish, even more so since He uses hyperbole. Anything is possible?

Jesus healed the sick, even raising people from the dead. He did not focus on the limitations of the flesh, but the unlimited capacity of God.

Ellen White says this:

> If you have faith like this, you will lay hold upon God's word, and upon all the helpful agencies He has appointed. Thus your faith will strengthen, and will bring to your aid the power of heaven. The obstacles that are piled by Satan across your path, though apparently as insurmountable as the eternal hills, shall disappear before the demand of faith. "Nothing shall be impossible unto you."[95]

If we would but grasp what has been made available to us instead of dwelling on ourselves, lifting our eyes to Christ, where the very power of God is to work in us, we would come off more than conquerors and would know that heaven is indeed ours. Life would be lived from victory to daily victory.

---

[95] Ellen G. White, *The Desire of Ages* (Mountain View, CA: Pacific Press, 1898), p. 431.

FAITH PART 2

May 31

Isaiah 49:15, "Can a mother forget the baby at her breast and have no compassion on the child she has borne? Though she may forget, I will not forget you!"

It happened one Sabbath. My wife and I had taken two cars to church since I had to be there early. When services were over, I took my car and she took hers, but we each had assumed that the other had our eight-year-old, Jenny, with them.

When I arrived home, I went about my business and shortly noticed that Jenny was not there. I asked my wife where she was. She said, "I thought you had her!"

I sped back to the church, (about 10 minutes away). The building was locked, but I searched around it on the side and back. At a house just beside the church, a friend's home, I heard her voice.

I ran to get her. But she did not run to me. She was furious! "How could you forget me?!" she cried. She began sobbing in my arms and I carried her back to the car and took her home. But her world had changed.

She had implicit trust in us. She lived a life of faith that, up to that time, had never known failure. She rested in our love for her, and she never doubted.

We had forgotten her. And the trust she had, had been betrayed.

Yet she demonstrated what real faith is. The faith of a little child.

It is this implicit trust that God longs for. When we trust in Him, He prompts us to trust and obey, a combination that will bring us to the portals of heaven and the pleasure of God.

THE DAILY LIFE
June 1

Galatians 2:20, "I have been crucified with Christ and I no longer live, but Christ lives in me. The life I now live in the body, I live by faith in the Son of God, who loved me and gave himself for me."

Romans 6:11, 13, "In the same way, count yourselves dead to sin but alive to God in Christ Jesus. Do not offer any part of yourself to sin as an instrument of wickedness, but rather offer yourselves to God as those who have been brought from death to life."

> *The key to heaven is to go to Christ, confess our sins and turn to Him to teach us His way.*

This crucifixion of self seems a difficult matter.

This crucifixion is the daily surrender to God of our wills and very persons to do His will. We put our will on His side. Rather than choosing to follow our inclinations, we follow where He leads us.

An example is what a student must do to learn the piano. The teacher instructs the student on what to do. He is to practice an hour a day. The teacher gives certain exercises, etc. The student wants to do something else but puts his will to practicing. He thus gains the power to do what he could not have done otherwise.

The rich young ruler asked Jesus how to have eternal life (Matt. 19:16). Jesus in the end invited him to sell his goods and come follow Him (Matt. 19:21). The real need was to put himself under the tutelage of Jesus that he might learn the way of life. But the young man refused (Matt. 19:22).

The choices God asks us to make may feel like cutting off a hand or plucking out an eye. But if we will surrender ourselves to Him, He will work to do His good will in us, and it will be accomplished.

The key to heaven is to go to Christ, confess our sins and turn to Him to teach us His way. He never turns away one who seeks Him. Like the ruler, we may demur, but if we do not let something separate ourselves from Him, heaven is assured.

THE STRENGTH OF THE LORD
June 2

Nehemiah 8:10, "Nehemiah said, 'Go and enjoy choice food and sweet drinks, and send some to those who have nothing prepared. This day is holy to our Lord. Do not grieve, for the joy of the LORD is your strength.'"

Nehemiah's advice was given to the Israelites who had returned to Judah after the Babylonian captivity. They gathered for a holy convocation and the law was read to them. It was then that they realized the gravity of the situation, Israel's utter failure to obey God even as He had made return possible. It brought them to tears. They lost all hope and began wailing at the inadequacy of their and their fathers' performance (Neh. 8:9).

Then Nehemiah stood and encouraged them with this advice. "Go, and have a festival! Celebrate, rather than weep at your failure." "For," he says, "the joy of the Lord is your strength" (Neh. 8:9–10, paraphrase).

We usually think of the joy of the Lord in more abstract terms than what is written by Nehemiah. We think more of enjoying the presence of God in our lives. And that is one way to look at it. When one is full of the love of Christ, realizing that he is beloved, that his sins are overlooked, the way to heaven is made secure and he is secure in God's love, then his life is full of joy.

But there is a concrete side as well. Celebrating! Eating choice food and drinking sweet drinks rather than mourning our shortcomings. In fact, mourning your shortcomings is probably the worst you can do, for it concentrates your mind on the negative rather than the power and will of God to give you success.

The *joy* of the Lord *is* your strength.

PERSONALIZING THE PROMISES
June 3

Isaiah 41:10, "So do not fear, for I am with you; do not be dismayed, for I am your God. I will strengthen you and help you; I will uphold you with my righteous right hand."

Philip Samaan tells of his anxiety while working as a religious book salesman in a small town in Idaho. Somehow, one hot morning, he could not force himself to leave the safety of his car to start knocking on doors. He ended up driving up and down the main (and only) street so many times that the people became suspicious and called the police to investigate. After explaining his predicament, the sheriff said, "Young man, make up your mind! Either start selling your books or get out of town!"

> *The Bible and all that is there is ours. God has given it to us.*

Scurrying home, he painfully reflected on his experience so far and his intense need for God's help. He opened his Bible to the above verse, and spent a long time praying and meditating. He projected himself into every word and took it to heart as if it were addressed to him personally. The promise became his very own as he filled his mind with the fact that God was the same as ever ... and that He was indeed there with him. He left his hotel room a changed person.[96]

We may do the same. The Bible and all that is there is ours. God has given it to us. Satan cannot take it from us, for the promises were made to us, not him. And God will fulfill them if we will let Him. And we may excitedly begin each day knowing that God has something good for us, even if there is trial and temptation.

---

[96] Philip Samaan, *Christ's Method Alone* (Joplin, MO: College Press LLC, 2012), pp. 1–2.

PUBLIC PRAISE
June 4

Psalm 149:1-2, "Praise the LORD. Sing to the LORD a new song, his praise in the assembly of his faithful people. Let Israel rejoice in their Maker; let the people of Zion be glad in their King."

There is something else that must be done that we may become the people of God, that we may be prepared to enter through the gates of the New Jerusalem.

We must openly and publicly testify about our God.

Why is this necessary? Are we not saved one on one and often in private, meditating and reading God's Word that convinces us of His enduring love and care?

> *Jesus is fearless. Though we may be faulty, if we confess our deep love for Him before men—an open risky confession—He will acknowledge us.*

Unless there is a public confession of our devotion to Him, there is a sense that it is actually not real!

This may seem a strange statement, but it is in fact the truth. Without a public declaration, love is only theory.

I recall falling in love as a youth. I was a shy suitor, afraid of rejection or humiliation. But to love without actually confessing love was not to love at all. She never really knew.

And our love for Jesus, in order to be real, must be made known. It is not that Jesus does not know, but He knows that without it, we will not become genuine lovers.

"I tell you, whoever publicly acknowledges me before others, the Son of Man will also acknowledge before the angels of God" (Luke 12:8).

Jesus is fearless. Though we may be faulty, if we confess our deep love for Him before men—an open risky confession—He will acknowledge us.

And our love will become real and meaningful.

Acknowledged before the heavenly hosts! What a privilege.

RETAINING THE BLESSING
June 5

Philippians 4:8, "Finally, brothers and sisters, whatever is true, whatever is noble, whatever is right, whatever is pure, whatever is lovely, whatever is admirable—if anything is excellent or praiseworthy—think about such things."

I have heard several, especially young people, note sadly that after a spiritual high point in their lives, the blessing seemed to fade away and they were left bereft.

Such thinking is addressed by Ellen White in the following passage:

> Many attend religious services, and are refreshed and comforted by the word of God; but through *neglect of meditation, watchfulness, and prayer, they lose the blessing*, and find themselves more destitute than before they received it. Often they feel that God has dealt hardly with them. They do not see that the fault is their own. By separating themselves from Jesus, they have shut away the light of His presence.
>
> It would be well for us to spend a thoughtful hour each day in contemplation of the life of Christ. We should take it point by point, and let the imagination grasp each scene, especially the closing ones. As we thus dwell upon His great sacrifice for us, our confidence in Him will be more constant, our love will be quickened, and we shall be more deeply imbued with His spirit. If we would be saved at last, we must learn the lesson of penitence and humiliation at the foot of the cross.[97]

Is your spiritual life barren and dry, dear reader? Do you desire the presence of Jesus? Then will to contemplate the life of Jesus, using, as she says, your imagination. We can visualize the episodes of Christ's life and the Spirit will be with us to apply each to our own needs. You will not be unhappy with the result.

---

[97]Ibid., p. 83, emphasis added.

WATCHFULNESS AND PRAYER
June 6

Luke 21:36, "Be always on the watch, and pray that you may be able to escape all that is about to happen, and that you may be able to stand before the Son of Man."

Most of us understand much about prayer, but what is this watching about? What are we to watch for? Why would God warn us about doing this?

There is a clue in Jesus' warning to the disciples in the garden, "Watch and pray so that you will not fall into temptation. The spirit is willing, but the flesh is weak" (Matt. 26:41).

Watchfulness is the characteristic of being attuned to the situation, of not being asleep to the wiles of the devil so that he may catch us unawares, and we fall to his temptations.

We have weaknesses that God has revealed to us, points of character that we know Satan has taken advantage of before. We must pray over and over for forgiveness because we fall to these.

Watchfulness means knowing and preparing for such attacks so that we meet them and gain the victory rather than falling to them.

The disciples were not watchful in the garden and missed the opportunity to support Christ in His most trying time, and to remain faithful rather than fail like Peter did in humiliation.

I do not see very many practicing this virtue. I do not do it enough myself. But if we are to be victorious in the Christian life, more time must be spent assessing our own weaknesses and preparing for the attacks of the devil at just those points of weakness. He knows where success lies, but if we prepare, he will be required to flee from us (James 4:7).

BOWING IN HUMILIATION AND PENITENCE
June 7

"If we would be saved at last, we must learn the lesson of penitence and humiliation at the foot of the cross."[98]

As we draw closer to Jesus, the defects of our own character will become visible in stark contrast to His. We will become more and more conscious of our own shortcomings. This can lead to discouragement even as we are making real progress in the path of light.

> Many who sincerely consecrate their lives to God's service are surprised and disappointed to find themselves, as never before, confronted by obstacles and beset by trials and perplexities. They pray for Christlikeness of character, for a fitness for the Lord's work, and they are placed in circumstances that seem to call forth all the evil of their nature. Faults are revealed of which they did not even suspect the existence.[99]

And the realization of these faults which we did not even suspect is a call to penitence and humiliation at the foot of the cross. We may bow in shame at our errors, but need not be discouraged, for there has been made a sure and safe place for us to confess and receive forgiveness for them. Instead of discouragement, these faults may, if we are willing, bring us into an even more intimate relationship with our Savior. After all, it was for this very reason that He came and died here, that He might be able to forgive and receive us unto Himself.

Lift up your head! The Savior is waiting for you to come to Him, even in penitence and humiliation. He will raise you up and set you at His right hand (Ps. 16:8).

---

[98]Ibid., p. 83.
[99]Ellen G. White, *The Ministry of Healing* (Mountain View, CA: Pacific Press, 1905), p. 470.

SECTION 8

God and the Jews

God demonstrated His ways by His dealings with the chosen people. The choice He made had a profound impact on the world ever since that time.

"On Jordan's stormy banks I stand,
And cast a wishful eye
To Canaan's fair and happy land,
Where my possessions lie."[100]

---

[100]Samuel Stennett, "On Jordan's Stormy Banks," *The Seventh-day Adventist Hymnal* (Hagerstown, MD: Review and Herald, 1985).

THE CALL OF MOSES PART 1
June 8

Exodus 3:1–3:

> Now Moses was tending the flock of Jethro his father-in-law, the priest of Midian, and he led the flock to the far side of the wilderness and came to Horeb, the mountain of God. There the angel of the LORD appeared to him in flames of fire from within a bush. Moses saw that though the bush was on fire it did not burn up. So Moses thought, "I will go over and see this strange sight—why the bush does not burn up."

God will often come to us when we least expect Him. We may feel we are far from Him, but He is ever present, and will reveal Himself to us even when we are going about our business unaware that He is so near.

God has holy ground everywhere where He will meet with His people unexpectedly. His condescension to come to us at such places shows His intense interest in us. He will surprise us with His presence and then invite us to follow Him.

Moses' experience at the bush is just such an encounter. It is a lesson for us of the omnipresence of our loving God who sees us even in the most discouraging of circumstances and will visit us when we may least expect Him.

Moses was leading his flock in the desert, doing the humble work at hand when he saw a bush burning, not something so unusual in that place. He went over to investigate.

There was no premonition that God was there. Moses' interest in the bush was mere curiosity. And yet that ground on which he trod was holy ground!

God has holy ground everywhere where He will meet with His people unexpectedly. His condescension to come to us at such places shows His intense interest in us. He will surprise us with His presence and then invite us to follow Him.

It is our privilege to enjoy such encounters. They give us hope even when we are hopeless or downhearted. Do not underestimate the God of Moses, One who speaks from burning bushes.

THE CALL OF MOSES PART 2
June 9

Exodus 4:13, "But Moses said, 'Pardon your servant, Lord. Please send someone else [to do it].'"

The story of Moses at the bush is almost comical and if it were not so serious, it in fact would be.

Moses, while herding his flock on a warm day, comes upon a bush, burning. This was not so unusual because the bushes of Sinai were dry and flammable. But the bush did not burn up, so Moses, out of curiosity, went to take a look.

Why did God come like this, and why not a more formal call?

When God calls a man or woman, it is as individuals. Isaiah was called in the temple (Isa. 6:4). Levi in his toll booth (Matt. 9:9) and James and John while they were fishing with their father (Mark 1:19–20). They left their nets immediately, while Moses instead of obeying, argued with God for some time, and at the end he asked God to find someone else! Yet in spite of his reluctance, and in spite of himself, he became one of the world's greatest lawgivers, honored even today by a place on the facade of the United States Supreme Court building![101] Three thousand plus years later! It is amazing what God can do with a man, even a one such as Moses, who asked, in the end, to be excused.

Ellen White says, "The divine command given to Moses found him self-distrustful, slow of speech, and timid. He was overwhelmed with a sense of his incapacity to be a mouthpiece for God to Israel …. The greatness of his mission called into exercise the best powers of his mind. God blessed his ready obedience, and he became eloquent, hopeful, self-possessed, and well fitted for the greatest work ever given to man."[102]

Will you, dear reader, allow the Lord to have His way with you? God's commands are enablings.[103]

---

[101]"Building Features," Supreme Court of the United States, https://1ref.us/1ih (accessed January 19, 2021).
[102]Ellen G. White, *Patriarchs and Prophets* (Mountain View, CA: Pacific Press, 1890), p. 255.
[103]Ellen G. White, *Christ's Object Lessons* (Washington, DC: Review and Herald, 1900), p. 333.

THE EXODUS

June 10

Exodus 5:1, "Afterward Moses and Aaron went to Pharaoh and said, 'This is what the LORD, the God of Israel, says: "Let my people go, so that they may hold a festival to me in the wilderness."'"

The Exodus reveals many things about God. It has been a story of hope for countless captive peoples, giving them a vision for the future and pointing them to heaven rather than earth.

But God did not keep the people from suffering the results of the will of Pharaoh. Pharaoh had power over them and used it to persecute them. His cruelty was so severe that the Israelites gave up hope for a time. They even turned their backs on Moses, the one who had come to deliver them.

We must be careful that we do not let the troubles of this life derail us from following God in all things. We will not get all we wish for, nor will things in life always be easy. Others who are not following God will take a different course and that course may result in our suffering pain and even harm and even death.

The Israelites faced death at the Red Sea. But God delivered them out of the hand of Pharaoh, whose body washed up on the shore of the sea. It may not always be that way for us.

But God gives us an assurance of victory over sin and even the trials and temptations of our lives. There will be an ultimate victory even if we do not experience a complete one today. The Israelites' example is for us, as Paul says (1 Cor. 10:1–6). And it is an example of hope.

Let us not let hope slip; it can save us from despair.

THE THEOCRACY
June 11

Exodus 19:5–6, "Now if you obey me fully and keep my covenant, then out of all nations you will be my treasured possession. Although the whole earth is mine, you will be for me a kingdom of priests and a holy nation."

Some among us have longed to make America a Christian nation, a nation ruled by God like Israel of old. On Mount Sinai, God covenanted with Israel to be their God and they His people. They would like to have the same relationship with Him. But when we study the history of Israel, we find that in the end it did not work.

Yes, God did agree to be their God, but within three months, Israel had lost faith and began worshiping a golden calf. Within three months! (Exod. 12–34).

When Samuel was prophet and judge, the people demanded a king. God noted that they had not rejected Samuel, but Him (1 Sam. 8:4–9). And then in 587 BC, the Babylonians took the king captive, and a new king was never instated. The monarchy never returned (Jer. 52:7–11. A king was never crowned after this).

Did God fail? No, but the people did. They never gave themselves completely to His rule and never abided by the covenant that they had sworn to keep.

It is no different now. A nation cannot keep any covenant that God would propose. So, He now deals with us as individuals. We are saved one by one. God calls us to join His people as a church but has not thought it wise to reinstate a theocracy, that is, become the Head of a nation. There are just too many who would not submit to His rule. And He will not force people to submit.

So, the idea of a theocracy is impossible at this time.

THE BOOK OF JUDGES
June 12

Judges 18:1, "In those days Israel had no king."

When I was in my first year of medical school, we were required to take a religion class. I chose one by Dr. Maxwell, a class where we would read each book of the Bible and then discuss its teachings. Dr. Maxwell asked us to answer one question about each book: what does this book say about God?

We read the first books of the Bible that showed the power of God and the frailty of men and then we came to the book of Judges.

God had brought the people of Israel to the land of promise and they had settled there and they followed God all the days of Joshua. But when Joshua died and the elders that outlived him also passed, the people were led by judges. And what a sorry lot!

All the weaknesses of men were demonstrated in the lives of these leaders. The people would follow God for a time, led by a judge who was seldom a paragon, and then slip back into their fallen ways. It was such a sad demonstration of human weakness.

And as I read, I was strangely comforted. Why did God put up with these people who could not seem to stay focused on His will or on the gifts He had promised?

And I said to myself, "If God could take these people as His own, then He could take me as His own as well."

The trouble seen in Judges is an example to us of the love of God for sinners who struggle with success in living the life of God. He gives grace to all—even the weak and unworthy. It was a wonderful revelation.

JEPHTHAH
June 13

Judges 11:30–32, 34–35:

> *And Jephthah made a vow to the LORD: "If you give the Ammonites into my hands, whatever comes out of the door of my house to meet me when I return in triumph from the Ammonites will be the LORD's, and I will sacrifice it as a burnt offering." Then Jephthah went over to fight the Ammonites, and the LORD gave them into his hands .... When Jephthah returned to his home in Mizpah, who should come out to meet him but his daughter .... She was an only child .... When he saw her, he tore his clothes.*

What are we to make of this? Why is it even in the Bible? Did God give victory because Jephthah made his rash vow? Would He have refrained if Jephthah had not?

The Israelites had forsaken God, and He had given them over to their enemies. But when they called on Him, He could "bear Israel's misery no longer" (Judges 10:16).

From earlier in the chapter, we learn that Jephthah, son of a prostitute, had been driven from his home by his legitimate brothers. He had gathered a band of adventurers around him and had become a man of valor.

> *It is not perfect men that God calls, for there are no such men. God will call and use anyone who is willing.*

He was the available "resource" to free Israel from their oppressors, and God did not hesitate to use him to save His people.

God will use even flawed men and women, crooked sticks, and on occasion He seems to prefer them. Paul had been killing God's followers before he was converted. Peter was impetuous and strong willed and Elijah failed at the critical moment.

I am so thankful for stories such as this. God did not turn from a man who was rash and foolish. God does not endorse such acts, but wanted to save Israel and called the man in spite of them.

It is not perfect men that God calls, for there are no such men. God will call and use anyone who is willing.

HIM WILL I HONOR PART 1
June 14

1 Samuel 2:30, "Those who honor me I will honor, but those who despise me will be disdained."

John 12:26, "Whoever serves me must follow me .... My Father will honor the one who serves me."

The verse in Samuel was spoken by a prophet sent to warn Eli.

He had allowed his two wicked sons, Hophni and Phinehas, to forcibly take the offerings God had ordained for the priests and to even sleep with the women who served at the tabernacle!

Though He rebuked them, He did not remove them from priestly office. God sent a prophet to warn him, and finally Samuel, a beloved child, was called to deliver a message a child should never have to deliver. But Eli would not act.

Unbeknownst to him, the law of reciprocal honor had been secretly working and now would come the time of reckoning.

The Israelites had just lost 4,000 men in a battle with the Philistines. Thinking the ark a mere totem, they called for it to be brought into battle with them this time. They brushed past the spineless priest and robbed the Most Holy Place of its treasure (1 Sam. 4:3).

Israel fell before their enemies and the ark was captured. Hophni and Phinehas were both slain (1 Sam. 4:10–11).

Eli waited anxiously at the empty tabernacle for news. When the report of the loss came, he toppled backward, breaking his neck and dying instantly (1 Sam. 4:18).

Learning of the defeat, the wife of Phinehas went into labor and with her dying breath named her son Ichabod, "The Glory has departed" (1 Sam. 4:21).

Such is the warning to us if we refuse to honor Him who has bestowed such honor on us as to call us to His service. It is a sobering message.[104]

---

[104] A.W. Tozer, *The Pursuit of God* (Camp Hill, PA: Christian Publications, 1993), p. 97.

HIM WILL I HONOR PART 2
June 15

2 Samuel 12:7–8, "This is what the LORD, the God of Israel, says: 'I anointed you king over Israel, and I delivered you from the hand of Saul. I gave your master's house to you, and your master's wives into your arms. I gave you all Israel and Judah. And if all this had been too little, I would have given you even more.'"

"Now over against Eli, set almost any Bible character who honestly tried to glorify God in his earthly walk. See how God winked at weakness and overlooked failures as He poured upon His servants grace, and blessing untold. Let it be Abraham, Jacob, David, or Elijah or whom you will, honor followed honor as harvest the seed."[105]

Abraham is spiritual father to half the world's population. Peter is revered as the foundation of the church by more than a billion. And Mary, a humble teenager from Nazareth who, to honor God, was willing to bear the scorn of her contemporaries, is exalted to the heavens.

It is not that they were perfect, but holy intention made the difference.

In Jesus, this law was seen in simple perfection. He gave all glory to His Father and said, "I always do what pleases him" (John 8:29).

"If I glorify myself, my glory means nothing. My Father ... is the one who glorifies me" (John 8:54).

And how did God honor Jesus?

He was exalted to the heavens, and to Him every knee will bow to the glory of God the Father (Phil. 2:9–11).

Do you desire to be honored by those around you? Do you crave respect? God has revealed the secret: those who honor God, He will honor.

---

[105]Ibid.

THE STILL SMALL VOICE
June 16

1 Kings 19:11–12, "The LORD said, 'Go out and stand on the mountain in the presence of the LORD, for the LORD is about to pass by ....' After the earthquake came a fire, but the LORD was not in the fire. And after the fire came a gentle whisper."

The importance of this episode in Scripture cannot be overestimated.

So many of us are looking for a God of power to set all things right in the world and deliver us from all that annoys or harasses. We want a superhero.

But God comes as a gentle influence, a quiet whisper in our ear to walk in His way (Isa. 30:21).

Elijah had fled from Jezebel and bemoaned the fact that he alone was faithful in all Israel (1 Kings 19:10). The miracle on Mt. Carmel had been unsuccessful in changing the people's minds and they had not stood with him. And God had failed to restrain the hand of the wicked queen, who seemed to have been unimpressed by fire from heaven. His only apparent choice was to flee.

He was the "only one left" and was on the lam. Where was God?

God came, but not as he expected and not with the power he expected. The mighty wind, the powerful earthquake and the raging fire did not reveal God.

Instead, He came as a gentle whisper, a seemingly impotent force against the fury of the sinful ruler.

But such quietude was how Jesus stood before His tormentors, a rock unmoved by the powerful tide of evil raised to oppose Him. His kingly bearing was noted by all.

Elijah's experience teaches us that God may not reveal Himself in power for our salvation. We are still to trust Him and we may speak to others through our demeanor as a gentle whisper to their consciences.

SOLOMON'S OTHER TEMPLE
June 17

1 Kings 8:10, "When the priests withdrew from the Holy Place, the cloud filled the temple of the LORD."

Solomon's temple was a beautiful structure, described in the Bible in such detail that models have been built to represent it. It was constructed of the finest marble, roofed with beams of cedar such that the building had the most delightful aroma upon entry even without incense. Two named pillars of bronze, Boaz and Jachin, flanked the cedar doors that stood at the entrance. And the altar and laver of bronze stood outside, exquisitely wrought (1 Kings 6 and 7:13–22).

But Solomon built another place of worship, the high places for his wives who worshiped Ashteroth, Chemosh, god of the Moabites, and Molech, the detestable god of the Amorites (1 Kings 11:7–8). He built high places for all his wives across the ravine from the temple mount on the Mount of Olives (the Mount of Corruption). We do not know how these looked, but there is one thing we do know, they stood there for over three centuries no matter who was king of Judah. They stood during the reigns of good King Asa, Jehoshaphat, Joash and Hezekiah. They stood during the time of Elijah, Elisha and Isaiah. It was not until the reforms of Josiah, perhaps twenty years before the first Jews were taken into captivity in 605 BC, that these high places were destroyed as described in 2 Kings 23:13.[106]

So, during the entire history of the southern kingdom of Judah, pagan altars were visible from the courts of the temple of God, built by the great King Solomon. How is it that God endured the insult of this, Satan throwing it up in His face day and night?

In spite of this daily affront, God did not abandon His people. He continued to meet them at the temple though they had built high places for competing gods just across the valley.

And He will meet with us. We may have sinned and been unfaithful. We should not withdraw from Him, but seek Him. His patience was astounding and remains to this day. If He endured that, He can endure us.

---

[106]"Babylonian captivity," Wikipedia, https://1ref.us/1ii (accessed January 19, 2021).

JOB PART 1: THE FREEDOM OF CREATURES
June 18

Job 1:8, "Then the LORD said to Satan, 'Have you considered my servant Job? There is no one on earth like him; he is blameless and upright, a man who fears God and shuns evil.'"

The enigmatic book of Job gives us insight into God's rule of the universe and how He feels about us.

At the beginning of the book God called the "sons of God" (Job 1:6, NKJV) together for one of His periodic meetings to discuss the issues of the day. During this one, Satan appears, apparently unbidden. His credentials are questioned and he answers that he represents earth, administers it and is prepared to give a report.

Before Satan can start, God asks a troubling question about Job, "Have you considered my servant Job ... a blameless and upright man, one who fears God and shuns evil?" (Job 1:8, NKJV). Of course, this individual is an outlier, one Satan would just as soon forget. But Satan has an intimate knowledge of him.

We know what happens later in the book. In light of that, why does God do this, especially to one so faithful and beloved? Would it not have been better to have kept quiet? And what about the children and flocks and servants, all involved in a horror of destruction, when left to Satan's whims? If God is concerned about the sparrows that fall, how can His unleashing of Satan not reflect negatively on His character?

God has several reasons, but we must notice first how free God's creatures are in His presence. God does not muzzle Satan. He is able to speak without restraint, even challenging God. We have the same freedom. Let us not fear to approach God with our cares, complaints and passions. If He will listen to Satan, He will listen to us.

JOB PART 2: THE HEDGE OF GOD
June 19

Job 1:8–11:

> *Then the LORD said to Satan, "Have you considered my servant Job? There is no one on earth like him; he is blameless and upright, a man who fears God and shuns evil." "Does Job fear God for nothing?" Satan replied. "Have you not put a hedge around him and his household and everything he has? You have blessed the work of his hands, so that his flocks and herds are spread throughout the land. But now stretch out your hand and strike everything he has, and he will surely curse you to your face."*

When God brings up Job, Satan's first act is to accuse God of unsportsmanlike conduct. "You have protected him so much that I cannot get near him! You are completely unfair."

This is a revealing conversation. God's enemy, Satan, admits to God's default setting for us: He builds a wall around us. Even the wicked are protected to a certain extent. When a friend or ally gives a complement, we may be skeptical at times, but when an enemy admits such a thing, it has to be the truth.

Here Satan freely confesses that God shields His beloved. That is what He always does and will do. It is such a problem for Satan that when he first opens his mouth in heaven, he complains about it.

If we only had the willingness to believe as Satan does about our Protector, it would save us much fretting and anxiety! We can even believe Satan's words on this one.

JOB PART 3: THE UNMASKING OF SATAN
June 20

Job 1:12,14–15:

> *The LORD said to Satan, "Very well, then, everything he has is in your power, but on the man himself do not lay a finger." Then Satan went out from the presence of the LORD .... [A] messenger came to Job and said, "The oxen were plowing and the donkeys were grazing nearby, and the Sabeans attacked and made off with them .... and I am the only who has escaped to tell you!"*

This episode is unusual because Satan is formally given permission to do anything he wants.

God's purpose here was to show exactly what Satan is like. He is a master of deception and has blamed God for all the evil here on earth. But in this instance, Satan reveals himself in spite of himself.

God seldom allows for such freedom on Satan's part. It would be too destructive. But God knows that there is no way for others to perceive Satan's real character except to allow him to do his will.

In this case, he reveals himself as the monster he is, going on a killing spree of utter destruction. There is no doubt about his motives when given free reign: death to all. It was only God's restraint that had prevented him from sweeping away the whole family before.

But when Satan shows up the second time, he has a retort: "Skin for skin! ... A man will give all he has for his own life" (Job 2:4). So, God lets him take Job to death's door, again revealing what Satan's will for us is: disease, suffering and death. And these are in stark contrast to what God's will was, a wall of protection around His man.

There is no more clear revelation of Satan's character than in the prologue of Job. Let us take warning from our loving Lord.

JOB PART 4: WHY JOB?
June 21

Job 1:8, "Then the LORD said to Satan, 'Have you considered my servant Job? There is no one on earth like him; he is blameless and upright, a man who fears God and shuns evil.'"

Job 2:10, "In all this, Job did not sin in what he said."

Why Job? Here is a man upright in heart who loved God. In fact, Job 31 is the highest statement of morality in the ancient world before Christ. Job was indeed blameless and one who shunned evil.

So why Job, a righteous man of such sterling character that even God bragged about him? Why allow Satan to have his way with *him*?

The simple answer is because there was no one else on earth that could have endured what Job did and remain faithful. Job's great faith allowed God to reveal the profound evil of Satan's character.

A lesser man would have given up, cursed God and died, and Satan's assertions would have proved true. But Job's faithfulness allowed for Satan's unmasking, a wonderful revelation to men and angels alike.

Many have thought God's treatment of this most faithful of servants scandalous. How could He do such a thing? But God had, at the beginning of Scripture, to reveal the character of Satan. Satan had clothed himself with such deception and men's hearts so loved wickedness that it was impossible any other way. So, Job was called on to endure real hardship for God's sake.

It was a high honor.

Job has been an example of righteousness, and his book is a treasure of truth for the ages, admitted so even by wicked men. We too may be so used by God if we will. Faithfulness in the little things draws us daily closer to Him who can preserve us from the evil one, even in the most trying of circumstances.

JOB PART 5: THE WAGER WON
June 22

Job 2:8–10, "Then Job took a piece of broken pottery and scraped himself with it as he sat among the ashes. His wife said to him, 'Are you still maintaining your integrity? Curse God and die!' He replied, 'You are talking like a foolish woman. Shall we accept good from God, and not trouble?' In all this, Job did not sin in what he said."

At the end of the second chapter, Job has lost all and even his life is in jeopardy. Sitting on an ash heap, he scrapes at the sores covering his body. His wife encourages him to curse God and be done with it.

She comes to him, one that is to be his helpmeet as was God's plan in the beginning, but she has no comforting words for the sufferer. "Integrity? Bah! Curse God and die!"

But even here, Job does not sin. He doesn't call her a fool, but says she is merely *speaking* like one. A kind retort to the bitterness of her soul.

Satan has done all he is allowed to do. He has utterly destroyed Job, taken his wealth, his family and his health. He sits on a pile of ashes scratching the scabs on his back. His wife derides him, calling him to curse God and give up.

But Job does not sin in anything that he says.

The wager seems to have been won.

So, why is there any more to the book at all? Had not God proved His point?

God had something more to prove, and something very important.

There was more at stake than just the "Grand Wager."

JOB PART 6: THE ARGUMENT
June 23

Job 4:7, "Consider now: Who, being innocent, has ever perished? Where were the upright ever destroyed?"

The rest of Job, until God appears in chapter 38, is a discussion between Job and his three friends, with a monologue by Elihu that adds little.

The conversations are repetitive and seem to drone on and on. At the end both sides are exhausted and stale. But the interesting thing is that both Job and his friends really believe the same thing, that God will reward the righteous and punish the wicked.

They differ in this: Job insists he has done nothing to deserve the treatment he has received and his friends feel that if he would only confess his sins, the suffering would end. Both believe God is righteous and just.

During much of the book, Job bemoans the loss of the feeling of God's closeness and fairness. He complains bitterly of that loss.

His friends become less and less compassionate and in the end refuse to speak to him anymore (Job 25; 32:1. Bildad's answer was very short and Zophar never answered a third time).

Why is so much time spent on this issue? Because it is so important in the understanding of God's character, especially so early in the world's history.

In this world, it is not always the good that prosper and the wicked that suffer. Satan has influence here. He is the prince of the air and will cause his people to prosper. He will also bring suffering to the righteous.

It is not a truism that wealth means the blessing of God. God wanted us to know this at the very beginning to save us from such a deception.

He thus allows for seemingly interminable discussion of the issue until He comes to speak from the whirlwind.

JOB PART 7: GOD SPEAKS
June 24

Job 38:1–2, "Then the LORD spoke to Job out of the storm. He said: 'Who is this that obscures my plans with words without knowledge?'"

In a brilliant stroke of literary genius, the author of Job allows God to speak at the end. But what a God speaks!

God treats Job like a man, in the end, not offering sympathy but challenging him to answer a string of probing questions. "Where were you …?" as if Job should have been available to give counsel when all the realm of nature was brought into being.

Job remains silent except for two short comments humbling himself before the God who bragged on him at the beginning (Job 40:3–5; 42:1–6).

The harsh words of God are a surprising comfort to those who face suffering and the loss of family, friends, health and wealth.

We do not have insight into the workings of nature and should leave the mysteries of this world to Him who created it all. The Creation is truly wonderful and amazing in complexity. Those who have the keenest knowledge stand awed at what God has done. From the workings of the universe to the intricacies of atomic physics, the Creation speaks of the wisdom of its Creator.

We puzzle at the complexities of life and our inability to understand its seeming vagaries of life and evil. How can God let us face such difficulties? How could God let Job suffer as he did?

But God knows the end from the beginning. He has given us this wonderful book to show the secret of His ways that we might not stumble over them.

Will we bow with Job at the end or refuse to put our faith in the One whose hand holds the scepter? He bids us put our trust in Him.

JOB PART 8: THE PARADOX
June 25

Job 38:1–4, NKJV, "Then the LORD answered Job out of the whirlwind, and said: 'Who is this who darkens my counsel by words without knowledge? Now prepare yourself like a man; I will question you, and you shall answer Me. Where were you when I laid the foundations of the earth? ...'"

Job 42:7, "After the LORD had said these things to Job, he said to Eliphaz the Temanite, 'I am angry with you and your two friends, because you have not spoken the truth about me, as my servant Job has.'"

Huh? How can God say what He has said here? Job is the one who has darkened God's counsel with words without knowledge, yet in the end, it is *he* who has spoken what is *right*!

When Pilate met Jesus, he immediately knew he was a righteous Man. But Job's three friends did not discern true virtue as Pilate had. They condemned Job as a sinner rather than giving comfort. They added to Job's suffering.

Job had spoken rashly, asking for an interview with God that he might complain of the injustice shown him. But when God appears for the interview, it was Job who fell silent, confessing that there were things that he did not know, things too wonderful for him.

In the end, God is so proud of Job, that He, too, might seem to speak a bit rashly: "[Y]ou have not spoken the truth about me, as my servant Job has" (Job 42:7). God loved Job and restored all to him.

We have not heard of Satan since chapter 1, but Job receives the accolades of God who calls him righteous and does so that the ages might see and know of His feelings for a man who will honor God in all circumstances.

TASTING AND SEEING
June 26

Psalm 34:8, "Taste and see that the LORD is good; blessed is the one who takes refuge in him."

I don't know if you have ever been to Baskin-Robbins®. The only ice cream really worth eating—at least in my humble opinion.

They do something interesting there, a clever gimmick to get you to buy some ice cream. They have a little pink plastic utensil called a "taste spoon." I saw this advertisement in the store recently: "Free tastes until you choose!" It is apparent this offer is not putting them out of business.

But there is a wonderful truth behind the taste spoon. When tasting, you are not committing to anything yet. Just tasting.

And our God puts up with that sort of behavior. He actually invites it!

He is not demanding a commitment to Him, but to just taste and see. Check it out. No commitment required.

How can He do that?

He knows His product. It is the best on earth and if first tasted, it will be desired.

He knows that we are skittish when it comes to commitment. We are afraid, for we have been burned before. It is painful, so we are cautious. And God knows that we need this "tasting" so that we can become comfortable.

And it shows how gracious He is with His children. We are sinful, fickle and easily distracted. A taste of real pleasure or love or any of the other gifts He has to offer has a chance at least of alluring us to Him. And He is willing to suffer the rejection after some taste and decide not to buy and walk out of the store.

Those Baskin-Robbins® people are on to something. They just didn't know that God has been in the business for millennia.

THE PROBLEM OF TRUST
June 27

Proverbs 3:5–6, "Trust in the LORD with all your heart and lean not on your own understanding; in all your ways submit to him, and he will make your paths straight."

Some years ago, when a young man was learning to fly, his instructor told him to put the plane into a steep and extended dive. He was totally unprepared for what was about to happen. After a brief time, the engine stalled and the plane began to plunge out-of-control. It soon became evident that the instructor was not going to help at all. After a few seconds, which seemed like eternity, the student's mind began to function again. He quickly corrected the situation.

Immediately he turned to the instructor and began to vent his fearful frustrations on him.

The instructor very calmly turned and said, "There is no position you can get this airplane into that I cannot get you out of. If you want to learn to fly, go up there and do it again."[107]

Are we willing to give God that kind of leeway? Let Him have control? He is experienced with lives that are totally given to Him. And He has shown His care and skill.

He says to acknowledge Him and to trust Him, and He will bring it to pass. There may be days of stress and difficulty, but He knows, just as this instructor did.

Do you want to learn to fly? Fly with the angels, see the world from the sky? Then do as this young man did; trust God with all that is in your life.

---

[107]"Trust," #3, Sermon Illustrations, https://1ref.us/1ij (accessed January 19, 2021).

PSALM 88

June 28

Psalm 88:3, 18, "I am overwhelmed with troubles and my life draws near to death .... You have taken from me friend and neighbor—darkness is my closest friend." (Read the whole Psalm.)

This Psalm is one of the darkest in Scripture. In fact, there is not a single verse in the Psalm that expresses a positive thought! Why would God allow this to be put in His book?

Some time ago, a young woman in my congregation had gone through a divorce that was not her desire and she had become quite depressed. A daughter of her husband had become a beloved child to her (she had no children) and she was taken from her. It had broken her heart.

She called me one night very depressed and crying. She pleaded with me to just read the Bible to her. I read several chapters including this one, thinking it might comfort her.

After the reading she hung up somewhat relieved.

Later she spoke to me about the reading, and amazingly, this chapter was one of the most comforting for her. Why?

She said that the feelings expressed there were ones that resonated with her and her deep feelings of loss. Here was someone who had gone through the same things she had. The expressions of loss and darkness there helped her realize she was not the first to experience such things and that God understood.

God is aware of our sorrow and pain and has put chapters such as this there for us. We have friends even from centuries past that can comfort us. It is a wonderful gift.

PSALM 103

June 29

Psalm 103:1–5, "Praise the LORD, my soul; all my inmost being, praise his holy name. Praise the LORD, my soul, and forget not all his benefits—who forgives all your sins and heals all your diseases, who redeems your life from the pit and crowns you with love and compassion, who satisfies your desires with good things so that your youth is renewed like the eagle's."

"Forget not all his benefits!"

What are the benefits? When inquiring about a new job or renewing health insurance, we all want to know, what are the benefits? Why should we change jobs or insurance companies?

What are the benefits God offers?

> *If God were offering policies, His would be the only one worth signing. Let us not forget all the benefits.*

The psalmist enumerates the ones that have meant the most to him.

First, He forgives all of our sins. God has made a way to escape guilt. He forgives us. He has borne the penalty and we are free. We can live free of the evil that our sins have begotten in us. We may cast it on Him.

He heals all our diseases. As a surgeon, I can testify that I did not cure anyone. I would remove impediments to the wonderful healing power that God has given us. He healed the wounds.

He redeems us from the pit. Some of us have sunk so low that our lives are as pits of filth and disgrace. God is even there wading into the muck to save us.

He satisfies our desires. Desire is a wonderful thing. God gave us these that He might have the pleasure of satisfying them. And such satisfaction causes us to soar like the eagles.

If God were offering policies, His would be the only one worth signing. Let us not forget all the benefits.

DESIRE

June 30

Psalm 37:3–4, "Trust in the LORD and do good; dwell in the land and enjoy safe pasture. Take delight in the LORD, and he will give you the desires of your heart."

While reading Psalm 103, I began musing on the problem of desire.

Why did God put desires in our hearts, and such personal desires that we often will not reveal them for fear of embarrassment? To tell of our inmost desires makes us vulnerable to ridicule. It is often sensed initially as the awakening desire for that first sweetheart, a secret longing that one dare not utter even to the beloved for fear of exposure.

Buddhist thinking on desire, though not completely negative, sees it as that which brings suffering. This suffering is repeated over and over until all desire is abandoned and one reaches a state of nothingness or emptiness, nirvana.[108]

The Bible seems to take a completely different tack.

Adam is called to name the animals that a desire might be awakened for a companion, a desire that God moves to wonderfully fulfill.

"Bone of my bones ... flesh of my flesh" (Gen. 2:23). "[A] man ... shall cleave unto his wife: and they shall be one flesh" (Gen. 2:24, KJV). The passion cannot be missed.

Jacob loved Rachel so much that the seven years he served for her seemed but a few days (Gen. 29:20).

> **God here invites the redeemed to quench their burning thirst by drinking deeply of the river of life that flows eternally for them. And it is there forever for the taking.**

God implants a desire that He might satisfy it.

In Revelation, "The Spirit and the bride say, 'Come!' .... Let the one who is thirsty come; and let the one who wishes take the free gift of the water of life" (Rev. 22:17).

God here invites the redeemed to quench their burning thirst by drinking deeply of the river of life that flows eternally for them. And it is there forever for the taking.

Yes, desire is not sinful, but God-given.

---

[108]"nirvana," Merriam-Webster, https://1ref.us/1ik (accessed January 19, 2021).

SINFUL DESIRE
July 1

Galatians 5:19–21, "The sins of the flesh are obvious: sexual immorality, impurity, and debauchery; idolatry and witchcraft; hatred, discord, jealousy, fits of rage, selfish ambition, dissensions, factions, and envy, drunkenness, orgies, and the like."

But what about sinful desire, lust, pride, envy, gluttony? They are desires. Did God accidentally build sin into the world He created?

If you examine sinful desire carefully, you will discover that these are not actions or attitudes that stand on their own. They are actually corruptions of noble desires or attitudes.

Envy is admiration that has been corrupted by selfishness. Gluttony is appetite taken to extreme. Lust is normal sexual desire that has become selfish and wishes to use another individual for one's own purposes without consideration for that person's worth.

Sinful desire is corruption of that which is good. God implanted desire in us that we might have the delight that the satisfaction of desire brings. And as the psalmist says:

"You have made known to me the path of life;
you will fill me with joy in your presence,
with eternal pleasures at your right hand" (Ps. 16:11, NIV 1984).

When our desires are under the control of a will that has submitted itself to God, they will not become destructive, but will impel us to higher and nobler actions. Lofty aspirations will be satisfied with lofty achievements and God will invite us to come up higher and be holier still.

Unbridled passions are powerful things. And the desire to rule oneself, to be the one in charge is an alluring and enticing prospect. So alluring, in fact, that when Satan offered such self-rule, a third of the angels jumped at the chance—and this in the very presence of the Almighty!

THE DESIRE TO RULE ONESELF
July 2

Revelation 12:3–4, "Then another sight appeared in heaven: an enormous dragon with seven heads and ten horns and seven crowns on his heads. Its tail swept a third of the stars out of the sky and flung them to the earth."

Many commentators see this verse as the result of Satan's rebellion. He swept a third of the angels out of heaven with him.

But what a wonder! How is it that a third of the angels in heaven, in the very presence of the Holy One, the King of love, would choose to leave?

It is the allure of self-rule. The idea of being the boss, that no one will call the shots but me. It was such a seductive temptation that they gave in to it, even though God warned them of the destructive results of such a course of action.

And so they were cast to earth. And here, our father Adam sided with the rebels, choosing to do it his way.

But we are unable to rule ourselves. The passions, desires and cravings of our minds and bodies are beyond our skill. We are powerless before them.

The lives of men testify to this fact. Alexander the Great was a master strategist, but could not rule himself, dying in a drunken stupor at age 32 years.[109] The combatants in WWI marched into war with joy and pride, but millions were cut down in the trenches of Flanders. Addicts, mastered by their craving for pleasure, ruin their lives and the lives of their families and friends.

And think of the woe, death and destruction that Satan's desires have wrought! Billions ruined! What a legacy!

God let him and us freely choose so that the universe might know, and so knowing might turn to Him only who gives true freedom.

---

[109] "Alexander the Great," Wikipedia, https://1ref.us/1il (accessed January 20, 2021).

PSALM 109: A CURSE ON THE WICKED
July 3

Read Psalm 109.

Jesus told us to love our enemies and bless them that curse us (Matt. 5:44). But in this Psalm, David calls down curses on those that have hurt and abused him. He is unstinting in his condemnation and desire for their destruction. He calls for their children to become beggars (Ps. 109:10) and their sins to remain unforgiven (verses 14–15)!

If this were the only set of such curses in Scripture, they might be excused as an aberration, but there are other Psalms expressing similar sentiments. Jeremiah lashes out at his enemies in Jeremiah 18 and the saints under the altar call to God to avenge their blood (Rev. 6:9–10).

What are we to make of this apparent repudiation of God's will as expressed by Jesus? He said to pray for those who despitefully use us and bless those who curse us, yet David is doing just the opposite.

The Psalms express the feelings of sinful human beings. They may not always reflect the will of God in all matters. And this one is especially difficult. David had befriended the person cursed and had been repaid evil for good. This is very hard to take. David responded by displaying hurt and angry curses. He was human just like us.

And he was not God. Jesus was the perfect example of His command to bless those that cursed Him. He demonstrated such love, a love that we have a difficult time emulating when experiencing such abuse.

God did not erase this Psalm of personal hurt from Scripture. It is right there along with Jesus' command.

The Bible is not about perfect men, but real ones, ones that struggle with love for those that torment them. Praise God for His willingness to expose the dark side of His saints that we might not become discouraged.

The Bible is not about perfect men, but real ones, ones that struggle with love for those that torment them. Praise God for His willingness to expose the dark side of His saints that we might not become discouraged.

PSALM 139: THE PRAYER OF KNOWLEDGE
July 4

Psalm 139:23–24, NIV 1984, "Search me, God, and know my heart; test me and know my anxious thoughts. See if there is any offensive way in me, and lead me in the way everlasting."

At the end of time, Jesus tells of some of His followers who come to Him saying, "Lord, Lord, did we not prophesy in your name and in your name drive out demons and in your name perform many miracles?" (Matt. 7:22, NIV 1984). They seem to have been active in carrying out God's program by doing many wonderful things.

But Jesus answers them, "'I never knew you. Away from me, you evildoers!'" (Matt. 7:23).

This prayer, found at the end of Psalm 139, if prayed with a sincere heart, is the answer to the problem displayed by these people at the end of time.

It invites God into the inward parts, into the mind and heart, asking Him to *examine* it and *know* it to see if there are errors of practice that will keep me from walking in the way of life.

I have taught for several years and if a student comes to me, asking me to review their papers and the work that they have done so that they may do better, I am delighted and will work harder with them to help them succeed.

If an individual goes to their physician asking for an examination because of some concern with their health, the doctor will do all he can to find the cause for anxiety.

God will do no less for us if we come to Him with an open heart. He longs to know and be with us. His answers to our prayers may result in testing, but it is better to be tested now than to suffer eternal loss at the judgement.

WHITE AS SNOW

July 5

Isaiah 1:18, NIV 1984, "'Come now, let us reason together,' says the LORD, 'Though your sins are like scarlet, they shall be as white as snow.'"

Job 38:22, "Have you entered the storehouses of the snow ...?"

It snowed yesterday and the landscape was transformed. In the winter, of course, the vegetation has died back and only the gray-brown trunks and branches remain. The ground is littered with debris from the stems of summer, in chaotic disarray, piled one upon another in heaps of ugly brush. They had been full of leaves and flowers, but now, only decay.

Then in the middle of the darkest days, when the sun is at its nadir—it snows! Everything is made new. The covering of white, when the sun shines on the crystal flakes, sparkles in beauty hiding all that is unsightly and dead. In the depths of winter, God sends a vision of life. It is just water, after all, but it is better magic than the most skilled magician can produce.

That is why God has it in His storehouse. It is His to use to encourage His children in even the darkest of days. When we are discouraged because of the seeming deadness of all that we are and do, God sends the snow of His loving care to cheer us on the way.

And He uses it as a symbol of what He does for the inmost soul of those surrendered to Him. Like the winter vegetation, we are dead and unlovely, but with His robe of righteousness, we become beautiful and are able to reflect His love to all around us.

What a gift! Just water! Our God is the Master Magician.

BOWING AT THE TEMPLE OF RIMMON
July 6

2 Kings 5:18–19, NIV 1984, "But may the LORD forgive your servant for this one thing: When my master enters the temple of Rimmon to bow down and he is leaning on my arm and I have to bow there also—when I bow down in the temple of Rimmon, may the LORD forgive your servant for this. 'Go in peace,' Elisha said."

What are we to make of this?

Naaman had just been cured of leprosy—a wonderful miracle. But before he leaves, he asks that he may be excused from complete devotion to Jehovah. He will be in the temple of the pagan god, Rimmon, bowing with his master.

And Elisha allows it! Or at least bids him, "Go in peace." Is this the way of God? Does He let converts continue their pagan practices even after they have become His followers?

This story shows the profound grace of God toward us.

He takes us where we are. Naaman was not yet prepared to stand up to the king. The previous verses show that he asked for an amount of earth that two donkeys could carry. He believed Jehovah must be worshiped on ground from Israel, so he was taking back some so that he might worship aright. It was evidence that he had turned from his idols to the living God, even though he did not understand all that that entailed.

There would one day come a showdown between Rimmon (Satan) and Jehovah for Naaman's complete allegiance. Although God is gracious, Satan is not. He would eventually force the issue.

But God would grant grace to His newborn child.

Do you need such grace? It is there for you. Satan will plague you with doubt and worry, but God will grant you grace. There you can get all you need.

GOD'S WILL FOR US
July 7

Jeremiah 29:11, "'For I know the plans I have for you,' declares the LORD, 'plans to prosper you and not to harm you, plans to give you hope and a future.'"

How often I have not believed that God's plans were going to bring prosperity and success! Rather I worried and fretted about what would happen if I did as He thought best.

But as time has passed, I have become more comfortable with God and His will.

There is the story of a man who was crossing the Mississippi River. He walked out onto the ice, but when he reached the center of the river, he became frightened that the ice might break through. He began to crawl on all fours and finally began to creep across the ice on his belly, fearful that it might crack open under him. He could hear the water flowing beneath and see the bubbles rushing along.

> *Study carefully the experience of the prophets. They gave themselves to God and were used mightily by Him to change the world. We may have the same experience if we will move forward in faith.*

After several minutes, in the distance, he heard a team and wagon approaching. The driver was singing loudly. In a moment it raced by him and on to the other bank.

How foolish he felt when he realized the ice was thick enough to support a team of horses and a loaded wagon while he crept on his belly! He stood up and walked cheerfully to the yonder shore.[110]

We are often as foolish as this man. We fail to realize that God's purposes are best and that if we would trust Him with ourselves completely, He would direct us in unfailing paths. So much anxiety could be avoided!

Study carefully the experience of the prophets. They gave themselves to God and were used mightily by Him to change the world. We may have the same experience if we will move forward in faith.

---

[110] "Faith," Sermon illustrations, https://1ref.us/1im (accessed January 20, 2021).

HOLY, HOLY, HOLY
July 8

Isaiah 6:1–3, "I saw the Lord, high and exalted, seated on a throne; and the train of his robe filled the temple. Above him were seraphim, each with six wings: With two wings they covered their faces, with two they covered their feet, and with two they were flying. And they were calling to one another: 'Holy, holy, holy is the LORD Almighty; the whole earth is full of his glory.'"

These verses tell of Isaiah's vision of God's throne. He was so impressed with the holiness of God that he felt he would be destroyed because of his unclean lips. But an angel came and touched them, anointing them with a message for Israel (Isa. 6:5–6). He became the greatest of the writing prophets.

However, the words of the angels are astonishing. While viewing the earth from heaven, they cry out, "Holy, holy, holy is the LORD Almighty, the *whole earth* is full of his glory" (Isa. 6:3, emphasis added).

When I look out over our world, I miss what they're seeing. How can the whole earth with all its pain, sorrow, war and destruction be full of His glory? How can they see glory when such things as plagues, death and abuse fill the planet? It is a prime argument of the atheists.

The angels are holy beings. They are sensitive to evil, yet it is the glory of God that they notice.

When Moses asked to see God's glory, God passed before him and said, "The LORD, the LORD, the compassionate and gracious God, slow to anger, abounding in love and faithfulness, maintaining love to thousands, and forgiving wickedness, rebellion and sin" (Exod. 34:6–7).

When the angels see our world, they see the graciousness of God in action. They are astounded by the depths of it and proclaim loudly that the earth, even with its wickedness and sin, most fully reveals it.

Let us strive to see what they do.

UNCLAIMED FREIGHT
July 9

Isaiah 55:1, "Come, all you who are thirsty, come to the waters; and you who have no money, come, buy and eat! Come, buy wine and milk without money and without cost."

Some delivery companies have a room of goods that have been left by people that ordered what was sent but never collected it. Amazing. There's even a furniture store called Unclaimed Freight, though that is not all they deal in.

It is wonderful what God has done for us in His Son. He has given us righteousness as a gift without requiring us to pay some terrible price or go on some arduous pilgrimage or do some great feat of power.

Listen to what Ellen White says:

> Not by painful struggles or wearisome toil, not by gift or sacrifice, is righteousness obtained; but it is *freely given* to every soul who hungers and thirsts to receive it. "Ho, every one that thirsteth, come ye to the waters, and he that hath no money; come ye, buy, and eat, ... without money and without price." Isaiah 55:1; 54:17; Jeremiah 23:6.
>
> No human agent can supply that which will satisfy the hunger and thirst of the soul. But Jesus says, "Behold, I stand at the door, and knock: if any man hear My voice, and open the door, I will come in to him, and will sup with him, and he with Me." "I am the bread of life: he that cometh to Me shall never hunger; and he that believeth on Me shall never thirst." Revelation 3:20; John 6:35.[111]

It is a gift, and with gifts, all that is required is to accept it. But many do not and will not. The gift is thus unclaimed.

There is a huge store of righteousness left, enough to supply the whole world and cover all the unrighteousness that the devil has managed to manufacture. What a tragedy!

We, however, may have it for free! Oh, the blessing and wonder of God's love.

---

[111] Ellen G. White, *Thoughts From the Mount of Blessing* (Mountain View, CA: Pacific Press, 1896), p. 18, emphasis added.

HOSEA

July 10

Hosea 1:2-3, "When the LORD began to speak through Hosea, the LORD said to him, 'Go, marry a promiscuous woman and have children with her, for like an adulterous wife this land is guilty of unfaithfulness to the LORD.' So he married Gomer."

One of the strangest commands in the Bible is the one given to Hosea: "Go marry a prostitute!" Such a command is akin to that given Abraham to sacrifice his son on the mountain or when Jesus commanded the paralytic to carry his mat through Jerusalem on the Sabbath (Jer. 17:21). Such commands are given that God might reveal Himself in a profound way, a way that could be done in no other way.

The command to Hosea comes because His people have fallen into idolatry, a kind of prostitution. They have sold themselves to other lovers for nothing, as Ezekiel had noted in chapter 16 of his book.

God wants to give a living example of what they have done and the love He has for them. He asks Hosea to marry one that none of us would marry, one that we would never want one of our children to marry—a prostitute! It is a shocking command.

And yet Hosea's book is so full of love, compassion and the yearning of the soul of our loving God.

"How can I give you up ...?" he asks. "My heart is changed within me" (Hosea 11:8). These are the words of a wounded lover who still loves in spite of betrayal and the terrible pain of rejection. God desires Israel to see the feelings He has for them and knows of no better way than to send a prophet that has gone through the same pain, rejection and brokenness of heart.

Praise God that Hosea was willing to be God's servant here.

HABAKKUK: THE PROBLEM OF EVIL
July 11

Habakkuk 1:2, "How long, LORD, must I call for help, but you do not listen?"

The wonderful little book of Habakkuk gives an answer, at least partially, to the problem of evil and God's dealing with it.

Habakkuk had been living in the southern kingdom of Judah among God's chosen ones, but had noticed great wickedness. The poor were oppressed and the widow and orphan cheated. The law was paralyzed and the wicked surrounded the righteous (Hab. 1:4). But these were God's people! How could He allow such a travesty to continue without taking action? Was God a God of justice or was there none?

Habakkuk prayed earnestly for an answer to his dilemma and God responded to him in Habakkuk 1:5–6, 8–9, 11. God said:

"Look and be astounded, for I am doing what no one would have believed even if told!

I am sending the Babylonians that ruthless people ....

Their horses are swifter than leopards, fiercer than wolves at dusk ....

They all come intent on violence.

They sweep past like the wind and go on ....

guilty people, whose own strength is their god."

Habakkuk was shocked! How could God do such a thing using a pagan nation to discipline His "holy" people?

"How can you send for punishment a people that are more evil than we are? Your eyes are too pure to see evil. How can a holy God, the Judge of all, use unholy means? It seems things are even worse than before!"

Then Habakkuk waited for God's response.

HABAKKUK: GOD'S ANSWER
July 12

Habakkuk 2:12, "Woe to him who builds a city with bloodshed and establishes a town by injustice!"

God's answer to Habakkuk was not to tell him that the Babylonians would not invade Judah. There was not to be mercy for the years of sin they had committed. He was to expect the arrival of ruthless conquerors. But that was not the end of the matter.

God sang a song that was to be sung over Babylon. This song is an ancient form of literature called a "Taunt Song" (Hab. 2:6). In such poems, a foe receives a glimpse of the future they can expect because of their own wickedness. God showed that Babylon would not go unpunished for their sins.

The song has 5 stanzas and each starts with "Woe."

"Woe to him who piles up stolen goods …!" (Hab. 2:6).

"Woe to him who builds his house by unjust gain …!" (verse 9).

"Woe to him who builds a city with bloodshed …!" (verse 12).

"Woe to him who gives drink to his neighbors … till they are drunk …!" (verse 15).

"Woe to him who says to wood, 'Come to life!'" (verse 19).

So, although the Babylonians were to come and take Judah captive, they would, in the end, suffer for the evil things that they did, above the work that God had called them to do.

God's answer was not an answer of peace and hope, but one of death and destruction. He could not comfort Habakkuk with words that would have put his mind at rest. Rather, the future looked to be one of foreboding and ruin.

What was Habakkuk to do? All seemed lost. He responds in a beautiful poem of faith in Habakkuk 3.

HABAKKUK: THE PRAYER OF FAITH
July 13

Habakkuk 3:19, "The Sovereign LORD is my strength; he makes my feet like the feet of a deer, he enables me to tread on the heights."

With the realization that Judah was doomed to invasion by a ruthless nation of thieves bent on plunder and destruction, Habakkuk sings a song himself, instructing the musicians to use a certain tune, *shigionoth* (Hab. 3:1).

He describes the power of God to do as He wishes with the wicked, to send His armies to crush their leaders and to pierce their heads with their own spears. God is all-powerful, walking on the sea and bringing to naught the will of the destroyers (Hab. 2:4–20).

But Habakkuk has no delusions about the invasion: it will surely come.

"I heard and my heart pounded …. Yet I will wait patiently for the day of calamity to come on the nation invading us" (Hab. 3:16).

"Though the fig tree does not bud and there are no grapes on the vines, though the olive crop fails and the fields produce no food, though there are no sheep in the pen and no cattle in the stalls, yet I will rejoice in the LORD, I will be joyful in God my Savior" (verses 17–18).

Habakkuk comes to faith after listening to the answers God gave to his questions. He sees that the wickedness of the people of Judah will be met with punishment from Babylon who will be punished in turn by those that come after them. He comforts himself that the day of calamity will come on the nation invading them. In spite of all the trouble and sorrow that he knows he will see, when there is no food and the crops fail, he will rejoice in God his Savior.

Can we come to such a conclusion?

HABAKKUK: THE CONCLUSION
July 14

Habakkuk 3:17, "The Sovereign LORD is my strength; he makes my feet like the feet of a deer, he enables me to tread on the heights."

Habakkuk complained when he saw evil among the righteous and wondered why God did not punish that evil by judgment. "How long?" was his cry.

God would answer the injustice in Judah by bringing an evil nation against them, doing even worse evil. Is this really an answer?

Habakkuk did not think so. That God would compound evil with more evil did not solve anything, but rather made a bad situation worse. Could such action come from a holy God?

God seemed to ignore Habakkuk's objection, but showed that the evil nation coming to destroy Judah would itself be brought to judgment in time. This satisfied Habakkuk, but should it satisfy us?

The problem is the use God made of Babylon, a wicked pagan people. Why would a holy God use them, as servants so to speak, to do His will when they were evil people themselves? Evil increases rather than decreases. How can this be righteous? Do ends justify means?

When a people or nation leaves the way of God, He will often withdraw His protecting care from them. Though mercy may plead, judgement cannot be delayed forever. God does not shrink from this withdrawal; it is the natural consequence of sin. This removal of protection permits Satan to have his way, resulting in trouble and woe as Judah learned. God's retreat brought Satan's advance through the wicked Babylonians. They would be punished in turn for their wickedness.

God gave Habakkuk insight so that his faith might be anchored to a solid rock—God's character—during troubling times. Ours can be anchored as well, if we will heed Habakkuk's lesson.

WHY DO THE WICKED PROSPER? PART 1
July 15

Psalm 73:1–3, "Surely God is good to Israel, to those who are pure in heart. But as for me, my feet had almost slipped; I had nearly lost my foothold. For I envied the arrogant when I saw the prosperity of the wicked."

There are several reasons why the wicked might prosper and be successful.

1. They might develop the talents that God has given. He is the Giver of all good gifts, and they develop theirs to their best ability in spite of their wickedness.

2. They might follow God's laws of success. These involve diligence and hard work. They study the issues that impact their chosen careers and do not flinch from taking the time necessary to become experts in what they do. After all, if their goal is to gain wealth, they, if dedicated, will use all their resources to gain it.

3. Satan may give them opportunities to be successful. He offered Christ the kingdoms of this world if He would worship him. If Satan sees one who would be willing to sell his soul for such gain, he might choose to honor this request for his own advantage. Many accept the splendid bribe to gain the world! Jesus has warned us of such a transaction: "What good is it for someone to gain the whole world, yet forfeit their soul?" (Mark 8:36).

4. Luck. Some of us are just plain lucky. Solomon observed that time and chance happen to us all. Although we almost always think of these chance happenings as bad, they, by all the rules of probability, could be good as well. Some people are just lucky.

5. They may be good cheaters. They steal and defraud well, so become good at it. Mafia types would fit here.

There may be other reasons why the wicked prosper, but there is one other important one that we seldom consider.

WHY DO THE WICKED PROSPER? PART 2
July 16

Matthew 5:44–45, "But I tell you, love your enemies and pray for those who persecute you, that you may be children of your Father in heaven. He causes his sun to rise on the evil and the good, and sends rain on the righteous and the unrighteous."

The last reason that the wicked may prosper is that God prospers them!

Job's friends would have thought this ridiculous, but it is what God does.

It is a part of Jesus' sermon on the mount, and He is quite clear on the matter. The Father actually *causes* His sun to rise on the evil and *sends* His rain to the unrighteous. Why?

Because He is that sort of a God. There is no ill will on His part toward His human children even if they are wicked. He loves them and would save them from themselves. And He sends them the bounties of His creation out of the sheer generosity of His inner being.

Not just that, when He tells us in the same passage to love our enemies and pray for those that persecute us, He is merely asking us to join Him in the love that naturally flows from the depths of His character.

I have found this command to be most difficult in practice. To be ill-treated and to return love and concern for the perpetrator's success goes against the very nature of my being. It is just totally unfair. They should get what they deserve ….

But then I am reflecting the character of the accuser and not that of our Savior. He has shown mercy in all things, forgiving me for my petty selfishness and rebellion. And didn't Jesus say we are to pray, "Forgive us our sins, for we also forgive everyone who sins against us"? (Luke 11:4).

Praying to do that won't work. Only surrendering to Him who is love so that He might work His will in us will change us. Let us then give ourselves afresh to Him.

SHADRACH, MESHACH AND ABEDNEGO
July 17

Daniel 3:16–18:

> *Shadrach, Meshach and Abednego replied to him [the king], "King Nebuchadnezzar, we do not need to defend ourselves before you in this matter. If we are thrown into the blazing furnace, the God we serve is able to deliver us from it, and he will deliver us from Your Majesty's hand. But even if he does not, we want you to know, Your Majesty, that we will not serve your gods or worship the image of gold you have set up."*

The three Hebrew worthies were saved from the fiery furnace when they refused to bow to the idol of the king's power. They were unconsumed and were visited by "One like a son of the gods" (Dan. 3:25) who walked with them among the flames. What an honor was theirs!

But because of this miracle, their speech before the king is often overlooked. It was a speech of amazing faith and refusal to be cowed no matter what the result might be. And it was given before there was any inkling of their salvation from the flames. (It should be noted that even if they were not saved from the flames, they were "rescued" from the hand of the king!)

Their faith in God was not dependent on their deliverance. They would worship none but the God of heaven whether their lives were preserved or not.

"But even if he does not ... we will not serve your gods" (Dan. 3:18). Not all of God's saints are delivered from their trials. We must face that fact squarely as these men did. John the Baptist died in prison, Paul was beheaded and Peter was crucified. Our path may not end with our lives protected.

But though we may not be saved, we can rest in the arms of the One who is all-seeing and knows the end from the beginning, a way that ends with *eternal* life.

WEALTH PART 1
July 18

Deuteronomy 8:17–18, "You may say to yourself, 'My power and the strength of my hands have produced this wealth for me.' But remember the LORD your God, for it is he who gives you the ability to produce wealth."

Money, money, money! If we only had more money, we could be so much happier.

Surprising as it may seem to some, God does not wish poverty on us. He gives us the power to get wealth. He, after all, could have made us all poor, unable to make money or turn our labor into goods and services that allow us to prosper. In fact, He is so generous that He gives us talents that He freely allows us to use to support ourselves and even to support ourselves comfortably.

But many of us struggle to use our wealth wisely. Some of us spend it foolishly, buying shoddy products that do not endure. Others indulge in binges of buying those things that do not give lasting satisfaction.

And yet others invest their money wisely, but ignore the Giver of their talents. They think they are the ones responsible for what they have earned, and that no one else has any right to tell them what to do with it.

To each of these problems God has an answer: "I have given you the power to get wealth. Do not think that it is the result of your own hands, or minds, or bodies. I have given you these gifts and I have something to say about what you do with the gifts I have given you" (Deut. 8:17–18, paraphrase).

He knows where wisdom lies in this matter and has given us advice.

Let us see what He has to say.

WEALTH PART 2
July 19

Job 1:9–10, "'Does Job fear God for nothing?' Satan replied. 'Have you not put a hedge around him and his household and everything he has? You have blessed the work of his hands, so that his flocks and herds are spread throughout the land.'"

Before we discuss God's advice, there is another attitude that must be mentioned. Some feel that God does not really want us to be successful, that He does not have an interest in our prosperity, but only in hard discipline. That He is a hard taskmaster.

Satan, however, knows otherwise. When God bragged about His servant Job, Satan complained, "You have placed a hedge around him to protect him" (Job 1:10, paraphrase). That protection allowed Job to amass a huge fortune in flocks and herds. The very hedge that God had erected made it possible for him to become one of the wealthiest men in the Middle East at that time.

God does not work against the getting of wealth, but desires that we might prosper and be healthy (3 John 2). And, "'For I know the plans I have for you,' declares the LORD, 'plans to prosper you and not to harm you, plans to give you hope and a future'" (Jer. 29:11).

But there is danger. Paul warns us, "Those who want to get rich fall into temptation and a trap and into many foolish and harmful desires …. For the love of money is a root of all kinds of evil" (1 Tim. 6:9–10).

How then can we gain a proper balance when it comes to wealth? How can we avoid the temptation that wealth, a gift of God, presents?

He has not left us defenseless. He has a way to keep us from making wealth an idol.

WEALTH PART 3: WEALTH WITHOUT GUILT
July 20

Malachi 3:8–10, "Will a mere mortal rob God? Yet you rob me. But you ask, 'How are we robbing you?' 'In tithes and offerings. You are under a curse—your whole nation—because you are robbing me. Bring the whole tithe into the storehouse .... and see if I will not throw open the floodgates of heaven.'"

Robbery! Stealing is a serious affair, but robbing God? How could we break the ninth commandment more completely?!

But this protest by God shows how we might deal with our wealth legitimately.

Tithing and giving offerings is the way we show that we recognize God as the originator of our wealth. That portion is His. He claims it as His own. And if we honestly give Him what is His own, it means that the remaining is legitimately ours for any proper use to which we might put it.

Tithing and giving offerings legitimizes our wealth. It makes it actually ours, really ours. We are not keeping something that does not belong to us, but are accepting with thanksgiving the very thing, the portion that God wants to give. He knows that we are bedazzled by money and wealth, that we do not really know how to handle it properly. So, He gives a means of making it ours while checking our natural selfishness.

Actually, God wants us to be wealthy. In heaven, after all, the very streets are paved with gold (Rev. 21:21). So it is not that God desires us to be poor. But He knows our weakness and so gives us the opportunity to use our wealth for good and to do it without guilt.

That is what tithing and giving offerings does for us. Wealth without guilt. What a gift that is!

WEALTH PART 4: THE WIDOW AND HER TWO MITES
July 21

Luke 21:2–4, "He also saw a poor widow put in two very small copper coins. 'Truly I tell you,' he said, 'this poor widow has put in more than all the others. All these people gave their gifts out of their wealth; but she out of her poverty put in all she had to live on.'"

What are we to make of Jesus' comment?

The Bible does not tell us that we are to give all that we have to God's cause. He has said that He will bless us if we return our tithes and, out of our love for Him, give generous offerings to further His work in the world.

So, why this commendation? One could even argue that it was silly for her to give all she had. How was she to support herself now? And the amount would hardly fund a minute's work at the temple.

But this offering was so significant that Jesus saw it as the only real gift given that day.

These two small coins represented a heart devotion to God. It was a deep abiding love for God that prompted the widow to cast all of her livelihood into the treasury.

Like lovers who give all to each other, this widow gave all to God. Her whole heart was in her offering: it was not the practical performance of duty that tithing is, but the act of casting her whole self on her Beloved, giving her all to Him.

Such monetary giving is not required. But God longs for the love and devotion the gift represented. It is the deepest desire of His gracious heart, for it recognizes the loving act He has done in sending Jesus. He gave all He had.

WEALTH PART 5: HEAVEN FOR HALF PRICE
July 22

Luke 18:22–23, "When Jesus heard this, he said to him, 'You still lack one thing. Sell everything you have and give to the poor …. Then come, follow me.' When he heard this, he became very sad, because he was very wealthy."

Luke 19:8–9, "But Zacchaeus stood up and said to the Lord, 'Look, Lord! Here and now I give half of my possessions to the poor ….' Jesus said to him, 'Today salvation has come to this house.'"

These stories, almost next to each other in the book of Luke, seem to show inconsistency and bias. The rich young ruler was commanded to give up *all* his possessions and Jesus noted that when he left that he was missing the kingdom. But Zacchaeus only gave *half* of his goods, keeping half to himself. Was that fair? Did Jesus deal too severely with that young man?

On the surface, it appears Jesus was inconsistent. But there is something deeper here.

Jesus was not unfair. He knew the hearts of each and called them to do what was necessary to save their souls. The rich young ruler was so wedded to his wealth that Jesus had to sever the ties completely so that he might be saved. Zacchaeus, however, willingly gave of his possessions without even being asked, showing a different attitude towards his wealth. Jesus knew the hearts of each and acted accordingly.

Jesus told Peter when he asked about John's future, "If I want him to remain alive until I return, what is that to you? You must follow me" (John 21:22).

We are not responsible for others' duties, only our own. We too can leave the call and the reward with Him. Such an attitude will bring peace and rest and success in Jesus.

WEALTH PART 6: YES, YOU CAN TAKE IT WITH YOU!
July 23

Matthew 6:19–21, "Do not store up for yourselves treasures on earth, where moths and vermin destroy, and where thieves break in and steal. But store up for yourselves treasures in heaven .... For where your treasure is, there your heart will be also."

An old saying says: "You can't take it with you." But Jesus points out in His sermon on the mount that this is a lie of the devil.

It is as if Jesus, an investment strategist that has just opened His office, invites you in for an analysis of your portfolio.

"I have noticed that you are making a pretty good salary these days," He says, "It is time to talk about the future."

"Yes, I know about the stock market and those shares of Berkshire-Hathaway® you have been following. They have appreciated nicely over the past few years, haven't they? But I would like to advise you about another strategy. Crashes, depressions and stock failures come and even the best investments fail. But there is a place where deposits only appreciate, and where they are safe forever. Heaven itself. God oversees the investment, and He is a master strategist. I advise you to put whatever you can there. It is safe, and the returns are astounding. Nothing is guaranteed here. But all you put there will be there when you get there, with compound interest. There is no better portfolio that I can think of. Be wise with your money. Don't let the vagaries of the markets here steal what you have worked so hard to obtain."

You stand up to leave. Jesus shakes your hand and gives you His prospectus, explaining how it works.

What will you do with His advice?

THE IMAGE OF DANIEL 2

July 24

Daniel 2:31, "Your Majesty looked, and there before you stood a large statue—an enormous, dazzling statue, awesome in appearance."

We seldom realize what a wonderful gift to us was this dream of Nebuchadnezzar! Not only was the curtain of time pulled back that we might see that the future was one of hope, that God had it in His hand, and that regardless of the circumstances of our lives God would establish a kingdom founded on justice, but the dream presented a simple interpretation of the future.

First, it is easy to understand. The image of a great statue made of various metals decreasing in value in descending order is not complicated. And the idea of regression is clear (Dan. 2:32-35).

Then Daniel explains the meaning of each part, giving pride of place to the king, thus anchoring Babylon as the beginning of the sequence of kingdoms, that there may be no error in the vision's decoding.

Finally, the interpretation cannot be misunderstood. There is to be a progression of kingdoms through time, each inferior to the last, but each becoming increasingly stronger than its predecessor (Dan. 2:38-42). This historical method of interpretation is key to all the visions of Daniel and Revelation. The first, most simple vision gives a clue to understand all the rest. It was a brilliant stroke.

God wished to convey to us the hope that was in Him and that He was in control of the future. But how could He convey it so that we might not misunderstand? He used a vision of utter simplicity that could not be gainsaid.

He has given us a gift of surpassing value, a gift of hope, easy to understand. Let us rejoice in His love.

RAISING UP AND PUTTING DOWN KINGS PART 1
July 25

Daniel 2:20–21, "Praise be to the name of God for ever and ever; wisdom and power are his. He changes times and seasons; he deposes kings and raises up others."

What responsibility does God bear for the horror of the Holocaust? Or the purges of Stalin? Was it His will that Mao devise a "The Great Leap Forward" that caused the death of 45 million?[112] Is all this His fault?

Daniel praises Him after he has learned of the interpretation of Nebuchadnezzar's dream. "You are the one who raises up kings and puts them down," he said (Dan. 2:21, paraphrase). If that is so, does He bear the responsibility for their actions—good or bad?

God does raise up kings and princes and deposes them, but there are other issues here. He respects the wills of men, a gift He has given them at great cost to Himself.

First, God claims in several places in Scripture that He raises up and puts down kings.

Psalm 75:6–7, "No one from the east or the west or from the desert can exalt themselves. It is God who judges: he brings one down, he exalts another."

Isaiah 45:1, "This is what the LORD says to his anointed, to Cyrus, whose right hand I take hold of to subdue nations."

Job 12:23, "He makes nations great, and destroys them; he enlarges nations, and disperses them."

It seems then that God is responsible for the setting up of kings and the success of men of power. To deny that is to deny the plain teaching of God's Word.

But what about Hitler and Stalin and Mao? Is He responsible for their actions and evil ways?

---

[112]"Great Leap Forward," Wikipedia, https://1ref.us/1in (accessed January 20, 2021).

RAISING UP AND PUTTING DOWN KINGS PART 2
July 26

1 Samuel 8:6–9:

> But when they [the Israelites] said, "Give us a king to lead us," this displeased Samuel; so he prayed to the LORD. And the LORD told him: "Listen to all that the people are saying to you; it is not you they have rejected, but they have rejected me as their king. As they have done from the day I brought them up out of Egypt until this day, forsaking me and serving other gods, so they are doing to you. Now listen to them; but warn them solemnly and let them know what the king who will reign over them will [do] ...."

There is another consideration in the setting up of kings and rulers. God allows for the wills of men, of nations and of individuals.

He did not want Israel to have a king, He wanted to be their king, but when you read the story of Judges, the people even then were restless under God's rule and desired a man to lead them. So, in the end, God let them have what they wanted—a king.

In the chaos of history, groups of men, supporting one leader clash with others in war and strife, struggling to gain power that they might rule. It is not God's will that this happen, but He allows for it. He gives them what they want.

He may work behind the scenes to effect His will, but He has given us freedom and so allows us to suffer the consequences of our choices. And these can be terrible indeed.

Is God responsible for the evil of men like Hitler and Stalin? He must have had some part in their rise to power.

RAISING UP AND PUTTING DOWN KINGS PART 3
July 27

Daniel 2:37, "Your Majesty, you are the king of kings. The God of heaven has given you dominion and power and might and glory; in your hands he has placed all mankind .... You are that head of gold."

The example of King Nebuchadnezzar is given to us that we might know how God works in history.

God clearly claims to have put Nebuchadnezzar on his throne.

But when we read the book of Daniel, we learn that Nebuchadnezzar rebels against God. He builds an image of gold, commanding that all bow down to it to signify that his kingdom will never end (Dan. 3:1–5). His pride causes him to claim title as "Builder of Babylon," refusing to acknowledge that God is the One that has given him power (Dan. 4:30).

Secular sources show his ruthlessness on occasion and even his mental illness at the end of his life (Daniel 4).

Was God responsible for all this? Of course not.

God does take responsibility for putting a man on the throne and giving him the reins of power. God puts down and raises up kings.

But men are responsible and the people are responsible for their own acts. Especially is this so in America where we vote in our own leaders. God has allowed us this freedom and we are responsible for the use we make of it. He cannot be blamed if we make a hash of the whole thing by choosing wicked men.

Thus, Obama and Trump are "God's choice," but they were chosen through us. He has allowed the process to be put in place, but we do the choosing.

We must be serious then about how we vote. We and the world will suffer the results of those choices.

RAISING UP AND PUTTING DOWN KINGS PART 4
July 28

Daniel 10:12–13:

> *Then he [the angel] continued, "Do not be afraid, Daniel. Since the first day that you set your mind to gain understanding and to humble yourself before your God, your words were heard, and I have come in response to them. But the prince of the Persian kingdom resisted me twenty-one days. Then Michael, one of the chief princes, came to help me, because I was detained there with the king of Persia."*

The angel here pulls back the curtain separating the heavenly economy from the earthly one.

Daniel had been mourning for three weeks, when an angel appeared to him. He was sent to tell Daniel that his prayers regarding his people were answered. The angel, as an aside, spoke of his struggle with the king of Persia.

One would think that God could just make the king do what he wanted. But that does not appear to be the case. Rather, the angel had spent three weeks dealing in some way with the king who was resisting. It sounds as if the angel is using some type of persuasive power that was not overwhelming. The king withstood him. As the issue became critical, Michael was called in and the king relented.

These few verses reveal how God deals with the earthly rulers He has put in place. They seem to be quite free to resist Him. This would explain the great evil that some have inflicted on us. They, unlike the king of Persia, did as they would in spite of God's will for them.

We must take their freedom to act into account, even though God put them in place. God blessed them with power but they will often refuse to exercise it as God would have them. It is a critical distinction.

THE END OF TIME
July 29

Daniel 5:1–2, "King Belshazzar gave a great banquet for a thousand of his nobles and drank wine with them. While Belshazzar was drinking his wine, he gave orders to bring in the gold and silver goblets that Nebuchadnezzar his father had taken from the temple in Jerusalem, so that the king and his nobles, his wives and his concubines might drink from them."

God has given us warnings about the end of time, but this story in Daniel gives a clue as to why God brings the earth's history to an end.

Belshazzar was not a righteous man. The history of Nebuchadnezzar was known to him, but instead of humbling himself, he set himself against the God of heaven. His final act of defiance was to bring in the sacred articles from the temple to drink wine from them! At that point, his fate was sealed by the handwriting on the wall.

Our culture is a wicked one. The world has had some reverence for the sacred, but that has nearly disappeared from Western culture. We have become corrupt and full of sin.

But now some are beginning to mock righteousness and all that is good. Nothing is sacred and sacred things are dragged in the muck of sensuality and sexual innuendo as if God does not hear and see. Those that would stand for righteousness are derided in the public square. It is only a matter of time until the sacred vessels will be used to drink the wine of sin.

Anyone can read the results of such acts. Destruction will be swift and sure and Jesus will come to end the sacrilege and take His people home.

Let us prepare ourselves and turn from our sins that He might save us and make us His.

Section 9

God in Human Form Comes to Earth

God sent His Son to teach us the way of truth and to die for our sins. He was given as the Light of the world. And we can be as cities set on hills if we will allow Him to enlighten us.

> Once in royal David's city
> Stood a lowly cattle shed,
> Where a mother laid her Baby
> In a manger for His bed;
> Mary was that mother mild,
> Jesus Christ her little Child.[113]

---

[113] Cecil Alexander, "Once in Royal David's City," *The Seventh-day Adventist Hymnal* (Hagerstown, MD: Review and Herald, 1985).

JOSEPH, SON OF DAVID PART 1
July 30

Matthew 1:18, "This is how the birth of Jesus the Messiah came about: His mother Mary was pledged to be married to Joseph, but before they came together, she was found to be pregnant through the Holy Spirit."

His first wife had died several months ago, and he could just not shake the depression that gripped his soul.

Then one day, a young woman entered his shop seeking help with her father's rental property. Her smile caused his heart to skip a beat.

The job was a small one, but the two of them began to have feelings for one another, and as time went on, he realized she would perfectly fulfill the void in his aching heart. When an opportune moment came, he asked her for her hand in marriage and after confirming their plans with her father, a date was set.

Oh, how sweet it was to be in her presence! They spent time looking into each other's eyes longing for the time when they could love one another fully.

Then one evening while Mary was mending the garment of a neighbor child, an angel appeared and told her she was to become pregnant by the Holy Spirit (Luke 1:26–32). It was an amazing announcement. The angel also told her of her relative, Elizabeth, who was pregnant in her old age, and Mary decided a visit for the older woman's counsel would help (Luke 1:39–40). She left immediately.

But the time came to return home and she must tell Joseph.

"I'm pregnant," she said.

"I noticed," he answered sarcastically.

"Joseph! It's not what you think. I would never be unfaithful to you. An angel told me I would become pregnant with the King of Israel. And so I am! You must believe me, Joseph!"

"How could you do this? You turned my sad night into day. And now this! Mary, Mary," and his shoulders began to heave, sobbing. He turned and left.[114]

---
[114]Dramatization based on Matthew 1:18–24.

JOSEPH, SON OF DAVID PART 2
July 31

Matthew 1:18–20:

> His mother Mary was pledged to be married to Joseph, but before they came together, she was found to be pregnant through the Holy Spirit. Because Joseph her husband was faithful to the law, and yet did not want to expose her to public disgrace, he had in mind to divorce her quietly. But ... an angel of the Lord appeared to him in a dream and said, "Joseph, son of David, do not be afraid to take Mary home as your wife, because what is conceived in her is from the Holy Spirit."

What was Joseph to do? His sweetheart had just told him she was pregnant—er, by the, ah, "Holy Spirit." Really??

He didn't believe it either but loved her still. How could he expose her to the ridicule of the community? Though his heart was broken, he devised a plan to divorce her privately. With sadness he made the arrangements.

Then an angel came in a dream. A dream no less! (an angel had *spoken* to Mary in person). One can wonder whether he struggled to accept the prerogative God had taken with his betrothed. He had burst into their relationship in a most unorthodox manner. Did he resent it? There is no hint of that, but only of submission to God's will and the shouldering of the responsibility of raising a Child not his own.

How could God do such a thing? Break into a romance! But it was just what He had to do to bring His Son into the world. God needed a *couple* who truly loved one another so an earthly father could support and discipline the Christ (Heb. 5:8). He was chosen just as much as Mary.

Because he was willing to subordinate his manly privilege to the Father, Mary had a protector for the Child.

NO ROOM IN THE INN
August 1

Luke 2:4, 6–7, "So Joseph also went up from the town of Nazareth in Galilee to Judea to Bethlehem the town of David .... While they were there, the time came for the baby to be born and she .... wrapped him in cloths and placed him in a manger, because there was no room for them in the inn."

Micah 5:2, written centuries before Jesus' birth, says that the Ruler would be born in Bethlehem of Judah. That "Little Town of Bethlehem" mentioned in the carol.[115] Yet, when He arrived, there was no room, not so much as a bed in the local inn. God knew He was coming and yet He seems to have made no preparation for Him.

No one appears to have had an inkling. The innkeeper thought it gracious to offer the stable; they were poor after all and it would at least be shelter. It was the *best* he could do (if he had only known!) But he did not know. Why?

Had God dropped the ball? It's almost as if the trip was an afterthought. But Micah's words reveal it was certainly not that. *Centuries to prepare*, and yet when it is accomplished, there is not a whisper in Bethlehem until the angels appear above the startled shepherds.

What's going on here? Psalm 121:8 says, "[T]he LORD will watch over your coming and going both now and forevermore." Really? If He does, there seems to have been a glitch of some type.

The chief priests *did* know the place where the Messiah was to be born and told Herod when he asked. They knew. But they had made no effort to prepare the town or the people for the Messiah. Though they had studied the prophecies, when the time actually arrived, they had made no arrangements.

John 1:11 says, "He came to that which was his own, but his own did not receive him." God had given them warning but would not force Himself on them. They thus lost the opportunity to welcome their Messiah. He had given them notice, but they ignored it and their secular king set out to destroy the Upstart.

---

[115]Phillips Brooks, "O Little Town of Bethlehem," *The Seventh-day Adventist Hymnal* (Hagerstown, MD: Review and Herald, 1985).

So, it remains today. God will not force Himself upon us to save us. He gives revelation and resources, but does not force the will. This is a sobering realization. God will not be trifled with. His opportunities to accept salvation and to cooperate with Him come with judgement if we do not avail ourselves of them. He is gracious but cannot save us from ourselves if we will not act. May God bless us.

IN THE MANGER
August 2

Luke 2:12, "This will be a sign to you: You will find a baby wrapped in cloths and lying in a manger."

When the angels burst into song over the quiet hills of Bethlehem that night, the shepherds quaked with fear, and were surprised by the message (Luke 2:8–12). But if angels announce your birth, you must be a Person of real significance. How often do angels come and do such a thing?

So, the shepherds are expecting a personage of real dignity and outstanding importance. The angels had to prepare them for something different. No, it is not the palace in Jerusalem that you will go to find this King. No, not there.

You must go to that stable by the inn. There, in a feeding trough you will find the newborn King.

A feeding trough? How could this be? The contrast with what one would expect when angels make the announcement is astounding.

The angels had said that this Child would be "the Messiah, the Lord." The Messiah, the Anointed One. Yet He is born in a stable and cradled in a feeding trough. The Baby comes with nothing, that is, none of the trimmings and trappings of royalty. In fact, He is born in a stable. But He is the King of the universe.

When Paul says that Jesus emptied Himself (Phil. 2:7), He meant that He truly set aside all the prerogatives of God. He took the lowest place, even being without a cradle. He borrowed a manger from the animals! That is stooping as low as one can go.

God emptied Himself so that we might be able to endure His presence. He so wanted us that He became like us in all things. What a blessing is ours to have such a God!

THE SHEPHERDS

August 3

Luke 2:8–11:

> *And there were shepherds living out in the fields nearby, keeping watch over their flocks at night. An angel of the Lord appeared to them, and the glory of the Lord shone around them, and they were terrified. But the angel said to them, "Do not be afraid. I bring you good news that will cause great joy for all the people. Today in the town of David a Savior has been born to you; he is the Messiah, the Lord."*

When I learned that shepherds were so distrusted by the Jews of Christ's day because they had a reputation as liars, I wondered why the angels were sent to them. That reputation even prevented their testimony in courts of law.[116]

But God sent the angelic hosts to them on the plains outside Bethlehem. What could be the reason?

It may be that they were the ones most likely to spread the news of the Messiah's birth to others.

Jesus was born in a stable to a peasant girl engaged to a carpenter. These were from the lower classes of society.

The high-born would not have accepted the angelic announcement. They would reason that it was impossible for this to be the Messiah and would not be willing to endure the embarrassment of telling anyone such a thing.

But the shepherds? They had no such scruples to impede them. Luke 2:17–18 says that "When they had seen him, they spread the word concerning what had been told them about this child, and all who heard it were amazed."

God found someone who could be depended on to do the work He needed done. They told the story to all who would hear.

---

[116]John Fieldsend, "Shepherds' character reference," CHURCH TIMES, https://1ref.us/1io (accessed January 20, 2021).

DON'T BE AFRAID

August 4

Luke 2:9–10, "An angel of the Lord appeared to them, and the glory of the Lord shone around them, and they were terrified. But the angel said to them, 'Do not be afraid.'"

When I was young, I was afraid of my father. It was not that he beat me or anything like that, but I worried that he would withhold love. I longed for his approval and though he seldom said anything either for or against me and was approving of my behavior most of the time (I did get the occasional spanking as did my siblings), there were areas where we differed that he might find silly. And these areas were very important to me and I did not feel he understood.

It can be that way with God. He is all-powerful and we do sin so that we most certainly have earned His disapproval. The consciousness of our shortcomings and sins can make us afraid and feel He is unapproachable.

But God understands that. It is clear that He knows that we feel this way, so whenever a messenger from Him appears, they are quick to calm us with their words.

The angels that met the shepherds on Christmas did that very thing. When they manifested themselves, the shepherds were terrified. Scared to death, you might say. So, to calm their fears, even before delivering their message of great joy, they said, "Don't be afraid!"

"Don't be afraid!" How often we are filled with fear when our heavenly Father has no intention of harm whatsoever. His assurances from the past should make us realize His good will towards us now.

Let us then come boldly into His presence for there is no anger there (Heb. 4:16). He has taken care of that with Jesus.

THE WISE MEN PART 1
August 5

Matthew 2:1, "[D]uring the time of King Herod, Magi from the east came to Jerusalem and asked, 'Where is the one who has been born king of the Jews? We saw his star when it rose and have come to worship him.'"

The Magi were learned men from Persia, usually followers of Zoroaster. They were a well-known class to the ancients.[117] But these men came to Jerusalem with a startling question that was a political bombshell. They sought a baby King, but there was no baby to be found in Herod's palace. In fact, he had previously killed his beautiful wife, Miriam and their two sons for fear of their usurping the throne.[118] No, there was no baby cradled there. No wonder the whole city was troubled by the visitors!

The wise men had stepped into a situation of great peril. But their question was so simple and sincere that no one doubted their honesty. Being wise to the ways of the world, they now knew the danger their query had stirred. They quietly awaited the fate of strangers who had thrown the city into turmoil by their question. It was a fearful time.

Herod was not idle. He considered just killing these strangers, and that might have settled it, but what of that Baby? What *of* that Baby?

He hatched a scheme to use the wise men for his own ends. He asked the religious leaders where the Christ was to be born (Matt. 2:4). They answered: "'But you, Bethlehem, in the land of Judah, are by no means least among the rulers of Judah, for out of you will come a ruler who will shepherd my people Israel'" (Matt. 2:6).

He called the wise men privately and told them of his findings. He sent them on their way with the admonition to return and tell him of the new King that he might also worship.

---

[117] "Biblical Magi," Wikipedia, https://1ref.us/1ip (accessed January 20, 2021).
[118] "Herod the Great," Wikipedia, https://1ref.us/1iq (accessed January 20, 2021).

THE WISE MEN PART 2
August 6

Matthew 2:9–10, "After they had heard the king, they went on their way, and the star they had seen when it rose went ahead of them until it stopped over the place where the child was. When they saw the star, they were overjoyed."

They left Jerusalem less sure of their mission than when they had entered. Why this place of death and intrigue? Why a palace without a baby? Why had the star brought them there when no one knew of such a child?

Then, as evening fell they saw the star. The Bible says they were overjoyed, likely an understatement. But the amazing thing was that they left Jerusalem alone. *Alone!*

They followed it to Bethlehem, about a two hour's walk. The star stopped over a humble home. They knocked and a peasant girl answered, awakened from an untroubled sleep. A peasant girl!

Now these men knew the accoutrements of royalty: servants, soldiers for protection and a retinue of advisers like themselves. But here was a simple peasant, answering in her peasant ways, only she and her carpenter husband.

She invited them in, surprised at their presence. "Who sent you?" She asked. "What do you know of this Child?" They explained the story of the star, their quest and the visit to Jerusalem. She brought them to the cradle where Jesus lay.

Then to her amazement, they bowed in worship. First at the foot of the new King. Then, showing that they truly believed, they lay down their treasures: gold, frankincense and myrrh, likely a small fortune. They then left, disappearing into the mists of time.

But what a faith was theirs! And how God used them! He desires to use us as His messengers of peace as well. It only remains for us to submit to His leading for such a reality to occur. Let us then give ourselves anew as these men did.

THE GIFTS OF THE MAGI
August 7

Matthew 2:11, "On coming to the house, they saw the child with his mother Mary, and they bowed down and worshiped him. Then they opened their treasures and presented him with gifts of gold, frankincense and of myrrh."

The wise men were responsive to the leading of the Holy Spirit. They studied the starry heavens and beheld the glory of God seen there. They were not too proud to explore the Jewish Scripture though it had not been given to them. Turning to the prophecies, they were moved to follow the star that appeared at the birth of Jesus. To the light they had accepted, further light was given and they set out to find the King.

When they found the Savior, they lay their gifts at His feet and God used these to save His Son from the wrath of Herod.

Ellen White says this:

> The magi had been among the first to welcome the Redeemer. Their gift was the first that was laid at His feet. And through that gift, what privilege of ministry was theirs! The offering from the heart that loves, God delights to honor, giving it highest efficiency in service for Him. If we have given our hearts to Jesus, we also shall bring our gifts to Him. Our gold and silver, our most precious earthly possessions, our highest mental and spiritual endowments, will be freely devoted to Him who loved us, and gave Himself for us.[119]

And if we devote our gifts and ourselves to Him, He will use us and our gifts just as He used and blessed that of the Magi. We might have the same privilege they did! And the same blessing.

Let us then reconsecrate ourselves to the service of our Creator. He said, "Those who honor me I will honor" (1 Sam. 2:30).

---

[119] Ellen G. White, *The Desire of Ages* (Mountain View, CA: Pacific Press, 1898), p. 65.

THE REVEALING OF THOUGHTS
August 8

Luke 2:34–35, "Then Simeon blessed them and said to Mary, his mother, 'This child is destined to cause the falling and rising of many in Israel, and to be a sign that will be spoken against, so that the thoughts of many hearts will be revealed.'"

Ellen White comments on Simeon's cryptic message:

> In the light of the Savior's life, the hearts of all, even from the Creator to the prince of darkness, are revealed. Satan has represented God as selfish and oppressive, as claiming all, and giving nothing, as requiring the service of His creatures for His own glory, and making no sacrifice for their good. But the gift of Christ reveals the Father's heart. It testifies that the thoughts of God toward us are "thoughts of peace, and not of evil." Jeremiah 29:11. It declares that while God's hatred of sin is as strong as death, His love for the sinner is stronger than death. Having undertaken our redemption, He will spare nothing, however dear, which is necessary to the completion of His work .... The whole treasury of heaven is open to those He seeks to save. Having collected the riches of the universe, and laid open the resources of infinite power, He gives them all into the hands of Christ and says, All these are for man. Use these gifts to convince him that there is no love greater than Mine in earth or heaven. His greatest happiness will be found in loving Me.[120]

At the very beginning of Christ's life, the purpose of His mission is disclosed. Have you seen, dear reader, the love that has been bestowed on you? There is none greater. It requires our heart's devotion.

---

[120] Ibid., p. 57.

THE ESCAPE TO EGYPT
August 9

Matthew 2:13, "[A]n angel of the Lord appeared to Joseph in a dream. 'Get up,' he said, 'take the child and his mother and escape to Egypt.'"

When Jesus was born, the Magi with their gifts traveled through Jerusalem and met Herod who, after speaking to the priests, bade them go on to Bethlehem. They found Jesus there; but before they left, they dreamed of Herod's duplicity and took another route home (Matt. 2:12). Joseph too dreamed and left Bethlehem for Egypt, out of reach of Herod and his government.

Why did God protect His Son in this manner? Why not just bring Herod's life to a speedy end? Or send an army of angels to show that wicked ruler a thing or two? The answer is because God does not deal with us and the wicked in that way. Most men have chosen to align themselves with the evil one; we have free will and God respects our choices. *Almost always*, governments are allowed to act and do their wills and God does not interfere. He defers to the will of the people, the king or the president and allows them to follow whatever way they would go. He is always there to lead and guide, but only very rarely uses force.

In the same way, He will not overpower us and force us to do right. When we refuse, He allows the natural processes to work themselves out for good or ill.

Instead, as in this instance, He directs His people in the way they should go. Here, He gave a dream to the Magi and three messages to Joseph.

In other instances, prophets speak for Him, or His beloved receive messages by reading the Bible, praying or consulting together.

We should not expect God to remove the leadership of a country by force or power. He works in subtle ways, ways that respect our freedom of choice and our wills. Most governments are not run by godly men, and He will not communicate with them. In a sense, they are on their own, and we should not look to them for help or succor.

If we want God's guidance, it must be actively sought. He will reveal His will if we are willing to submit. Our duty is to humbly trust and obey.

A PATTERN FOR THE YOUNG
August 10

Luke 2:51–52, "Then he went down to Nazareth with them and was obedient to them. But his mother treasured all these things in her heart. And Jesus grew in wisdom and stature, and in favor with God and man."

How can young people gain the approval of God? He has not kept His will secret. Ellen White comments on Jesus' youth:

> Jesus is our example. There are many who dwell with interest upon the period of His public ministry, while they pass unnoticed the teachings of His early years. But it is in His home life that He is the pattern for all children and youth. The Savior condescended to poverty, that He might teach how closely we in a humble lot may walk with God. He lived to please, honor, and glorify His Father in the common things of life. His work began in consecrating the lowly trade of the craftsmen who toil for their daily bread. *He was doing God's service just as much when laboring at the carpenter's bench as when working miracles for the multitude.* And every youth who follows Christ's example of faithfulness and obedience in His lowly home may claim those words spoken of Him by the Father through the Holy Spirit, "Behold My Servant, whom I uphold; Mine Elect, in whom My soul delighteth." Isaiah 42:1[121]

Psalm 119:9, 11, "How can a young man stay on the path of purity? By living according to your word. I have hidden your word in my heart that I might not sin against you."

Jesus chose to live in poverty that He might be an example to us. The young in any circumstance may have Him at their side and gain the same approval that Jesus obtained from His Father.

---

[121]Ibid., p. 74, emphasis added.

RAIN ON THE JUST AND THE UNJUST
August 11

Matthew 5:45, "He causes his sun to rise on the evil and the good, and sends rain on the righteous and the unrighteous."

These indiscriminate actions of God have caused much confusion in the hearts of righteous and wicked alike. Job and his friends both believed God blessed the good and cursed the wicked and could not see God in the tragedies of Job and the apparent freedom from such that the wicked enjoyed.

The psalmist struggled as well. Psalm 73:1–3, "Surely God is good to Israel, to those who are pure in heart. But as for me, my feet had almost slipped; I had nearly lost my foothold. For I envied the arrogant when I saw the prosperity of the wicked."

The wicked become emboldened in sin because they do not see immediate justice for wrongdoing (Eccles. 8:11). The fields of the righteous and wicked both receive His sun and rain and their hearts are hardened. In Psalm 94:7 the wicked say, "The LORD does not see; the God of Jacob takes no notice."

But this characteristic of His being is so important to Him that He is willing to risk the confusion that ensues from its action. These gestures well up from the depths of His goodness. He must let the wicked know that He bears no ill will toward them and that He will bless them in spite of their evil ways. Paul sees it from a slightly different angle in Romans 5:8, "But God demonstrates his own love for us in this: While we were still sinners, Christ died for us."

And God would have His children reflect this love. Luke tells us that Jesus advised the rich of His day to invite to their banquets those that could not repay them with a return invitation (Luke 14:13). And Jesus after describing God's gifts of sun and rain to all, enjoins us to be therefore *perfect*, praying for our enemies and treating them with kindness (Matt. 5:44, 48). It is one of the most profound evidences that there is a God and that He rules in love.

Do you wish to be a witness to God's goodness? Then go and do as He would do on this matter.

A PROBLEM WITH THE INCARNATION PART 1
August 12

John 1:11, "He came to that which was his own, but his own did not receive him."

John 8:58-59, "'Very truly I tell you ... before Abraham was born, I am!' At this, they picked up stones to stone him."

There is a certain aspect of the incarnation that has always troubled me. It seems that God expected the Jews to realize that their Redeemer would come as a divine/human Figure. But when He came, they did not accept Him, assumed He was like other men and rejected His claims to divinity, even attempting to stone Him for blasphemy (John 8:59) and eventually crucifying Him as a blasphemer.

This rejection of Jesus has had huge repercussions. The Jews are outside the Christian fold and their children have almost uniformly turned from Jesus just as their parents did. Over the centuries, persecution has dogged their steps, driving them from their homes or forcing them to convert.

Was it reasonable to expect them to recognize their Redeemer as divine? Was there any clue in the Old Testament that there would come a divine Visitant and that He could call Himself God without sin?

There are several places in Scripture where God comes in human form, but the most telling is the visit to Abraham in Genesis 18. In this passage, Jehovah appears as a weary traveler and accepts Abraham's hospitality. He then asserts His divinity by confirming the promise, reading Sarah's mind and discussing the judgement on Sodom and Gomorrah with him. Abraham calls Him Jehovah, and the Visitor does not rebuke Abraham for this appellation (Gen. 18:22-24). It is a striking encounter.

There was thus precedent for a Human claiming to be a divine Figure and being called Jehovah. And this at a critical juncture in the history of Israel, the announcement of the birth of the promised Son. But that is not all.

A PROBLEM WITH THE INCARNATION PART 2
August 13

Isaiah 9:6–7, "For to us a child is born .... And he will be called Wonderful Counselor, Mighty God, Everlasting Father, Prince of Peace. Of the greatness of his government and peace there will be no end."

The Messiah, when He came, came gently and quietly but not without notice.

A Child was born in Bethlehem of a common laborer and his young wife. Yes, the shepherds heard angels and spread their tale which may have even reached Jerusalem. But shepherds? Their testimony, after all, was not even allowed in court. Was this really reliable information? Those strangers from the east, Magi, came looking for a newborn King, causing quite a stir, but left for Bethlehem and were never heard from again. Yes, Herod did kill some twenty or so infants, but he was becoming old and paranoid.[122] A couple of older folks who always hung about the temple had said something about a Child of promise, but that was it. What to make of it all? After this bit of excitement, things pretty much returned to normal.

This certainly could have been the thinking of most who knew anything about the birth of Jesus. Was God fair with the Jews? Did they really have a sufficient warning to understand the gravity of the situation? Were these happenings really adequate as an announcement for the Messiah? And did they have enough information to discern that He would be a divine Figure? Wouldn't a more vigorous engagement have served the better purpose of warning them? The messengers could be dismissed as unreliable or mere flukes.

Was God fair?

Who but a divine Figure could answer the description in Isaiah? To apply such verses to anyone else would suggest that the one doing so was making a blasphemous application.

And when Herod inquired about the birth of the King, the rabbis quoted from Micah 5:2. "But you Bethlehem ... out of you will come for me one who will be ruler over Israel, whose origins are from of old, from ancient times."

Who could fulfill such but a divine Figure?

---

[122] "Massacre of the Innocents," Wikipedia, https://1ref.us/1ir (accessed January 20, 2021).

A PROBLEM WITH THE INCARNATION PART 3
August 14

John 1:32–34, "Then John gave this testimony: 'I saw the Spirit come down from heaven as a dove and remain on him. And I myself did not know him, but the one who sent me to baptize with water told me, "The man on whom you see the Spirit come down and remain is the one who will baptize with the Holy Spirit." I have seen and I testify that this is God's Chosen One.'"

The Old Testament contains clues of Jesus' divinity. Jehovah came to speak to men in human form on serval occasions, but most clearly when He came to announce the birth of the promised Son to Abraham. Such an important message was delivered by Jehovah Himself in human form.

The shepherds and Magi had caused a commotion with their announcements, but there had been little after that to warn the people.

But then John appeared with his message: "Repent, for the kingdom of heaven has come near" (Matt. 3:2). And, "I baptize you with water for repentance. But after me comes one who is more powerful than I, whose sandals I am not worthy to carry. He will baptize you with the Holy Spirit and fire" (Matt. 3:11).

Who was this who was more powerful than the new prophet, John? Why was he not even worthy to carry His sandals?

The Jewish leaders sent priests and Levites to question him (John 1:19–27). He told them he was not the Christ but informed them that the Christ was among them. John later called this Man the "Son of God" (John 1:34, NKJV).

They thus had clues from the Old Testament, a commotion at the birth of the Jesus and then a forerunner who called Him the Son of God.

These were fair warnings but were not all.

A PROBLEM WITH THE INCARNATION PART 4
August 15

Luke 4:18–19, "The Spirit of the Lord is on me, because he has anointed me to proclaim good news to the poor. He has sent me to proclaim freedom for the prisoners and recovery of sight for the blind ... to proclaim the year of the Lord's favor."

Matthew 9:3–6:

> At this some of the teachers of the law said to themselves, "This fellow is blaspheming!" Knowing their thoughts, Jesus said, "Why do you entertain evil thoughts in your hearts? Which is easier: to say, 'Your sins are forgiven,' or to say, 'Get up and walk'? But I want you to know that the Son of Man has authority on earth to forgive sins." So he said to the paralyzed man, "Get up, take your mat and go home."

The last evidence given to the Jews was the words and actions of Jesus Himself. He proclaimed freedom to the captives, the favor of the Lord and restored sight to the blind. He forgave sins, a prerogative of God Himself, giving evidence that He could do so by curing a paralytic, proving that He had the power to do so.

He then claimed to be the I AM in John 8:58.

The evidence He gave previously confirmed His claim in this chapter. Only one more miracle remained, the raising of a man from the dead (John 11:43–44). It was the last straw for the Jews. They could not let such a man live who claimed to be God (John 11:53). They plotted to kill Him and carried out their plan. But Jesus had told them the result of such planning.

A PROBLEM WITH THE INCARNATION PART 5
August 16

Matthew 23:37–38, "Jerusalem, Jerusalem, you who kill the prophets and stone those sent to you, how often I have longed to gather your children together, as a hen gathers her chicks under her wings, and you were not willing. Look, your house is left to you desolate."

The last evidence of Jesus' divinity did not appear until after He was crucified.

Several years later, the temple was destroyed and not one stone was left upon another just as Jesus had foretold (Matt. 24:2). The destruction was so complete that the exact location of the temple on the Temple Mount is unknown.[123]

The laws of the Torah are not being carried out at this time. There have been no sacrifices for sin or cleansing of the temple on Yom Kippur since AD 70 or so. None of the laws of Moses described in Exodus or Leviticus are being performed. The slaying of the Passover lamb as prescribed by the law at the temple has not been done for millennia.[124]

During the last two millenia, attempts were made to rebuild the temple, but these all failed. The nation of Israel has forbidden such efforts because of the unrest that would ensue. A shrine of Islam is the building there.[125]

Although He is no longer among us physically, His words still speak truths that can be checked for authenticity. Evidence for His divinity is present for those who wish to examine the facts. Although some faith is required, there is ample evidence on which to base belief.

---

[123] "Temple Mount," Wikipedia, https://1ref.us/1it (accessed January 20, 2021).
[124] "Korban," Wikipedia, https://1ref.us/1iu (accessed January 20, 2021).
[125] "Third Temple," Wikipedia, https://1ref.us/1is (accessed January 20, 2021).

THE TEMPTATION

August 17

Mark 1:13, "[A]nd he was in the wilderness forty days, being tempted by Satan."

Jesus had grown up in Nazareth under the care of His parents, but then He was called to John for baptism. The Spirit of God descended on Him, and God spoke to Him acknowledging Him as His Son (Mark 1:11).

"At once the Spirit sent him out into the wilderness" (Mark 1:12). Surprisingly, by following the will of the Spirit, He meets Satan, who tempts Him 40 days.

At the beginning of His ministry, Jesus was sent to do battle with His adversary. It was single man to man combat. And the results would determine if Jesus could challenge the devil on his own turf.

From Job, we know that the world is under the authority of Satan. He walks up and down in it and rules over it (Job 1:7). He is the prince of the air. Satan has control of the earth.

The victory of Jesus led to the despoiling of the world. Satan had no power to resist Jesus after his defeat in the desert. Then, the devil could not prevent Jesus from doing whatever He wanted to do. He could not stop Him, for he had nothing in Jesus (John 14:30).

This can be seen by the response of the devils inhabiting the demoniacs (Mark 5:7–13; Matt. 8:29). All they could do was beg for mercy. They had no power to resist.

Thus, the whole world lay before Jesus to do all He desired, for Satan had been vanquished.

Jesus chose to follow the will of the Father. There was always the temptation to deviate from God's will and do it another easier way. This happened even after the devil was defeated, for Jesus was always free to turn from the cross.

He never did so, even when faced with its horrors, but steadfastly set His mind to go to Jerusalem (Luke 9:51). We can have such steadfastness as well, if we will give ourselves to Him unreservedly.

THE VICTORY

August 18

1 Corinthians 15:57, "But thanks be to God! He gives us the victory through our Lord Jesus Christ."

Romans 6:14, "For sin shall no longer be your master, because you are not under the law, but under grace."

We seldom appreciate the scope of the victory that Jesus has won for us and has offered to us.

Satan has been completely defeated. He has lost the battle. Jesus utterly defeated him as noted in the previous entry.

But there is more than that: Jesus has given *us* His victory. Though He won, He has allowed us to be partakers in it.

How can that be? How can *we* be victorious when we did not fight?

By grace as Paul said above. It is a gift.

Does Jesus have the right to give such a gift? Well, since He defeated Satan and died in our place, bearing our sins, taking them from us and receiving the just punishment we deserve, He has removed every impediment. He can do what He wants!

And His gracious will is to give us the victory over sin and over ourselves if we will let Him have His way.

Note the words of Paul in Romans 6:13, "Do not offer any part of yourself to sin as an instrument of wickedness, but rather offer yourselves to God as those who have been brought from death to life; and offer every part of yourself to him as an instrument of righteousness."

By giving ourselves to Him, we gain a victory that was won by Someone else—Christ our Lover and Redeemer.

It is a gift beyond price and with it comes life eternal. *Hallelujah!*

BEHOLD THE LAMB OF GOD
August 19

John 1:29, "The next day John saw Jesus coming toward him and said, 'Look, the Lamb of God, who takes away the sin of the world!'"

Revelation 5:6, "Then I saw a Lamb, looking as if it had been slain, standing at the center of the throne."

Why this Lamb of God? Why does God need a Lamb? Is He guilty of some sin such that a sacrifice is necessary?

In the Old Testament, repentant sinners came with lambs to atone for sin. 1 Peter 1:19 even says that Jesus was like a lamb without blemish or defect as the lambs for the Passover were described. But why would God present His own Lamb?

There are two reasons for God's providing a Lamb.

First, is to take away any accusation that He will not take responsibility for His act of making the universe, a place where sin has entered. Although He did not choose to allow sin here, it is here, and since He is the Creator, there is a sense that He is responsible. And though He did not choose sin, He, by His willingness to bear the consequences, has fulfilled His responsibility.

Secondly, by making this sacrifice of an unblemished Lamb, He is able to take all the sin of the world away from sinners and unto Himself. As John said, this Lamb takes away the sin of the whole world. All sin was placed on Him, so that we need not bear it ourselves.

God has taken the blame and borne all the sins that we have committed here. We are thus free from bearing the punishment for them. His Lamb has done it.

There is freedom from guilt because of Jesus' sacrifice. There is grace for our time of need. Let us turn from our guilt and take the freedom offered in Jesus.

THE INIQUITY OF US ALL PART 1
August 20

Isaiah 53:6, "We all, like sheep, have gone astray, each of us has turned to our own way; and the LORD has laid on him the iniquity of us all."

This verse tells us what God did on that day on Calvary, when Jesus bore the sins of the whole world. Merely stating it, however, hardly encompasses the enormity of the actual act. The sins of the *whole* world.

Think of the sin going on right now. Killings of people in Afghanistan and other places in the Middle East and around the globe. Murders, drive-by shootings in Chicago and other cities in America and the world. The drug trade and all the misery that it brings with it. The greed and corruption in government and by the business community. The lust and violence portrayed by Hollywood and the entertainment industries of the world.

Then there are our own peccadillos, the little sins we do every day, unconsciously, little lies or compromises. The indulgences that we do not tell others of, the secret sins of our carnal nature.

Multiply this for the millennia of the earth's existence. Jesus bore all of these. It was only because of His divine nature that He could do such a thing. But the Bible says that God saw fit to place them all on Him (Isa. 53:6). God took them all to Himself in the person of Jesus.

John said, "Behold! The Lamb of God who takes away the sin of the world" (John 1:29, NKJV). We add to the sin, but He subtracts it, carries it away from us so that it not ours anymore.

What a God we have that takes the burden of the whole world on Himself that we may live.

THE INIQUITY OF US ALL PART 2
August 21

Isaiah 53:6, "[And] laid on him the iniquity of us all."

There is another aspect of this that needs to be made clear.

Since Jesus has taken our iniquity and has borne it to the place of punishment, it is no longer ours. He has it and it is His by right. He bore it all.

We are thus free from "the accursed load"[126] as the old hymn says.

We just do not believe that it is as easy as God has told us.

If Jesus has borne our sins, they are His. We, in a sense, have no right to them. If we continue to believe that we must bear them, then we are taking something from Jesus that is His.

Now we can mope around, feel bad about our weaknesses and sins and our many shortcomings, but we are doing something that God has taken from our hands and given into the hands of the Son. He knew that we could not bear them. They would crush us and *will* crush us if we do not give them to the One who can bear them for us.

I have co-signed loans for some of my relatives. When you do that, you need to be prepared to pay the loan, even in full. And if you are required to do that, the other person goes free. Now of course, we can do so grudgingly and with malice. But maybe the other party failed for no fault of their own. Then we might bear it cheerfully from love.

Jesus does this and did it while we were yet sinners (Rom. 5:8). He loved first and bore our sins first. His attitude is love from beginning to end.

---

[126] Horatius Bonar, "I Lay My Sins on Jesus," *Seventh-day Adventist Hymnal* (Hagerstown, MD: Review and Herald, 1996).

HUNGERING AND THIRSTING AFTER RIGHTEOUSNESS

August 22

Matthew 5:6, "Blessed are those who hunger and thirst for righteousness, for they will be filled."

Ellen White has wonderful things to say about our ability to obtain righteousness and holiness: "Not by painful struggles or wearisome toil, not by gift or sacrifice, is righteousness obtained; *but it is freely given to every soul who hungers and thirsts to receive it.* 'Ho, every one that thirsteth, come ye to the waters, and he that hath no money; come ye, buy, and eat ... without money and without price .... This is his name whereby he shall be called, the Lord our righteousness.'"[127]

As we need food to sustain our physical strength, so we need Christ, the Bread from heaven, to sustain spiritual life and impart strength to work the works of God.

So, it is not striving or sacrificing or toiling that brings righteousness, but the accepting of it from Jesus. It is hard to fathom the gift that is ours. We may be holy. God bids us come up higher and be holier still. And if we will, He will give that precious gift to us: holiness and righteousness. We may then go out and fulfill the commands that He has given us, for He gives the wherewithal to do what He has said. Such a wonderful promise!

This does not mean that we sit idle, but that we obey the commands He has given. As a child obeys a parent he loves, so we obey our heavenly Father and He imparts the strength and will to do as He has said.

We will then know the way of salvation by experience.

---

[127]Ellen G. White, *The Faith I Live By* (Washington, DC: Review and Herald, 1958), p. 109, emphasis added.

BE NOT ANXIOUS PART 1
August 23

Matthew 6:25, "Therefore I tell you, do not worry about your life .... Look at the birds of the air; they do not sow or reap or store away in barns, and yet your heavenly Father feeds them. Are you not much more valuable than they?"

Ellen White writes: "All that was needed for existence would have been yours without the flowers and birds, but God was not content to provide what would suffice for mere existence. He has filled earth and air and sky with glimpses of beauty to tell you of His loving thought for you."[128]

If we could but keep our minds on the message of the flowers and birds, they forever speak of God's loving care.

But we often fill our minds with the care that comes to each of us. Ellen White also said this: "We may well have anxiety and anticipate danger and loss, for it is certain to befall us."[129] She is not unaware of the vicissitudes of life. They will certainly come.

But God points us to the birds and their lives. "God cares for us," they sing, "and He will care for you as well."

God has given us the gift of life and the gift of His dear Son. Paul says, "He who did not spare his own Son, but gave him up for us all—how will he not also, along with him, graciously give us all things?" (Rom. 8:32).

Satan would have our hearts full of care, focused inward at our weaknesses and the troubles we face, while God directs us to the birds cheerfully filling the air with their song.

It is not that we will be trouble-free but that God has anticipated it and given us an invitation to cast it on Him (Ps. 55:22). The birds bring the message to us each day.

---

[128]Ellen G. White, *Thoughts From the Mount of Blessing* (Mountain View, CA: Pacific Press, 1896), p. 96.
[129]Ibid., pp. 100–101.

BE NOT ANXIOUS PART 2
August 24

Matthew 6:34, "Therefore do not worry about tomorrow, for tomorrow will worry about itself. Each day has enough trouble of its own."

Ellen White says in *Thoughts From the Mount of Blessing*:

> If you will seek the Lord and be converted every day; if you will of your own spiritual choice be free and joyous in God; if with gladsome consent of heart to His gracious call you come wearing the yoke of Christ,—the yoke of obedience and service,—all your murmurings will be stilled, all your difficulties will be removed, all the perplexing problems that now confront you will be solved.[130]

In other words, your life would be one of blessing. Really?

Jesus' advice is to deal with one day at a time. "[D]o not worry about tomorrow" (Matt. 6:34). Most of our anxious thoughts focus on the trouble we see in the future. Usually the day is not something that we cannot face. The troubles are not so large that they seem unmanageable.

But instead, we spend our time borrowing trouble from the future. Jesus tells us to only consider the days' problems, for they are enough for us to bear.

Ellen White elaborates on Jesus' advice and tells us what we might do today to make tomorrow of little concern. It is to give ourselves to His joyous service, freely giving gladsome consent to His gracious call to wear the yoke of Christ, the yoke that is easy and the burden that is light (Matt. 11:29–30). Then it is that our murmurings will be stilled, our difficulties resolved and our problems solved.

Such seems to be beyond belief. But from experience, I can testify that such can be the case. It is only up to us to consent.

---

[130]Ibid., p. 101.

OUR DAILY BREAD
August 25

Matthew 6:11, "Give us today our daily bread."

Here Ellen White explains the broad scope of this verse:

> When you have thus made God's service your first interest, you may ask with confidence that your own needs may be supplied. If you have renounced self and given yourself to Christ you are a member of the family of God, and everything in the Father's house is for you. All the treasures of God are opened to you, both the world that now is and that which is to come. The ministry of angels, the gift of His Spirit, the labors of His servants—all are for you. The world, with everything in it, is yours so far as it can do you good. Even the enmity of the wicked will prove a blessing by disciplining you for heaven. If "ye are Christ's," "all things are yours." 1 Corinthians 3:23, 21.

All things are ours! Even all in the whole world as far as it can do us good.

What a wonderful thought and promise. Even the work of the wicked against us is turned back to a blessing on us!

If we could but grasp the depth of the thoughts of God toward us, that He is bending over us in love and will use all for our benefit, how much less would there be fretting and complaining about our situation. How much more would there be joy in the work He has given us.

Our daily bread and all things for us are sure. Let us rest in this promise and do His work with cheerful hearts. The blessing will be ours.

THE SNAKE IN THE DESERT
August 26

John 3:14–15, "Just as Moses lifted up the snake in the wilderness, so the Son of Man must be lifted up, that everyone who believes may have eternal life in him."

When Nicodemus came to Jesus that night, Jesus spoke some of the most profound and beloved truths of Scripture.

He also mentioned some amazing paradoxes.

Here He tells us that He must be lifted up as the snake was lifted up by Moses in the wilderness.

Now the snake is another name for the devil, the tempter, the one who, in the garden, usurped rule from Adam and is the prince of the air (Rev. 12:9). How is it that Jesus likens Himself to a snake?

Jesus is to be lifted up as the snake was. Not only that, the people were to *look* to the *snake* for healing! What could this mean?

Jesus, by dying, won the keys of hell and holds them in His hand (Rev. 1:18). The kingdom of death, ruled by the snake, is now His. He has won the throne of the snake-kingdom, so He may be considered as the snake was—the Ruler there.

The snake was a symbol of death and so was lifted up for the people to see. Jesus too has taken death to His bosom. He wears a robe dipped in blood (Rev. 19:13). In Revelation 5:6, He appears as a Lamb that was slain. In all these visions, death is portrayed as the preview of Jesus. He died, making death His and so is pictured as a snake, a means of death, the symbol of the usurper.

All of these show the intimate relationship that Jesus has with death. Since this is so, we need not fear it, for Jesus is there. He has wrenched the keys of that place from Satan. And when we enter there asleep, as each of us must, awaiting His return, we find our Lord in control.

THE CALL OF LEVI
August 27

Mark 2:14, "As he walked along, he saw Levi son of Alphaeus sitting at the tax collector's booth. 'Follow me,' Jesus told him, and Levi got up and followed him."

There is something wonderful about the call of God. We do not have a sense of purpose built into us and must discover or be told what our purpose should be.

But when God calls, wonderfully wrapped inside that call is a delightful kernel that then permeates the whole of life with its flavor. That flavor is a realization of purpose, that the thing that we are doing is what we were made for. God created us so that we might fulfill this thing He has called us to do.

This is very satisfying. It is a gift that makes life so much more worthy of living. It goes to the very soul of our existence and tints our acts and desires with a legitimate feeling of accomplishment of an eternal good. There is nothing like it.

However, it comes only through accepting the call of God, as Levi did. He left his toll booth and all its benefits so that he might have a life lived to the fullest, filled with the purpose of God. No other life has anything nearing this in satisfaction.

To accept such a call is to fill your life with blessing that comes from the throne of God Himself. He personally blesses such that will follow Him. Praise God for His unspeakable gift.

WHAT GOD DOES WITH A MAN
August 28

Luke 5:8–11, "When Simon Peter saw this, he fell at Jesus' knees .... For he and all his companions were astonished at the catch of fish they had taken, and so were James and John, the sons of Zebedee, Simon's partners .... So they pulled their boats up on shore, left everything and followed him."

Here we are introduced to the first disciples of Jesus. They were untutored in the schools of the rabbis. They, in fact, were fishermen, running a business on the shore of the Sea of Galilee.

But the youngest among them, John, became devoted to the Savior, calling himself the beloved disciple (John 20:2). And toward the end of his life, he wrote his Gospel, the Gospel of John.

But what a book! It is written in the most elementary Greek of the New Testament, the book beginning students start on, but it is one of the most profound. The book contains simple stories that when dwelt on contain deep spiritual truths garbed in plain clothes. The depths of its revelations are reserved for those who will meditate carefully on its words.

I recall my introduction to the book my first year at seminary. Several weeks were spent considering the first three chapters with their simple narrations and statements that plumbed the abyss of God's will and thought.

This man was a fisherman by trade, but he wrote a masterpiece of literature. The books written about his Gospel fill libraries!

"For God so loved the world that He gave His only begotten Son" (John 3:16, NKJV)—penned by a fisherman.

His life and work show what can happen to a man, even a fisherman, who is fully committed to the Master. He may be uneducated, but his talents will be developed to the full and used to bless the world.

IS THAT REALLY FAIR?
August 29

Matthew 13:10–12, "The disciples came to him and asked, 'Why do you speak to the people in parables?' He replied, 'Because the knowledge of the secrets of the kingdom of heaven has been given to you, but not to them. Whoever has will be given more, and they will have an abundance. Whoever does not have, even what they have will be taken from them.'"

This statement of Jesus has always seemed unfair to me.

Why would Jesus say that those getting the least would be robbed of the little they had, while those getting more would get in abundance? Really?

But Jesus was making a wonderful point.

He had just told the people the parable of the sower, more properly, the parable of the soils.

The sower scatters the same kind of seed everywhere. But it is not the seed that determines the outcome, it is the soil. Seed that falls on good soil sprouts to become a thirty, fifty or 100-fold increase, while that which falls on the path, or the weedy and shallow ground, disappears.

God has given His Word and blessings to all. But we determine whether there will be a harvest of good or dearth.

Ellen White says this:

> [T]he result is not beyond our control. True, we cannot change ourselves; but the power of choice is ours, and it rests with us to determine what we will become. The wayside, the stony-ground, the thorny-ground hearers need not remain such. The Spirit of God is ever seeking to break the spell of infatuation that holds men absorbed in worldly things, and to awaken a desire for the imperishable treasure.

Those that respond to the gospel are invited to take all of the water of life they desire, without cost. But those that refuse, lose the little they are given.

AND SOME FELL ON THE PATH
August 30

Matthew 13:3–4, "A farmer went out to sow his seed. As he was scattering the seed, some fell along the path, and the birds came and ate it up."

Why doesn't everyone accept the gospel message that we find so compelling? Is there something wrong with us that we believe so willingly and readily? Why doesn't my really smart brother or neighbor or father see the beauty in Jesus as I do? Or how about that really kind lady down the street?

Wilberforce, the British politician who drove slavery from the British Empire tried endlessly to get his friend, the prime minister, William Pitt, to attend a religious service with him. Finally, after months of pleading he acquiesced.

For Wilberforce, the speaker gave a most inspiring message. The Holy Spirit moved on his heart in a wonderful way. But as they walked out of the church, Pitt said he didn't understand a thing that that fellow was talking about.[131]

The seed had not fallen on fallow ground, but on a hard place, a place where there was no understanding. It was thus snatched by the devil with no thought at all.

Hard ground hearers do not receive the message of life but go about their business as if there were no eternity. They may enjoy life and become wealthy and appear to be happy and even be happy in their ignorance. Their apparently successful lives should not deceive us.

Such unbelievers may be moved by the lives of true followers of Jesus. But they, as the parable says, are hard as the paths of Palestine, trodden to stone by countless feet. Our lives and prayers may possibly soften them. But it is not the usual outcome.

---

[131] Paxton Wood, *The Sunday At Home: A Family Magazine for Sabbath Reading*, vol 27, p. 674.

A SEVERE MERCY
August 31

Mark 5:11–13, 17, "A large herd of pigs was feeding on the nearby hillside. The demons begged Jesus, 'Send us among the pigs; allow us to go into them.' He gave them permission, and the impure spirits came out and went into the pigs. The herd, about two thousand in number, rushed down the steep bank into the lake and were drowned. Then the people began to plead with Jesus to leave their region."

This episode occurred when Jesus cured two demoniacs, casting out the devils in them. Jesus allowed them to enter a herd of pigs, killing them all, resulting in great loss. The people, afraid of further loss, implored Jesus to leave them alone.

Ellen White says this: "It was in mercy to the owners of the swine that this loss had been permitted to come upon them …. Jesus desired to break the spell of selfish indifference, that they might accept His grace."[132]

How often do we see the mercy in loss? C.S. Lewis said, "[P]ain insists upon being attended to. God whispers to us in our pleasures, speaks in our conscience, but shouts in our pains: it is His megaphone to rouse a deaf world."[133]

When loss comes upon us, instead of falling into despair, we must recognize it as a call to come to Jesus. It may not be that we need to have the chains of selfishness broken as the owners of the swine needed. But God may still be calling us to look to Him rather than to the world for a solution to our problems.

If loss can bring us to turn to God and thus become prepared for the kingdom, how can it even be considered loss? In fact, it is great gain.

Let us seek to find God in all circumstances. He may be shouting because we would hear in no other way.

---

[132] Ellen G. White, *The Desire of Ages* (Mountain View, CA: Pacific Press, 1898), p. 338.
[133] C. S. Lewis, "Quotable Quote," goodreads, https://1ref.us/1iv (accessed January 20, 2021).

GOD IS SO UNFAIR

September 1

Read the parable of the vineyard in Matthew 20:1–15.

This is one of Jesus' difficult parables. The ideas He proposes go against the grain of human fairness and common sense. If a vineyard owner today had done as this man did, the workers would have hauled him before the labor relations board and accused him of prejudice!

But the parable gives keen insight into the ways of God and they are not our ways.

Jesus set the scene on a typical day during the Palestine grape harvest. The owner goes to market to hire workers to reap the grapes. He finds men at the beginning of the day and pledges to pay them the usual price for a day's work. He has a large harvest and visits during the whole day. At evening, one hour before dark, he hires more and says, "I will pay you whatever is right" (Matt. 20:4).

He then starts with the last crew, giving them a whole day's wage. Everyone gets the same amount even if they have labored for only a single hour.

As the workers realize what is happening, partying breaks out. The workers celebrate the generosity of the landowner. "Look how we have been treated," they shout as they dance in the streets.

But the first workers, getting a day's wage for a day's work, the amount they had agreed to, are miffed. "We thought we were going to get more," they say in exasperation (Matt. 20:12, paraphrase).

Jesus has the landowner answer: "Don't I have the right to do what I want with my own money? Or are you envious because I am generous?" (Matt. 20:15).

The parable teaches two things: grace is His and He is not bound by any ideas we may have of fairness in its distribution. Second, He will give it far and wide.

Revelation 22:17, "[A]nd let the one who wishes take the free gift of the water of life." Freely, mind you. We too often look over our shoulders to see if God is doing it all fairly, when we would do better plunging into the grace He has so freely offered each one of us.[134]

---

[134] Alareece Collie, "Strange. Not getting my fair share," *Adventist Review*, May 2, 2017.

THE ECLIPSE

September 2

Proverbs 4:18, NLT, "The way of the righteous is like the first gleam of dawn, which shines ever brighter until the full light of day."

In August of 2017, an eclipse of the sun occurred over a large swath of the North American continent. It was the first total eclipse in several decades that Americans could view easily. Thousands traveled to places where it would pass: Oregon, Wyoming, Missouri and Tennessee, etc. My family, scattered over America, viewed it in different places. My brother and I went to a small town in Oregon with some friends.

A friend, who lived in the path of the eclipse said to me, "It will be 95% totality where I live, why drive so many miles? I told him a partial eclipse is nothing and totality everything. He trusted my assessment and came with me to a place where it was total. When he saw the totality, he agreed.

Total eclipses of the sun are one of nature's most—if not the most—beautiful and spectacular phenomena. And even if the moon covers 99% of the sun's disc, one will not see the beauty of totality.

At totality, the sun's shimmering atmosphere becomes visible, something that cannot be seen unless the bright light of the sun's disc is completely blocked. That atmosphere is utterly beautiful. Pictures do not do it justice. It must be seen personally.

So it is with the Christian life. Unless commitment is total, the beauty and satisfaction of righteousness will not be realized. Serving with all your heart is the only way the real beauty and satisfaction found in Jesus can be known. The commitment allows the atmosphere of grace to be fully seen.

Such a commitment may feel like the severing of the hand or the plucking out of the eye as Jesus suggested (Matt. 5:29–30), but it is the only way to find true satisfaction in Him.

THE MIRACLE OF THE LOAVES AND FISHES
September 3

John 6:10–11, "Jesus said, 'Have the people sit down.' There was plenty of grass in that place, and they sat down (about five thousand men were there). Jesus then took the loaves, gave thanks, and distributed to those who were seated as much as they wanted. He did the same with the fish."

Ellen White says this about the miracle:

> In feeding the five thousand, Jesus lifts the veil from the world of nature, and reveals the power that is constantly exercised for our good. In the production of earth's harvests God is working a miracle every day. Through natural agencies the same work is accomplished that was wrought in the feeding of the multitude. Men prepare the soil and sow the seed, but it is the life from God that causes the seed to germinate. It is God's rain and air and sunshine that cause it to put forth, "first the blade, then the ear, after that the full corn in the ear."[135]

I have noted the same in my work as a surgeon. I will remove the impediments to healing: infection, abscesses or tumors and God will furnish the necessary powers for health in the restorative forces in our bodies. If these were not active, I could never lift a knife to provide relief from any illness.

We are the beneficiaries of miracles every day, even every hour. To acknowledge this and rejoice at His loving care is a duty, actually a privilege. To rejoice in them is to fill our lives with the joy of the love of our Creator. And the joy of the Lord is our strength (Neh. 8:10).

---

[135] Ellen G. White, *The Desire of Ages* (Mountain View, CA: Pacific Press, 1898), p. 367.

YOU GIVE THEM SOMETHING TO EAT
September 4

Matthew 14:15–18, "As evening approached, the disciples came to him and said, 'This is a remote place, and it's already getting late. Send the crowds away, so they can go to the villages and buy themselves some food.' Jesus replied, 'They do not need to go away. You give them something to eat.' 'We have here only five loaves of bread and two fish,' they answered. 'Bring them here to me,' he said."

With a small lunch at hand, Jesus tells the disciples to give the multitude something to eat. Why would He do that? His command seemed impossible.

But Jesus wanted to teach them and us something so important that He gave them this absurd command.

They noted their lack of resources—a child's lunch. Jesus said, "Bring it to me." And when they brought their meager store and placed it in His hands, it was sufficient for the huge crowd—with twelve baskets left over!

Christ has told us, "[S]hare your food with the hungry and to provide the poor wanderer with shelter" (Isa. 58:7). *"Go into all the world and preach the gospel"* (Mark 16:15). But we hesitate, unwilling to give all that we have, fearing to spend and be spent for others. But Jesus says, "You give them something to eat."

We often fail to perceive that behind the command is a promise, a promise of the same power that fed the multitude beside the sea.

Will we take counsel with our fears and unbelief or go forward in obedience to His instructions? Jesus here showed the result of obedience. He has entrusted His words to us for the world. Can we fail to do as He has asked—to cooperate for the salvation sufficient for all?

COME APART AND REST AWHILE
September 5

Mark 6:31, "Then, because so many people were coming and going that they did not even have a chance to eat, he said to them, 'Come with me by yourselves to a quiet place and get some rest.'"

Ellen White, commenting on these verses says, "The disciples came to Jesus and told Him all things. Their intimate relationship with Him encouraged them to lay before Him their favorable and unfavorable experiences, their joy at seeing results from their labors, and their sorrow at their failures, their faults, and their weaknesses."[136]

How often do we come to Jesus and do as the disciples did? How often are we reluctant to do so? We feel that if we reveal especially our weaknesses and failures that we will be rejected, as the world has rejected us and mocked our mistakes. But Ellen White's words encourage us to lay it all out before Him—even the worst that we have done.

And I confess the joy that is mine when I do such a thing. To let Jesus know of all that is in me: the faults, sinful desires and the falling to temptation, opens a way for Him to come and comfort me. As He said to the woman actually taken in adultery that very day, *"Then neither do I condemn you .... Go now and leave your life of sin"* (John 8:11).

We so often feel we must hide our sins from our Savior when He is a *Savior* and the very reason we should tell Him of them. There is certainly no help anywhere else.

"Come rest awhile" (Mark 6:31, paraphrase) is His invitation. That rest means rest from our self-condemnation and sorrow. A place at His side is the only place such rest can be found.

---

[136]Ibid., p. 359.

MAKING TROUBLE FOR OURSELVES
September 6

John 6:15–17, "Jesus, knowing that they intended to come and make him king by force, withdrew again to a mountain by himself. When evening came, his disciples went down to the lake, where they got into a boat and set off across the lake for Capernaum."

After the feeding of the 5,000, the people came to make Jesus king. He knew that such an action would result in war and loss for the gospel. So, He dismissed the crowd, sent the disciples across the lake and went up to be alone to agonize with the Father for the hearts of men and His disciples. He knew the disappointment they would face when He was crucified and felt He must prepare them.

But Jesus' command to leave was most difficult. The tide of public opinion had turned in His direction and the disciples resented that Jesus would not take advantage of it. Would they always be thought of as followers of a deceiver?

Ellen White says this: "Unbelief was taking possession of their minds and hearts. Love of honor had blinded them .... To be united with a teacher who could work mighty miracles, and yet to be reviled as deceivers, was a trial they could ill endure."[137]

They had witnessed the feeding of 5,000, yet disappointment absorbed their thoughts and His blessings were forgotten.

We, when faced with disappointment, can talk ourselves into unbelief as well. How easy it is to concentrate on the problems and trials. Yet Jesus has blessed our lives with so many things, and He does so continually. Dwelling on the blessings gives more of them.

Let us then think of them rather than our disappointments and sorrows. He is our all in all.

---

[137] Ibid., p. 380.

MARY AND MARTHA
September 7

Luke 10:38–42:

> *Jesus and his disciples … came … where a woman named Martha opened her home to him. She had a sister called Mary, who sat at the Lord's feet listening to what he said. But Martha was distracted by all the preparations …. [So she] asked, "Lord, don't you care that my sister has left me to do the work by myself? Tell her to help me!" "Martha, Martha," the Lord answered, "you are worried … about many things, but few things are needed—or indeed only one. Mary has chosen what is better, and it will not be taken away from her."*

There are two things about this story that we must learn if we are to be successful Christians.

First: Sometimes following Jesus means inconveniencing someone else. You must cease being afraid of this and follow Jesus wherever He might lead.

Martha was doing something good, opening her home to Jesus so that His needs might be satisfied and He might have rest, food and freedom from the press of the crowd. And Mary, instead of helping with this was at Jesus' feet, listening.

When Martha came to get Mary, Jesus did not thank Martha and tell Mary to go help, but told Martha that what Mary was doing was the best thing. In fact, He said that *only* **one** *thing* was needed and it was the thing Mary was doing.

Someday, someone will press you to do this or that when you know God is calling you to do something else, something that will inconvenience *them*. Jesus has already spoken on this matter: what He calls you to do is the only needful thing.

Second: What *you* choose makes a difference. Notice what Jesus said here: *Mary* has chosen what is better.

So, who did the choosing? It was not Jesus or Martha or custom that chose. No, Mary chose. She let nothing, even the inconvenience of Jesus, keep her from her desire.

It was Mary who chose. Jesus respected the choice she had made, defending her against her sister and societal convention itself.

Jesus would have us let nothing come between us and Him.

THE BEST SEAT IN THE HOUSE
September 8

Luke 12:37, "It will be good for those servants whose master finds them watching when he comes. Truly I tell you, he will dress himself to serve, will have them recline at the table and will come and wait on them."

Some years ago, I visited a restaurant in Boston where my daughter served as manager.

When we arrived, we did not have to wait, but were ushered right in and given a table in a corner that sat a little above the rest so that we had a view of the whole place. The servers were so solicitous! They brought delightful dishes prepared especially for us that had been approved by my daughter, the best that they had to offer. She herself was at our side at all times, introducing us to the staff and showing how happy she was to have us there. It was an experience I will never forget.

> *What a privilege is ours! The King stoops to serve us! But that is the way He is. Why would we have any other to rule over us?*

In this verse, Jesus pulls back the curtain of the future to show us the first great feast in heaven. He tells us that He personally will serve us just as my daughter did that night. We will be the ones that are given special attentions and the best in the house. And Jesus will be the head waiter!

In Revelation, the elders cast their crowns at Jesus' feet, and rightfully so (Rev. 4:10–11). He is the One who has gotten the victory for us.

But Jesus also knows that we have chosen Him at great cost to ourselves and He desires to honor us in front of the whole universe. So, He gives a banquet to celebrate our arrival and serves us Himself.

What a privilege is ours! The King stoops to serve us! But that is the way He is. Why would we have any other to rule over us?

A SINNER WITH JESUS PART 1
September 9

John 8:5, "In the Law Moses commanded us to stone such women. Now what do you say?"

As a youth, my shortcomings tormented me. I was acutely aware of my sins and failings. I thought God would view me as undeserving of His love. He is the holy God after all.

In reality, what does God actually think of us?

This question is answered decisively in a story from John's Gospel. It is a familiar one. The story of the women taken in adultery.

This woman is unique for an interesting reason: she had not sought Jesus but had been dragged into His presence unwillingly. Sinners, lepers and outcasts wanted to see Jesus, even the demon-possessed ran to meet Him. But this woman had no interest in seeking Him but had been brought against her will. She represents all sinners that dwell on this planet. All.

Her accusers state the case against her: she was caught in adultery, the very act. It was a capital offense. "What do you think?" they asked.

Jesus seems to accept the details presented, not saying a word in her defense, but instead stoops to write in the dirt of the temple court. The accusers become impatient and gather closer to see what He is writing (John 8:6–7).

He traces the sins of each from oldest to youngest and standing up says, "Let any one of you who is without sin be the first to throw a stone at her" (John 8:7). They slink away, their hypocrisy exposed.[138]

Jesus turns to the woman and asks about her accusers and she notes that they have disappeared. Jesus then says, looking on her with compassion, "Then neither do I condemn you …. Go now and leave your life of sin" (John 8:11).

That is the attitude of our God toward us. It consists of three acts on His part that we will discuss tomorrow.

---

[138]Ibid., p. 461.

A SINNER WITH JESUS PART 2
September 10

John 8:11, "Then neither do I condemn you …. Go now and leave your life of sin."

When Jesus deals with sinners, He does three things.

1. He dismisses their accusers. The first instance of this is found in Zechariah 3 where Satan accuses the high priest who is standing before God robed in filthy garments. The Lord rebuked Satan, sending him packing (Zech. 3:2).

How can God do that? Because He has the goods on Satan and knows his evil ways. He has no standing before God and cannot accuse us. Jesus did this with the accusing teachers and Pharisees as well.

But we have another accuser, sometimes even more persistent than Satan himself: our own hearts. They can accuse us and torment us unmercifully.

God has an answer for them as well: 1 John 3:19–20, "This is how we … set our hearts at rest in his presence: If our hearts condemn us, we know that God is greater than our hearts, and he knows everything."

God's first act then is to dismiss the accusers.

2. He then says, "Neither do I condemn you." Jesus was not sent into the world to condemn it, but to save it (John 3:17). He came to save us, not condemn us. There are plenty of accusers, but there is one Savior and He is here to save us from sin and ourselves.

3. He bids us, "Go and leave your life of sin." This is a command, but also a promise. He will give us the strength to fulfill the very thing He has asked us to do if we will let Him.

When I learned of Jesus' attitude toward us, I stopped concentrating on my sins and began concentrating on Him, the One altogether lovely. It is our salvation and remedy.

A SINNER WITH JESUS PART 3
September 11

John 3:17, "For God did not send his Son into the world to condemn the world, but to save the world through him."

There is another very important lesson to be learned from this story.

The adulterous woman was brought into the very presence of Jesus for condemnation. Jesus took this opportunity to teach a very important concept.

This woman was a rank sinner, caught in the very act of sinning and was brought *against her will* into the presence of God.

What would God do with such a one?

Instead of the expected condemnation, He bent in understanding and forgiveness, encouraging her to turn from her life of sin!

How foolish we are to let our sins keep us from the Savior! When Jesus died, the veil in the temple was rent from top to bottom, signifying that heaven was open to us (Matt. 27:51). Sin was now no hindrance to our entering there.

And Jesus, wishing to give more than this abstract symbol of the fact, acted out the principle in His dealing with the woman taken in the very act of adultery.

It is an error to think that when we sin, the way to heaven is blocked. Is there another place we can go for help? Would God rather we suffer the torture of guilt and shame for a season instead of coming right to Him?

Jesus met the woman where she was. Guilty, shamed and embarrassed. He did not chase her away until she had repented or made things right.

There in the temple court He endowed her with the forgiveness He would soon win at great cost to Himself.

We must not let our sins keep us from Him. He has shown us that He will receive us. Will we come?

HE ACCEPTS US AS WE ARE
September 12

2 Corinthians 5:19, "God was reconciling the world to himself in Christ, not counting people's sins against them."

In the story of the woman taken in adultery, though she had not sought him, Jesus did not count her sins against her. Instead of condemnation, He told her He did not condemn her, but admonished her in love, "[G]o and sin no more" (John 8:11, NKJV).

> *It is important to realize the scope of God's acceptance of us even with our sins. He truly does not count them against us. And it is not just once that He is willing to do that.*

It is important to realize the scope of God's acceptance of us even with our sins. He truly does not count them against us. And it is not just once that He is willing to do that.

The problem often occurs when we have followed Jesus for some time, but then fall into some sin and are ashamed to go to Jesus, thinking we have failed again or are really unworthy. We are always unworthy, but as the verse says, He does not count our sins against us. And He is willing to overlook our sins more than once in a lifetime.

Ellen White says this: "As you see the enormity of sin, as you see yourself as you really are, do not give up to despair. It was sinners that Christ came to save .... No earthly parent could be as patient with the faults and mistakes of his children, as is God with those He seeks to save."[139]

Each day we must come to Him as we are: weak, sinful, discouraged that we do not seem to be able to do as He wishes. He is there with us ready to forgive as He did the woman. Our mistake is to not come to Him. Satan will accuse us, but we can go to Jesus no matter what.

It is our birthright in Him. Let us take advantage of all He has done for us.

---

[139] Ellen G. White, *Steps to Christ* (Mountain View, CA: Pacific Press, 1892), p. 35.

THE PRODIGAL FATHER
September 13

Luke 15:11–12, "Jesus continued: 'There was a man who had two sons. The younger one said to his father, "Father, give me my share of the estate." So he divided his property between them.'"

I have read several books on child-rearing but have never read anything even coming near a recommendation to act as this father did. Give the boy his inheritance? What? He is rebellious and foolhardy and will certainly waste it all. One could even argue that the father enabled the boy in troublemaking. Most books on parenting would suggest a sterner hand and certainly not a division of the estate.

But that is the whole point of the story, the character of this father.

His generosity is unaccountable. And as the boy walks off, the father's last act is handing over the money!

And that is exactly how God has treated us. We have been rebellious and wicked, ignoring our Father and going our own way. Does He cease to bless or does He send curses on us? Does lightning strike us?

No. He gives us health, days of sunshine and the bounties of life. Each morning we awaken, whether sinner or saint, to the earth in its courses and the laws of nature working for our benefit. Even the rankest atheist, who has utterly ignored the Father, has the blessings of life and friends and fame, all in spite of his rebellion.

There is none more prodigal than our heavenly Father, who blesses the just and unjust and has given His own beloved Son for us. Heaven could bestow no greater gift, eternal life for sinners if they will have it!

Let's stop thinking the worst about God. He bends in love, stooping to help us find the way to Him and real life.

THE PUNCHLINE
September 14

Read the parable of the prodigal son in Luke 15:11–31.

A good joke ends with an unexpected punchline, something we did not anticipate.

Good stories are often the same and Jesus was a master storyteller. He charmed the people with His parables with unusual endings.

The parable of the prodigal son is of such a character. But the love shown to the rebellious son has obscured the punchline: the father's words to the older son. This parable was told to the Pharisees, the ninety and nine just persons who had complained about Jesus' custom of eating with sinners (Matt. 9:11).

The parable starts with the younger boy asking for and receiving his inheritance. He goes to a far country, falls into want and returns home. He is greeted by the father who elevates him again to sonship and throws a joyful celebration at his return.

The older brother finds out and refuses to come in, insulting the father. The father goes out to reason with the boy and the boy blasts him with complaints about his brother who has wasted the inheritance. He then lays into the father for not giving him any token of his love.

Then comes the punchline: the older brother represents the narrow and critical Pharisees. We expect Jesus to have the father tell them a thing or two, but instead he says, "Son, I am with you always, and all I have is yours" (Luke 15:31, paraphrase). No anger, no denunciation, but a pledge of love and patience, not anything near what we would expect.

We do not know if any Pharisees accepted Jesus' love at that time, but a large group joined the apostles after Pentecost—proof of Jesus' appeal to them.

The offer is for us as well.

THE CALL OF THE PHARISEES
September 15

Luke 15:31, "'My son,' the father said, 'you are always with me, and everything I have is yours.'"

Throughout the Gospels, the Pharisees seem always to be at loggerheads with Jesus. But in the parable of the prodigal son, Jesus appeals to them to take up the work of the gospel. His words are similar to His great commission given in Matthew 28:18–20.

In the story, the father throws a party to honor the return of his rebellious son. His older brother refuses to come into the feast, so the father goes out to convince the boy to join the festivities. The father's appeal to the elder son is a call to these critical men. Jesus has just been eating with sinners, celebrating their salvation. Jesus invites the Pharisees to unite with Him in this work of joy.

First: He calls them sons. Astounding! Even the Pharisees are sons!

Second: He says, "[Y]ou are always with me" (Luke 15:31). This is the same assurance given the disciples in Matthew 28:20: "And surely I am with you always, to the very end of the age."

Third: He says, "[E]verything I have is yours" (Luke 15:31). What a promise! This is akin to Jesus' words in John 14:13 to His disciples: "You may ask me for anything in my name and I will do it."

Jesus' love for the lost revealed in the father's love for the prodigal has cheered sinners for 2,000+ years.

But Jesus' love for these critical, narrow-minded men is more amazing still! He is unperturbed by their shriveled attitude. He catches them off guard, then appeals to them to join in His work of salvation even as He appealed to the disciples.

We are amazed at God's love for sinners, but for proud Pharisees? Only a God of real love could do so.

THE TRANSFIGURATION
September 16

Matthew 17:2, "There he was transfigured before them. His face shone like the sun, and his clothes became as white as the light."

Jesus had just told the disciples that He was to suffer many things at the hands of the religious leaders at Jerusalem. Peter, in shock, had rebuked such thinking, but Jesus turned to him and delivered his sternest reprimand, "Get behind me, Satan! ... [Y]ou do not have in mind the concerns of God" (Matt. 16:23).

What do you say after being told that?

The disciples lost hope and followed Jesus in sadness. Then at sunset six days later, Jesus took three of them (including Peter) to the top of a high mountain (Mark 9:2). There He prayed earnestly for several hours, the disciples praying with Him for a while before they were overcome with sleep.

Suddenly Jesus becomes as radiant as the sun, and Moses and Elijah appear with Him, chosen above even the angels near the throne to visit Jesus and encourage Him. The disciples awaken in a start and all discouragement leaves them. Their Master is the Honored of heaven.

This demonstration was given to establish the faith of the disciples and us. Jesus' humble mien veiled the real Jesus, the King of the universe. And in this instance, the King stood unveiled in majesty clothed in His rightful garb. The unveiling did not prevent the crucifixion. Jesus' words of His death had taken all hope from the disciples. But His passion and death were what He had come to do that the world might be saved.

Notice the mercy of Christ, unveiling Himself before them to restore their hope that they might be able to endure the future. That mercy has been given to us as well. Take hope! Jesus is the King!

THE WIDOW AND THE PROSTITUTE
September 17

Luke 6:38, "Give and it will be given to you. A good measure, pressed down, shaken together, and running over, will be poured into your lap. For with the measure you use, it will be measured to you."

At the temple in Jerusalem in Jesus' day, there was a courtyard where the offerings were given. Seven large metal horns, like cornucopias, protruded from a wall of the treasury where gifts were deposited.[140] The givers would line up with their money and cast it into these horns. And of course, since there was only metal currency, large gifts made quite the clatter.

When Jesus entered this place and observed the gift giving, He said nothing until a poor widow came and surreptitiously threw in her small contribution, two mites, equivalent to about two dollars in our currency (Mark 12:41–44).

He said something that sounds impossible: "She has put in more than all the others" (Mark 12:43, paraphrase). Two bucks? More than bags of money?

Then He explains: "She has put in all she had" (Mark 12:44, paraphrase).

These comments show us the mind of God and what is His great desire: the hearts of His children.

It is not the great acts or the great contributions, it is the heart that makes the difference to Him.

It was the same with the prostitute who bought the ointment for Jesus' feet. Her gift was extravagant, costing a year's wages, maybe $24,000 in our money. But with that gift came the heart of the giver. Both of these women gave gifts, one very small and one very large. Yet Jesus responded the same to both. It was not the size of the gift that mattered, but the heart of the giver. Behind the widow's mites and the bottle of expensive perfume were the love and passion of hearts that were given totally to God and an expression of love that could not be missed by Him.

The givers of large sums and their gifts at the temple are forgotten and the temple itself is gone; even its exact location is unknown. But the widow and her two mites and the bottle of perfume remain to this day. How impressive a gift they were! They touched the heart of God and He has made them an everlasting memorial.

---

[140]Leen Ritmeyer, "The Treasury of the Temple in Jerusalem," Ritmeyer Archaeological Design, https://1ref.us/1iw (accessed January 20, 2021).

THE TENANTS

September 18

2 Corinthians 5:19, *"God was reconciling the world to himself in Christ, not counting people's sins against them."*

I have been a landlord for several years now. My wife and I own a couple of apartment buildings in a local town; they are part of our retirement. There is something I have noticed about tenants, though. It is an attitude that almost all of them have when they have not paid their rent. They don't want to talk to me or see me.

I will call, write letters or go to their apartments to see them, but they try to avoid me if at all possible. Some of them will go to great lengths, sneaking out when they see me, so that we do not have to meet.

Their rent stands between us so that there can be no relationship.

This behavior is just like that of Adam and Eve when they ate of the forbidden fruit in the garden. They had sinned and then they did not want to see God. Their sin stood between them and God and they went, just as my tenants do, and hid, doing their utmost to avoid the "Landlord."

Now I have, on occasion, forgiven the rent. When this is done, the relationship is restored. They don't hide any longer. They are grateful and some have become my best tenants, making sure to pay on time.

God has removed the impediment that has separated us, just like me forgiving the rent. We have open access to Him, for He does not count our sins against us.

So, what are we waiting for? The way is open. The rent is paid. He has taken care of the problem. Let us go and open our hearts to Him. We will not be disappointed.

> *So, what are we waiting for? The way is open. The rent is paid. He has taken care of the problem. Let us go and open our hearts to Him. We will not be disappointed.*

THE LAWYER
September 19

1 John 1:9, NKJV, "If we confess our sins, He is faithful and just to forgive our sins and to cleanse us from all unrighteousness."

Several years ago, while I was working as a surgeon, a patient of mine died shortly after the surgery. The family was unhappy with my care and sued. I received a letter which I sent to my insurance company and they assigned me a lawyer.

I made an appointment with his secretary and went down to Boston on the scheduled date.

His office was a small three-room affair with an outer office and two rooms in back. The secretary invited me into a chair while I waited for him. The third room was a smaller one filled with an assortment of medical equipment, crutches, braces and various other items packed helter-skelter in a disorderly pile. I thought I was in real trouble. If the man could not keep his own things in order, what hope was there for me?

> *"There is no chapter in our experience too dark for Him to read; there is no perplexity too difficult for Him to unravel. No calamity can befall the least of His children … in which He takes no immediate interest."*

He came in several minutes later, a tall man dressed casually in a vest and tweed coat. He sat down after greeting me cordially, looked over my papers and started the interview.

He said sternly: "I want you to tell me everything about this case, all the mistakes and errors you made, everything. You must hide nothing from me. Even if you think you made a mistake, it is important that you tell me of it. If I find out about it at the trial, it will be much harder for me to defend you. Tell me it all."

So, I confessed everything, every error and misstep.

He looked up pensively, "I think we can win this. I can tell you are hiding nothing."

We went on to win the case.

Jesus tells us to do the same, to hold nothing back. It is only as we reveal our deepest secrets that He can cleanse and cure us of our sins. He has dealt with sinners for thousands of years. He knows all of us and unless we tell Him all, even our darkest deeds, He cannot win in the end.

"There is no chapter in our experience too dark for Him to read; there is no perplexity too difficult for Him to unravel. No calamity can befall the least of His children ... in which He takes no immediate interest."[141]

---

[141]Ellen G. White, *Steps to Christ* (Mountain View, CA: Pacific Press Publishing Association, 1892), p. 100.

PETER AND JUDAS
September 20

Luke 22:56–57, "A servant girl saw him seated there in the firelight. She looked closely at him and said, 'This man was with him.' But he denied it. 'Woman, I don't know him,' he said."

Luke 22:3–4, "Then Satan entered Judas, called Iscariot, one of the Twelve. And Judas went to the chief priests and the officers of the temple guard and discussed with them how he might betray Jesus."

The sins of Peter and Judas, though not the same in every aspect, were very nearly the same. Judas betrayed his Lord for thirty pieces of silver (Matt. 26:14–15). Peter denied his Lord when called to confess allegiance, though he had pledged his life a few hours before. He called curses down on himself rather than confess (Matt. 26:74)!

In spite of the similarities, the courses of their lives deviated sharply after their sins. Judas went out and hung himself in despair, while Peter went out and wept bitterly (Matt. 27:5; 26:75).

Why such a difference in behavior?

There seems to have been two reasons these two men came to such different ends: one a hopeless suicide, the other a leader of the apostles.

First of all, Judas gave himself up to his sin. He planned this betrayal, going to the chief priests deliberately, intentionally. Peter, on the other hand, did not plan such an act, but did not realize the deficiencies of his own soul and he ignored Jesus' warning that Satan would like to sift him as wheat (Luke 22:31).

Secondly, Judas had not developed faith in a loving, forgiving God, while Peter had. Judas could have been saved. But he could not see beyond the horror of his sins to the grace of Christ. He thought salvation impossible. And disbelief made it impossible. It was not that the arm of the Lord was shortened, it was that he did not believe it could save. Peter, however, remembered the love of Christ for sinners and though devastated by his weakness, he believed.

The path of each is open to us. Will we entertain dark thoughts, believing that God will not forgive and we are hopeless? Or will we cling to the words of Christ, "Turn to me and be saved" (Isa. 45:22)?

Section 10

The Installation of King Jesus

Like any earthly king, Jesus was installed on His throne. Only this installation was like no other and was full of irony.

> Throned upon the awful tree,
> Lamb of God, Your grief we see.
> Darkness veils Your anguished face;
> None its lines of woe can trace.
> None can tell what pangs unknown
> Hold You silent and alone.[142]

---

[142]John Ellerton, "Throned Upon the Awful Tree," *The Seventh-day Adventist Hymnal* (Hagerstown, MD: Review and Herald, 1985).

THE TRIUMPHAL ENTRY
September 21

Zechariah 9:9, "Shout, Daughter Jerusalem! See, your king comes to you, righteous and victorious, lowly and riding on a donkey, on a colt, the foal of a donkey."

The event initiating Jesus' ascension to His throne, the cross, was His entry into Jerusalem the capital on a donkey, the seat of royalty. Such an act signaled that the King had arrived.

Jesus had never taken such a step before. The disciples were delighted when He chose to do this. Jesus was finally moving to take His rightful seat, they thought. But they could not see what would be the result of such an act.

> *Jerusalem had not realized the day of her visitation. The King had come, but the rulers strove to prevent His entry. It was the beginning of the end.*

However, the rulers could. This method of entering the city was Jesus' declaration of kingship. It could not be missed.

"Hosanna to the Son of David!" (Matt. 21:9) cried the crowd. Who else could this be but the King?

Lazarus led the donkey and the tumult included many that Jesus had healed of their dread diseases.[143] The children rejoiced that One who understood them and loved them had come to rule in Jerusalem, the city of peace.

But the rulers would have none of it. They went out to halt the proceedings. "Stop your followers," (Luke 19:39, paraphrase) they cried as if they could hinder the will of God. But Jesus, pointing to the rocks at the side of the road, said they would cry out if human voices failed to make the proclamation (Luke 19:40).

As Jesus entered for the last time, He paused at the brow of the hill overlooking the temple and wept for the city He loved, the city shortly to be abandoned by its Redeemer. "I have longed to gather your children together as a hen gathers her chicks under her wings, and you were not willing" (Matt. 23:37).

Jerusalem had not realized the day of her visitation. The King had come, but the rulers strove to prevent His entry. It was the beginning of the end.

---

[143]Ellen G. White, *The Desire of Ages* (Mountain View, CA: Pacific Press, 1898), p. 572.

AT THE TEMPLE: THE BOOK OF THE LAW
September 22

Luke 19:47–48, "Every day he was teaching at the temple. But the chief priests, the teachers of the law and the leaders among the people were trying to kill him. Yet they could not find any way to do it, because all the people hung on his words."

After entering Jerusalem as its King, Jesus repaired to the temple.

Just as a Jewish king received a book of the law when taking the crown, that he might dispense justice to the people (2 Kings 11:12), so Jesus entered the temple to discuss the law of the new kingdom.

But before He could set up rule there, He had to remove those that were there illegitimately. If one is to rule, imposters and usurpers must be cast out.

Jesus drove out the money changers and sellers of sacrifices, those who were desecrating the temple with their wares (Luke 19:45). And none of them questioned His authority. They fled before the face of the King.

"My house [claiming ownership as well as divinity] will be a house of prayer; but you have made it a den of robbers" (Luke 19:46) Jesus cried as He sent them packing.

The priests and teachers of the law then came to ask questions of the King. Jesus answered their questions showing that He knew the law and would give the people the proper interpretation of it. As the king would dispense wisdom and judgement to the people, so did King Jesus when He entered the temple (Luke 19:47).

The leaders came first with a question of authority. Who was Jesus that He should ride into Jerusalem on a colt and take control of the temple as if He ruled the place? "By what authority are you doing these things?" they asked. "And who gave you authority to do this?" (Mark 11:28).

AGNOSTICISM
September 23

Matthew 21:23–25, 27:

> [T]he chief priests and the elders of the people came to him. "By what authority are you doing these things?" they asked .... Jesus replied, "I will also ask you one question. If you answer me, I will tell you by what authority I am doing these things. John's baptism—where did it come from? Was it from heaven, or of human origin?" ... So they answered Jesus, "We don't know." Then he said, "Neither will I tell you."

Why did Jesus reply with this evasive answer to these inquiring leaders?

Because they would not have believed any answer He gave. Jesus had given ample evidence of His divine mission. His teachings were profound. His miracles were many and performed not to ease His way on earth, but to help the poor, sick and downtrodden of society. He had fulfilled the predictions of the Old Testament prophets regarding the Messiah (Isa. 61:1–3, etc.).

When He came into the presence of Pilate, the pagan magistrate recognized His divine character immediately. Here was a Man of striking integrity and kingly bearing. A few questions forced from his lips the declaration to the murderous crowd, "I find *no* fault in this Man" (Luke 23:4, emphasis added). If a pagan could recognize divinity, the elders could have as well. But they would not.

Theirs was the position of agnosticism. When asked about divine things, the existence of God, the Creation of the universe, such individuals will not say that there is *no* God, but that they just don't know.

Jesus showed the foolishness of such thinking.

Agnosticism is a type of blindness to evidence. As the psalmist says, the very heavens declare God's glory, testifying daily of His divine power to the whole world (Ps. 19:1). Paul notes that men are without excuse because they suppress the knowledge of God, ignoring the power revealed in the Creation (Rom. 1:18–20).

And Jesus said even one returning from the dead would not persuade these cavilers (Luke 16:31). Such individuals refuse to recognize the evidence that is before them and we will have little success convincing them by it if they do not recognize it for themselves. The best argument in this situation is a holy life lived in strict integrity. Such a life cannot be gainsaid. Actions by such a one will speak louder than any words or discussion since a wall has already been built that is near impossible to breach.

THE PARABLE OF THE TENANTS
September 24

Luke 20:9, "He went on to tell the people this parable: 'A man planted a vineyard, rented it to some farmers and went away for a long time.'"

Read Matthew 21:33–46.

On entering the temple, He first showed the fearful future for the Jewish nation when it had rejected Jesus.

The parable told of a rich landowner who planted a vineyard and of farmers who would not return rent due to the owner and what these wicked tenants would do in the end. The owner sent many servants to collect the rent, but the farmers mistreated them and still refused to pay. The owner then sent his son and they seized him and cast him out of the vineyard and killed him.

Jesus then asked the people what the owner should do? The leaders replied, "He will bring those wretches to a wretched end" (Matt. 21:41). Before they realized it, they had condemned themselves.

Jesus then speaks of the future: "Therefore I tell you that the kingdom of God will be taken away from you and given to a people who will produce its fruit" (Matt. 21:43). And a little later, "Jerusalem, Jerusalem, you who kill the prophets and stone those sent to you, how often I have longed to gather your children together, as a hen gathers her chicks under her wings, and you were not willing" (Matt. 23:37).

Jesus would not let the leaders sin their great sin, rejecting their Messiah, without giving them warning of what they were doing. But they would not listen or take heed.

These warnings are for us as well. By rejecting the leading of the Spirit, we too can sin against God. Let us then be careful to follow wherever He leads.

THE CURSED FIG TREE
September 25

Matthew 21:18–19, "Early in the morning, as Jesus was on his way back to the city, he was hungry. Seeing a fig tree by the road, he went up to it but found nothing on it except leaves. Then he said to it, 'May you never bear fruit again!' Immediately the tree withered."

Jesus had just taken possession of the temple, driving out the money changers and managers. Little children had filled its courts with their lisping praise and the lame and blind had flocked there to be healed. And He healed them all.

But in the face of all this, the chief priests and teachers protested and began plotting to kill Him.

The next day, as He passed by, a fig tree full of leaves portending ripe fruit stood by the road. But there was no fruit. Jesus cursed the tree and it withered, a living example of the fate of the Jewish nation.

Many today look to the nation of Israel as a fulfillment of prophecy. But the Jewish people since the time of Jesus have been hardened to the gospel. Their house has indeed been left desolate and on the Temple Mount stands a shrine of Islam (Matt. 23:38).

God labored with the Jewish people for more than 1,000 years, but when their Redeemer came, they received Him not. In the parable of the tenants, Jesus said, "Therefore I tell you that the kingdom of God will be taken away from you" (Matt. 21:43). It could not have been made clearer. They did indeed embrace Caesar as their king, and he ruled cruelly.

They are an example of those that turn from God to themselves. Jesus would have gathered them under His wings as a hen gathers her chicks, but they would not (Matt. 23:37).

PAYING TAXES
September 26

Matthew 22:21, "Then he said to them, 'So give back to Caesar what is Caesar's, and to God what is God's.'"

When Jesus said this to the Jews of His day, they were amazed, but we often miss the profound insight that Jesus gave us in these few words.

The Pharisees had teamed up with the Herodians, an unlikely alliance, to trap Jesus. They came with a question on taxes. But Jesus, in a brilliant statement, set before them the proper relation between the governments of men and God.

He asked for a coin, questioning them about Caesar's inscription thereon. He then gives the penetrating answer in the above verse.

First, Jesus recognizes and legitimizes earthly rulers and their administrations, even to the collecting of hated taxes. They are not outside of God's will. He allows for their authority. We are to render to them respect and even submit to their power to collect money from us in the form of taxes. Odious though this practice seems, even to the sapping of financial support for the gospel, Jesus saw it as legitimate.

Second, governmental authority is limited. God has a sphere where His will is supreme and earthly governments have no right to infringe on it. He has given us His requirements in His laws and rules. Even if governments tell us to ignore His commands, we are to follow them regardless of the demands of Caesar (Acts 5:29).

Jesus saw the conflict that could arise and met it simply: give to Caesar what is his, but to God what is His. God can overrule Caesar, but we must be careful to respect Caesar's realm.

It was an amazing insight, preventing His followers from taking radical stands that would hurt the heavenly kingdom on earth and yet recognizing that God's authority is the ultimate one.

MARRIAGE IN HEAVEN
September 27

Matthew 22:23, "That same day the Sadducees, who say there is no resurrection, came to him with a question. 'Teacher,' they said, 'Moses told us that if a man dies without having children ....'"

Read Matthew 22:23–33.

Next the Sadducees came to question Jesus. Although they had great power because they controlled the priesthood, they were deeply cynical and did not believe in the resurrection.[144] Theirs was a question of unbelief, thinking they had believers in the resurrection trapped by the rules of Moses.

It was a rhetorical question of possibilities rather than realities and involved Moses' law of the levirate. "Seven brothers," they said, "each died in order. The first had married a woman, whom the second, and third married, each in turn, until after all had married her, she, too, died. Who will have her as wife in the resurrection?" (Matt. 22:25–28, paraphrase).

Jesus rebuked them for their lack of scriptural knowledge and failure to appreciate the power of God.

He then quoted from the story of the burning bush in Exodus (a book they accepted as from God) where God says, "I am the God of ... Abraham, the God of Isaac and the God of Jacob" (Exod. 3:6). "He is not the God of the dead but of the living [for to him all are alive]" (Matt. 22:32).

"Some of the teachers of the law responded, 'Well said, teacher!'" (Luke 20:39) just as we should. For God is the God of the living. Jesus revealed that God sees believers in Him, though they have died, as living, anticipating the resurrection. It is a comfort to know God's thinking on His sleeping saints. They are as if they were alive to Him. He only waits to bring them forth from the grave whole and new.

That Jesus would take a question to trap Him and turn it to give hope shows His skill and knowledge.

---

[144]Ibid., p. 603.

THE GREATEST COMMANDMENT
September 28

Mark 12:28, "One of the teachers of the law came and heard them debating. Noticing that Jesus had given them a good answer, he asked him, 'Of all the commandments, which is the most important?'"

The Jewish teachers often debated about which commandment was the most important. If one could determine this, then its obedience would trump all others and they would know how to act to please God.

Unfortunately, there was no surety among them and each had his own opinion on the matter. Jesus, on the other hand, spoke with authority and the people were astonished at His teaching.

When asked directly by this lawyer, Jesus gave this answer: "'Hear, O Israel: The Lord our God, the Lord is one. Love the Lord your God with all your heart and with all your soul and with all your mind and with all your strength.' The second is this: 'Love your neighbor as yourself.' There is no commandment greater than these" (Mark 12:29–31).

The lawyer was impressed and complemented Jesus on His answer. Jesus noted that he was not far from the kingdom of God (Mark 12:34).

Jesus silenced all of the Jewish teachers with His answers. He understood the law, because He had given it, and so taught us its true meaning. We need not dispute as the Pharisees and Sadducees did, not knowing what God's thinking was on the matter. We now have His own interpretation and can be sure of His meaning.

But then Jesus had a question for them. It was a question regarding the Messiah and who He was. Jesus asked ….

WHOSE SON IS CHRIST?
September 29

Matthew 22:41–45:

> While the Pharisees were gathered together, Jesus asked them, "What do you think about the Messiah? Whose son is he?" "The son of David," they replied. He said to them, "How is it then that David, speaking by the Spirit, calls him 'Lord'? For he says, "'The Lord said to my Lord: "Sit at my right hand until I put your enemies under your feet."' If then David calls him 'Lord,' how can he be his son?"

Jesus gave them one last chance to turn from the terrible sin they were about to commit. If the Messiah was David's son, how could he at the same time call Him "Lord"?

There are two problems. If the Messiah is David's son or offspring, He could not be alive during David's lifetime, yet David calls Him 'Lord.'

And He must be greater than David, for David calls Him 'Lord.'

Jesus knew of their plans to kill Him. He would save them from this act that would destroy the nation and the temple. He would rather have sent these men as His messengers to the world with the gospel just as He would send His disciples.

But they were heedless of His warnings and hardened their hearts. In the end they stirred the crowd to call a curse down on themselves, saying, "His blood is on us and on our children!" (Matt. 27:25). And so it was!

Jesus never ceased loving His people, but sin separated Him from them and the separation was sealed by the cross. It was not His will that such a thing come to pass. He wept over their stubborn ways but would not violate their wills. He left the temple the last time, sorrowful.

THE ANOINTING AT BETHANY
September 30

Mark 14:6, "'Leave her alone,' said Jesus. 'Why are you bothering her? She has done a beautiful thing to me.'"

A necessary part of any Jewish coronation was the anointing of the king (see 2 Kings 11:12). But who would anoint King Jesus?

The priests had no interest in such a thing but were plotting to kill the King. Any recognition by an anointing from that quarter was ridiculous.

The disciples were so busy thinking of their own places in the new regime that it never occurred to them.

Where could God turn?

He could turn to one who loved Jesus. So, the Spirit moved on the heart of a woman of disputable reputation to do the duty that no legitimate power was willing to perform. And she did it with amazing elegance.

She purchased the best oil possible, even better than any other king had received. She bought an extravagant amount and poured it all on His head and feet, signifying that His thinking and actions were both blessed.

The fragrance filled the room and spoke to the disciples of their stingy ways.

But that is not all.

The scent went with Jesus through the trial and all the way to the cross. It was to let all know that this was indeed the King of the Jews, One who had been anointed in proper fashion with the best the earth had to offer.

It was also one of the few reminders for Jesus of the results of the work He had come to do: the saving of humanity by His sacrifice. Its pervasive presence perfumed His work on the cross.

And when Jesus rose from the dead, He wanted to see Mary first. She was the only one who even partially understood.

THE SHEEP AND THE GOATS
October 1

Matthew 25:31–32 "When the Son of Man comes in his glory, and all the angels with him, he will sit on his glorious throne. All the nations will be gathered before him, and he will separate the people one from another as a shepherd separates the sheep from the goats."

Standing before God during the judgement seems a fearful thing. That our pasts would be brought up before the holy God is a frightful prospect. But God has a different view on the matter.

Ellen White says this:

> Those whom Christ commends in the judgement may have known little of theology, but they have cherished His principles. Through the influence of the divine Spirit they have been a blessing to those about them. Even among the heathen are those who have cherished the spirit of kindness .... Among the heathen are those who worship God ignorantly ... yet they will not perish .... [T]hey have heard His voice speaking to them in nature, and have done the things that the law required .... How surprised and gladdened will be the lowly among the nations, and among the heathen, to hear from the lips of the Saviour, "Inasmuch as ye have done it unto one of the least of these My brethren, ye have done it unto Me"! *How glad will be the heart of Infinite Love as His followers look up with surprise and joy at His words of approval!*[145]

God is not looking to condemn or destroy, but to welcome His lowly ones into fellowship. Our lives and the sin around us must not absorb our thoughts, but we must turn our thoughts heavenward. There we will see the smiling face of our Redeemer, longing to give us His approving glance.

---

[145]Ibid., p. 638, emphasis added.

JESUS' PRAYER FOR US
October 2

John 17:20, "My prayer is not for them alone. I pray also for those who will believe in me through their message."

Some of us have a hard time believing that God will hear our prayers. We are full of turmoil and sin and lack the will that we think we should have to overcome sin and do what God would have us to do.

Why would God hear our prayers? Why would He listen to ones such as us with all of our faults and shortcomings?

We can take hope because Jesus our Savior prayed for us. He prayed for us just as He prayed for the disciples that were with Him that night before the crucifixion when they all abandoned Him to die alone. We can read His prayer in John 17. It is a wonderful prayer.

He prays for Himself, then He prays for His disciples. And there is not a whisper of their future actions at the cross, their abandoning of Him in the time of crisis. He overlooks it but instead pleads with the Father to protect them in His absence.

> *Now we often feel that God does not hear us, but He certainly heard His Son. And if the Father listened to the Son, who prayed that the Father might remember us and protect us, certainly He will hear us as we pray.*

Then He prays for us, for you and me, we who have listened to the testimony of the disciples that He called. He prayed for us!

Now we often feel that God does not hear us, but He certainly heard His Son.

And if the Father listened to the Son, who prayed that the Father might remember us and protect us, certainly He will hear us as we pray.

Jesus even said that He did not need to speak to the Father about us, for the Father loved us (John 16:27).

Let us then go to the throne of grace, for Jesus has prayed for us. And God already said He would hear Him (John 16:23).

WHY A BETRAYER?
October 3

Matthew 26:14–16, "Then one of the Twelve—the one called Judas Iscariot—went to the chief priests and asked, 'What are you willing to give me if I deliver him over to you?' So they counted out for him thirty pieces of silver. From then on Judas watched for an opportunity to hand him over."

I have often wondered why betrayal was necessary to take Christ. Couldn't the priests just arrest Jesus at some haunt and bring Him to trial? Why did they need someone to lead them to Gethsemane?

But actually the situation was far from simple for several reasons.

First, the people considered Jesus a prophet and any open action would have resulted in an immediate riot, a risky option in the tinder box that was Palestine at the time.

Second, there were the disciples. They were armed and would defend Jesus to the death (John 18:10)! Even with the midnight arrest, Peter sprang into an active defense. These men were serious and committed. They presented a real obstacle.

Why not just have a spy follow the group until it was safe to arrest Him? Again, the disciples were watching for just such an individual who would have been accosted and cared for in an "appropriate" fashion.

No, the arrest had to be secret.

They had come to an impasse when Judas approached them that day, an inside man who knew every plan the Savior was making! He was completely unexpected.

They could now plan a secret arrest, away from the crowds. He changed the whole situation.

So, men schemed to destroy the One who had come with eternal life in His hands. How fallen is our nature that we would use our powers to do such a thing!

THE ARREST
October 4

Matthew 26:47, "While he was still speaking, Judas, one of the Twelve, arrived. With him was a large crowd armed with swords and clubs, sent from the chief priests and the elders of the people."

Now the Jewish leaders could plan for the arrest of Jesus. It could not be bungled. They gathered enough strength to overpower any resistance the disciples might muster. Jesus would be taken without too much difficulty. However, if there was to be a fight, they would be ready.

The betrayer approached the Savior and signaled with his kiss (Matt. 26:49).

The disciples sprang to defend Jesus. Peter had said he would die for his Savior and drew his sword to fulfill the promise. But the fisherman was so clumsy with his weapon, he could only sever an ear (John 18:10).

Blood splattered everywhere (ears are quite vascular organs). The disciples surrounded Jesus, ready for a last stand. But He stepped out from among them and faced the mob.

He picked up the severed ear and replaced it, healing it instantly (Luke 22:51).

"Those who use the sword will die by the sword" (Matt. 26:52, NLT), Jesus said as He moved from the healed man and addressed the mob, "If you are looking for me, then let these men go" (John 18:8).

The disciples were stunned. Would there be no resistance?

The mob closed in on the Savior and bound Him with ropes—as if it were necessary. They took Him away as the disciples stood speechless. Then, realizing that all was lost they fled for their lives (Matt. 26:56).

Jesus would not allow the disciples to risk their lives to save Him. He had warned them of this hour. They must live that they might give the good news to the world. To be cut down here would have frustrated the purpose of God. There was a better battle to be fought in the future. They would be then ready when they were not now.

Jesus sought to smooth the way for them. He would give His life to save them as well as us.

"I FIND NO FAULT IN HIM"
October 5

John 18:38, "With this he [Pilate] went out again to the Jews gathered there and said, 'I find no basis for a charge against him.'"

Some time ago, I was stopped by a policeman for speeding. I think I was going 75 mph in a 55-mph zone! He came up to the car and asked me if I knew why I was being stopped. "It may have been speeding," I answered sheepishly.

He looked at me and said, "You seem like a nice guy. I'll let you off with a warning."

I turned to him. "Wait a minute," I said, "How do you know I'm a nice guy? You just met me and have not known me for more than ten seconds. How *could* you possibly know that I am a nice guy?"

He cocked his head and bent down, "I have been doing this for thirty years. I know a nice guy when I see one. Now be on your way."

He was intimately acquainted with people that were not nice and he could tell in a heartbeat.

Pilate was the same. He was used to evaluating those that came before him. He knew the criminal class well, like my policeman friend. And when he met Jesus, it was as clear as day that He was not part of it. And so, after a few questions to confirm his assessment, he walked out and faced those crafty Pharisees and announced, "I find no fault in Him at all" (John 18:38, NKJV).

It was an astounding statement of truth, occurring after a few moments' encounter with Jesus.

Here God gave another warning to the ones He loved. But they were intent on murder, the murder of God Himself! Even a pagan knew when He met Jesus. But His own people would not acknowledge Him.

THE CORONATION
October 6

Mark 15:16–19, "The soldiers led Jesus away into the palace ... and called together the whole company of soldiers. They put a purple robe on him, then twisted together a crown of thorns and set it on him. And they began to call out to him, 'Hail, king of the Jews!' Again and again they struck him on the head with a staff and spit on him. Falling on their knees, they paid homage to him."

When a man is made king, there must be a coronation. So it was with Jesus. But His coronation was surely the most ironic of all time. The Roman soldiers thought they were mocking this "King of the Jews," and their disdain for the Jewish people was poured out on the Savior. But in reality, *in reality*, they were performing the coronation necessary for Jesus to take His throne: His cross.

Crucifixion was a dehumanizing process. A man lost control of himself and was considered more like a thing than a human. Jesus underwent this very real change from human to thing and was treated as such. He was beaten, then dressed in a discarded robe and handed a staff. A crown of thorns completed the costume.

The soldiers blindfolded Jesus, took the staff, struck Him and asked Him to prophesy who had done it, then spit on Him (Luke 22:64). They would bow in mock obeisance and hit Him in the face. After they had exhausted themselves with their derision, they took Him off to be crucified.

That the Creator of the universe would submit to such treatment without retaliation is shocking. Peter expressed our horror when he remonstrated with Jesus about this very thing (Matt. 16:21–23). How could He allow it?

Satan was given free rein in his treatment of Jesus. Every act pressed on the mind of the King to shake off the shame and allow humans to bear their own just fate and destruction. But it would have led to the loss of the universe as well.

The prize was too precious. He would endure it all for us and His other creatures.

THE ATTRACTION OF THE CROSS
October 7

John 12:32, "And I, when I am lifted up from the earth, will draw all people to myself."

I am amazed that I find the cross so attractive. I am drawn to it. And I am not the only one who is so moved. Unbelievers are drawn just as believers are. The devout Hindu, Gandhi, found the cross attractive, though put off by some of his followers.[146] But the cross and its Victim? There is a strange fascination.

Why?

Others have been crucified; the Romans filled the hills around Jerusalem with them in AD 70, as they did with Spartacus' followers outside Rome.[147]

It is the reaction of Jesus that makes His cross such an attractive thing.

Jesus goes to the cross, an innocent man, admitted so by the judge who tried to acquit Him. He is mostly silent, not railing against His accusers, but rather in resigned dignity meeting them. His kingly bearing is noted by all.

Then, He forgives those who are abusing Him, for they have no idea what they are doing. He is surrounded by ravening wolves but has the calm demeanor of One in complete control.

And then He has the audacity to promise a dying criminal a place in the kingdom He is claiming as His own (Luke 23:43).

But what is really attractive is the character of the One dying there. His whole life was devoted to doing good. He went about healing the sick, raising the dead and forgiving sin. Then He is taken out, mocked, beaten and killed in the cruelest way. And yet He does not retaliate even then! If He can do that, He will accept and treat me that way, for I am just like they were.

He is not a threat. He is a Savior. And He showed it there like it could not have been shown anywhere else.

So, they took the humiliated Christ for the last humiliation, the crucifixion. Why did God allow such a thing as this?

---

[146]Pascal Alan Nazareth, "Gandhi, Christ and Christianity, https://1ref.us/1ix (accessed January 20, 2021).
[147]Simon Sebag Montefiore, "DELANCEYPLACE.COM 11/8/11 - FIVE HUNDRED JEWS WERE CRUCIFIED EACH DAY," Delanceyplace.com, https://1ref.us/1iy (accessed January 20, 2021).

TAKING THE THRONE PART 1
October 8

John 19:19–22:

> *Pilate had a notice prepared and fastened to the cross. It read: JESUS OF NAZARETH, THE KING OF THE JEWS. Many of the Jews read this sign, for the place where Jesus was crucified was near the city, and the sign was written in Aramaic, Latin and Greek. The chief priests of the Jews protested to Pilate, "Do not write 'The King of the Jews,' but that this man claimed to be king of the Jews." Pilate answered, "What I have written, I have written."*

When a king begins his reign, he is free to exercise the power that he has received at the coronation when he is proclaimed king.

What powers did Christ exercise upon taking His throne, the cross? His words tell us of the power that He would exercise as the newly installed King.

First, it should be noted that an announcement regarding the reason He was being crucified was placed above His head: a sign told in three languages that he was the King of the Jews.

Pilate had put it there in irony and anger because of the cunning of the Jewish leaders and he refused to change the wording despite their protests.

But even in their protest, they state plainly that that is what He claimed to be.

This public announcement of His claim gave credence to the proclamation of John the Baptist and Jesus that the kingdom was at hand (Matt. 3:2). Now the King had taken His throne publicly, and it was acknowledged even by a heathen official.

No other person had been crucified with this epitaph above their head. Only Christ.

TAKING THE THRONE PART 2
October 9

Matthew 27:45–46, NKJV, "Now from the sixth hour until the ninth hour there was darkness over all the land. And about the ninth hour Jesus cried out with a loud voice, saying, 'Eli, Eli, lama sabachthani?' that is, 'My God, My God, why have You forsaken me?'"

This cry is not the cry of One who appears to have taken the throne of the kingdom. How can it be evidence that Jesus was King? It is rather a cry of abandonment.

Yet, when Jesus prayed to the Father that Their shared glory might be revealed, part of that answer was this cry (John 17:1–5).

How so?

It shows the utter length to which God would go to save humanity and thus any creatures that He had created.

The choice of the Father, by the agreement from the beginning, was either us or Jesus. Both could not be saved.

Jesus was abandoned to death that we might live. This abandonment was not some sham or plaything, but a real thing. It occurred as Christ was hanging on the cruel cross. God left Him, and He cried out in the agony of utter loneliness and death.

And so the glory of God's love was shown to the whole universe. Just how far the Godhead would go was seen clearly.

Sometimes a woman is pursued and loved by two men, but only one can be chosen to enter a marriage. As the vow says, "forsaking all others." The one unchosen knows the depth of such forsaking. Though his love may have been deep, he is left out.

So it was with Jesus. We were chosen and He was left. That choice is proclaimed from the throne that we might know the depths of that love.

TAKING THE THRONE PART 3
October 10

Luke 23:40–43, "But the other criminal rebuked him. 'Don't you fear God?' he said, 'since you are under the same sentence? We are punished justly, for we are getting what our deeds deserve. But this man has done nothing wrong.' Then he said, 'Jesus, remember me when you come into your kingdom.' Jesus answered him, 'Truly I tell you, today you will be with me in paradise.'"

Although Jesus forgave all of mankind at the cross, there was one case that was particularly important: the thief.

This man had lived a wicked life and now came to a wicked end and was hours away from the judgement that comes to all men (Heb. 9:27). It appeared that there was no hope. He had led a life of crime and admitted that the punishment he was receiving was just. There was no indication that mercy was available.

But this man, on the very edge of eternity, who had been unrepentant to this very moment, as he was about to die, asked to be forgiven and allowed into the kingdom.

It was an audacious request.

But Jesus did not hesitate. "Truly I tell you, today you will be with me in paradise" (Luke 23:43).

This man shows the scope of Jesus' ability to forgive. Even a man who was wicked and sinned up to the very last hours of his life, a life given to sin and destruction could have his sins forgiven and even be promised at that moment that he could be in Paradise! If this man could be forgiven of a life of sin, we can as well.

> *We are too timid in asking forgiveness. Jesus has made a way of escape for us and is able to bring us into His kingdom in spite of ourselves. And it is His right to do so.*

We are too timid in asking forgiveness. Jesus has made a way of escape for us and is able to bring us into His kingdom in spite of ourselves. And it is His right to do so.

I THIRST

October 11

John 19:28, "Later, knowing that everything had now been finished, and so that Scripture would be fulfilled, Jesus said, 'I am thirsty.'"

The early church was wracked by disputes about the nature of Jesus. Was He man? Was He a divine figure? Was He a spirit? Did He leave His body here and go to heaven when He died?

Jesus met all these arguments on the cross. There he cried out, "I am thirsty" (Ibid.).

It is a clear indication that He was fully human.

How could One thirst who was not thoroughly human? Such a sensation is not one experienced by a spirit. One who was not human would not feel such a need nor would they cry out to be given water.

So it is certain that Jesus was human. This was in opposition to the Gnostic view that Jesus did not take a human body but was a pure spiritual Being.

But what difference does it make?

A great deal. That Jesus was fully human, experiencing what it really means to be human is so important to us. If He was not human, He did not really enter the reality of human experience and is unable to understand what it means to be like us.

And if God did not take on flesh, He has not humbled Himself as Paul said in Philippians 2, where the emptying of Christ is described.

I take great comfort in the idea of Jesus' coming in flesh. He knew exactly what it is to be thirsty and tired and hungry and tempted. And the One who knows by experience has made a way of escape through His own actions here. And this Man of flesh stands before the throne of God in heaven itself.

We are thus secure.

IT IS FINISHED
October 12

John 19:28–30, "Later, knowing that everything had now been finished, and so that Scripture would be fulfilled, Jesus said, 'I am thirsty.' A jar of wine vinegar was there, so they soaked a sponge in it, put the sponge on a stalk of the hyssop plant, and lifted it to Jesus' lips. When he had received the drink, Jesus said, 'It is finished.' With that, he bowed his head and gave up his spirit."

What exactly was finished?

Although the world has continued for another 2,000+ years, the great controversy was ended. Satan was defeated and permanently cast from heaven. His place had apparently been in the throne room of heaven at God's right hand accusing us day and night (Rev. 12:10). Christ proclaimed Satan's "ministry" finished; he would never enter heaven again to rail against the saints.

The plan agreed on before the foundation of the world was complete. The debt was paid and we were free.

The temple veil was torn from top to bottom signifying the end of the services there (Matt. 27:51). The way into the Holy of Holies was now open to all, sinner and saint alike. The veil symbolizing that separation was torn asunder.

The Jewish ceremonial system ended as well. We need not bring lambs for sacrifice for our sins, for they have been borne by Him who was the Lamb of God. The Jews of Jesus' day continued the sacrifices for another forty years, but they were meaningless and have not been reinstated since then.

The Abrahamic covenant also ended that day. The Jewish people proclaimed that their only king was Caesar and with the death of the divine party to the covenant, the sign of that covenant—circumcision—became meaningless as well (John 19:12–16).

THE MEANING OF THE CROSS PART 1
October 13

1 Peter 2:24, "He himself bore our sins in his body on the tree, so that we might die to sins."

I read an article some time ago that told of Bishop Eva Braunen of Freeport, Sweden, taking down the cross in the Seaman's Chapel so as to be more inclusive. Who wants to go into a building with a cross on it, anyway?[148]

She understood the offense of the cross.

What is the cross? It was an instrument that Rome used to subdue and torture people. It had nothing to do with religion. The Menorah, the symbol for Judaism, is a lamp giving light. As the Psalm says, "[A] light unto my path" (Ps. 119:105, KJV). But a cross?

When we do executions nowadays, they are done in private so as not to offend. But Rome knew the value of public display. Hanging naked, dying a slow painful death that all could see sent a message. And that is how we treated God when He came among us.

The cross reveals several things.

1. It reveals the utter wickedness of humanity. That we would nail the God who made us to the cross, like a butterfly mounted on a board, shows our unmitigated sinfulness, depravity and ingratitude. We did it. It is the dark blot that exposes our inadequacy and need for redemption. It shows the depths to which we have fallen. God reaches out a hand of mercy and we pin it to a cross so that it might not move. Astounding ingratitude.
2. The reality of our salvation. It is not an ethereal thing, but a down and dirty flesh and blood reality. We are dealing with stark naked truth with no glossing over to make it more palatable. What took place there took place on our planet with its clumsy violence and rude behavior. A behavior we are all too familiar with.

---

[148]"WORLD'S FIRST OPENLY ..." ORTHODOX CHRISTIANITY, https://1ref.us/1iz (accessed January 20, 2021).

THE MEANING OF THE CROSS PART 2
October 14

3. The cross also reveals the distance that God would go to save us. Astounding. It will take eternity to plumb the depths of the condescension of Christ. The God of unapproachable light hangs naked on a cross! God reaches over the chasm that separates us from Him and participates with us in death, the very thing we so fear, and makes it His! He embraces it. 2 Corinthians 5:21 says He was made sin for us. We know what sin is. It is part and parcel of who we are when we stand before the mirror and are truly honest with ourselves. He became that for us. And we know what that means. This is another sign we are not dealing with a fantasy.
4. Because the cross is so real, so believable, so characteristic of life here, it gives us a base on which to ground belief in something that seems so less real: the fact that we can be saved. We are sinners, the ones who are not faithful, who casually compromise with evil and betray others, not living up to the light that we know. We know who we are and think it is impossible to be any different. But the cross shows that we are known of God and nevertheless loved. He reaches down and says, "Take My hand, I can save you. SEE, I know."

The cross is thus the very basis for our faith. Someone who did that can be trusted to fulfill what He has promised. If He did that, then I can cast myself on His mercy and rest in Him.

The cross shows the fullness of God's love. Oh, I love it, though it is a repugnant thing. And to take it as the symbol of our salvation is to truly accept what God has done for us.

I don't like the cross. I don't like what it says about me. But I am so happy that God decided to take it to Himself, for it means that He has taken me to Himself as well. I have a real God who understands the real me and my needs.

A SABBATH REST
October 15

Luke 23:56, "But they rested on the Sabbath in obedience to the commandment."

Jesus had passed into the rest of death. A rest from the torture of the cross and the battle He had won there.

At the Creation, God saw that all was very good and He rested on the Sabbath. Jesus had just accomplished the salvation of mankind and it too was very good. Jesus' rest gave new meaning to the day celebrating the good done by God.

But Jesus was the only one who was resting that Sabbath. The Sabbath proclamation was made from the temple court as usual, but the torn veil could not be hidden, a premonition of some future woe. The priests performed their duties with nervous trepidation.[149]

> *Jesus had sought to warn the disciples of His death, but surprisingly, it is the Jewish leaders who remembered, not the disciples. They set a guard that only helped confirm the resurrection.*

The disciples spent the day in hiding. Would they be the next to be called before the Sanhedrin? Would their lives be forfeited as well? They cowered in fear, afraid to venture from the upper room.

Hope had fled. The One they had committed their lives to was dead. All that they had longed for died when Jesus breathed His last. They fell into deep despair.

And Peter! Not only had all hope vanished, he had betrayed the One he loved and there was no asking forgiveness. Jesus had known all along, but Peter had refused to listen and correct his weakness. Now he had failed. Depression like a dark fog blotted out all hope.

Jesus had sought to warn the disciples of His death, but surprisingly, it is the Jewish leaders who remembered, not the disciples. They set a guard that only helped confirm the resurrection.

The disciples forgot, the priests remembered! How dull we often are as well.

---
[149]Ellen G. White, *The Desire of Ages* (Mountain View, CA: Pacific Press, 1898), p. 774.

THE RESURRECTION PART 1
October 16

Matthew 28:8–10, "So the women hurried away from the tomb, afraid yet filled with joy, and ran to tell his disciples. Suddenly Jesus met them. 'Greetings,' he said. They came to him, clasped his feet and worshiped him. Then Jesus said to them, 'Do not be afraid. Go and tell my brothers to go to Galilee; there they will see me.'"

There is something a little strange about the resurrection story. Jesus shows up, often unexpectedly, speaks to a minor character, Mary or these women, and then disappears before finally meeting the disciples privately.

Why not a trip to the temple where He drives the priests out, takes control like before and spends a couple of days healing and teaching so that the resurrection is known by all?

Or better yet, an appearance at the palace of Herod or Pilate or Caesar? Now that would settle the issue. No one today could doubt that Jesus rose. So, why not? He certainly could have.

Jesus did not do that so that probation might be extended. A day will come when as Revelation 11:15 says, "The kingdom of the world has become the kingdom of our Lord and of his Messiah." Such an appearance means the end of time and of any chance for anyone to join the kingdom and be in heaven. When Jesus appears at the White House or on Capitol Hill, it is the end.

God would give the human race more time. He longs to fill His kingdom with subjects but knows that to force the issue would mean war. So, He holds off, giving all of us a chance to take advantage of His grace so that we do not fall under judgement.

That's why He did not make a grand entrance.

THE RESURRECTION PART 2
October 17

John 20:10–16:

> *Then the disciples went back to where they were staying. Now Mary stood outside the tomb crying. As she wept, she bent over to look into the tomb and saw two angels in white, seated where Jesus' body had been, one at the head and the other at the foot. They asked her, "Woman, why are you crying?" ... At this, she turned around and saw Jesus standing there, but she did not realize it was Jesus .... Thinking he was the gardener, she said, "Sir, if you have carried him away, tell me where you have put him, and I will get him. Jesus said to her, "Mary."*

This touching encounter shows how Jesus loved one whom He loved. There is a certain gentleness shown here. He does not want to unduly surprise her but wants her to know that He is indeed alive.

This is who He wanted to see first at the resurrection. She had loved Him as no other and had shown that love openly in the face of ridicule and criticism. She made herself vulnerable to the rebukes of the disciples with her extravagant gift at Simon's feast. She is the one who really showed the Savior what the love of the redeemed would be like for eternity and He took that memory to the cross.

So when He arose, He remembered her. He would see her before He returned in triumph to the Father, having fulfilled the pledge made from the foundation of the world.

She was His emissary to the disciples with the message of hope and life. That was her privilege.

THE RESURRECTION PART 3
October 18

Luke 24:36–39, "Jesus himself stood among them and said to them, 'Peace be with you.' They were startled and frightened, thinking they saw a ghost. He said to them, 'Why are you troubled, and why do doubts rise in your minds? Look at my hands and my feet. It is I myself! Touch me and see; a ghost does not have flesh and bones, as you see I have.'"

This conversation is an amazing one.

Jesus had told the disciples He would die in Jerusalem and would then rise again (Luke 18:31–33, etc.). But even with this assurance, and even after the women had reported the empty tomb, and even after the pair who had walked to Emmaus and met Jesus told of their experience (Luke 24:13–35), when Jesus shows up, they did not believe it was Him, but rather a ghost.

In other words, their belief in ghosts was stronger than their belief in the words of Jesus spoken on more than one occasion!

Jesus does not deny that there are ghosts or spirits. He hints at another world that is not apparent to us, the world of the spirits. He does not elaborate here, but in other places clearly speaks to those who inhabit that world (Mark 5:1–20, etc.) and exercises His control over them.

But the disciples, expressing their faith in the reality of that world, forget the comforting words of Jesus. They believed in ghosts more than they believed in Him.

We have the same problem. It may not be ghosts that are convincing, but we do not believe God could actually raise us to life. It just seems too good to be true.

But He has given evidence of His power. The very existence of Christianity, growing from a despised cult within Judaism, attests to His power. The miracles and complexities of life attest as well.

Let us then choose faith and not doubt. It is God's will for us.

THE BODY OF CHRIST PART 1
October 19

Hebrews 10:5–7, "'Sacrifice and offering you did not desire, but a body you prepared for me; with burnt offerings and sin offerings you were not pleased.' Then I said, 'Here I am—it is written about me in the scroll—I have come to do your will, my God.'"

The body of Christ. I am reluctant to write on this subject for it is such a profound reality and I am such a weak sinner. And the body of Christ was a holy thing.

But we humans, when allowed, abused and finally murdered Him, treating His body as a cheap and common thing to be pierced and nailed to a cross. God was in human flesh and we did our best to cruelly degrade and dehumanize Him until He died, abandoned by all He loved..

And yet, God, wanting to be with us and to save us from our utter wickedness, consented to come to this planet and live among us. As Paul says with astonishment, "He became a servant and humbled himself even to the death on a cross!" (Phil. 2:8, paraphrase). It is to this reality into which I wish to delve.

The author of Hebrews quotes from the Septuagint version of Psalm 40:6–8 when he writes the above verses. God was not happy with burnt offerings, but desired instead to prepare a body for Jesus.

Why was this so important to God? More important than the sacrifices? Why was a body for Jesus a divine passion or yearning?

There are several reasons full of deep meaning. But the most important to realize is that Jesus, God, the Creator of all, stepped from the throne of heaven and became one of us. He had a body like we do.

His body carried out the same functions that ours do: He ate, He slept, He worked, He sweated, He was weary and spent. He was uncomfortable and tired. And He even had to go to the bathroom.

And He, unlike us, was under attack from the devil 24/7. And yet, He had a body. Like us. A body. An amazing fact in itself.

THE BODY OF CHRIST PART 2
October 20

Hebrews 2:14,17, "Since the children have flesh and blood, he too shared in their humanity …. For this reason he had to be made like them, fully human in every way, in order that he might become a merciful and faithful high priest in service to God."

This verse and the following emphasize the sacrificial aspects of Jesus' incarnation.

John noted when He saw Jesus for the first time, "Behold! the Lamb of God!" (John 1:29, NKJV).

In order for there to be an actual sacrifice, a body was necessary. Without the shedding of blood, there is no forgiveness (Heb. 9:22). There had to be a body, or forgiveness was not possible. Is this really so? Why? Why does God need the shedding of blood for forgiveness?

Sin is a corporal matter. It is done in the flesh. We are fleshly creatures and when we sin, it is our flesh, ourselves that sin. We are sinners and we pay for sin by suffering in our flesh, our bodies, us. We are destroyed by death.

God could not let us off without putting the sin on a body to bear it for us. So, Jesus had to have a body. This body was He Himself.

He was like us in this respect. We are body and spirit. So was He. Without a body, He could not be the Bearer of sin.

BUYER'S REMORSE
October 21

Isaiah 53:11, *"After the suffering of his soul, he will see the light of life and be satisfied."*

A friend of mine, a real estate broker, tells me that first-time buyers can get quite excited about the purchase of a new home. They have never owned one before and look with great anticipation to moving in. It's ours! We own it!

But then when they actually do move in, the home does not meet their expectations in some important way. They begin to see the defects in the walls, the creaking of the floors and the smallness of the rooms, or perhaps the inadequacy of the house as a whole.

They develop buyer's remorse. Excitement gives way to disappointment.

Jesus and His Father have paid a huge price for us. It was not merely silver or gold, but the rending of the Godhead, the loss of the loving communion They had had with Each Other from the beginning. Jesus died and it was not an easy death but a death by torture, especially when you factor in the way that those He came to save treated Him.

> *We can walk into heaven happy in the realization that our Savior has no regrets. We are worth every penny of the price He paid for us.*

It would not be a stretch to imagine that at some point the Godhead would look over the saints, a motley crew to say the least, and say to Themselves, "This was just not worth the trouble. What did We get for all Our pain? Wow!"

But if we are tempted by the devil to think such things, God has put our minds to rest. Isaiah tells us that when Jesus reviews the suffering He endured, He is satisfied (Isa. 53:11). His soul rejoices at the results.

We can walk into heaven happy in the realization that our Savior has no regrets. We are worth every penny of the price He paid for us.

Section 11

Women

How has God dealt with women, the often despised of this earth?

> "God of the women who answered your call,
> Trusting your promises, giving their all,
> Women like Sarah and Hannah and Ruth—
> Give us their courage to live in your truth."[150]

---

[150] Carolyn Winfrey Gillette, "On our search for meaning …" Wagga Wagga Uniting Church, https://1ref.us/1j0 (accessed January 20, 2021).

GOD AND WOMEN
October 22

Genesis 2:21–22, "[A]nd while he was sleeping, he took one of the man's ribs …. Then the LORD God made a woman from the rib."

Genesis 3:16, "Your desire will be for your husband, and he will rule over you."

The Old Testament has an agrarian outlook. In such cultures, women have a subordinate role. This has led to their abuse on a large scale since men are not inherently good, but have evil natures. Their superior strength has allowed them to control those with less power.

This is not to say that women are righteous either, for they too are capable of great evil.

What has God said about the relationship the sexes should have with one another? What is God's will on the matter? How does He advise us?

At the beginning, it appears there was to be a relationship of equals. Adam's rib was from his side, not his head or foot.

Then, at the tree of knowledge, Eve took a dominant role, speaking to the serpent while Adam stood silently by, making no move to remonstrate with her about her act of disobedience. She seemed to be the one in charge while he followed her cue.

That evening, when God returned, He announced the results of the fall: woman would have pain with childbirth, her labor, and would be ruled by men.

This was certainly not God's will, but the consequences of the fall. It was stated as a matter of fact, a sad comment on the reality of the life of toil, misunderstanding and suppression women would have.

But there was not only sorrow. Women would bear children whose love for their mothers would endure for a lifetime. Fathers do not usually receive such devotion.

God was gracious even in the fall.

WOMEN IN THE NEW TESTAMENT
October 23

1 Corinthians 11:3, "But I want you to realize that the head of every man is Christ, and the head of the woman is man, and the head of Christ is God."

The New Testament does not have a very different view of the role of women than the Old Testament. They are to live in a subordinate role under the headship of men.

There are three household conduct codes written in the New Testament, two by Paul (Eph. 5:22–6:9; Col. 3:18–4:1) and one by Peter (1Peter 2:18–3:7). These codes were not uncommon in Roman society. Others are known from antiquity by various thinkers of the time (Aristotle wrote one).[151]

In the codes of the New Testament, women are to take a subordinate role and to be respectful of their husbands. Sarah, who called Abraham "lord," is held up as a worthy example by Peter (1 Peter 3:6).

However, the Bible contains a subtle difference from the pagan codes. There is a mutual submission enjoined by Paul (1 Cor. 7:4; Eph. 5:21) that is not like male rule commanded in the pagan codes. Women are not told to obey as children are told to obey.

This idea does not depose the father as head of the home but does add a tone of mutuality that the Roman codes do not have. It also gives women a place of their own, one that a husband is to respect even as he receives headship over the household.

God would restore a mutuality to the marriage relationship, but He also takes into account the results of the fall. He is a God of mercy, but order as well.

---

[151] Ian Paul, "Aristotle and the Household Codes," Psephizo, https://1ref.us/1j1 (accessed January 20, 2021).

WOMEN'S ORDINATION PART 1
October 24

Mark 3:14, "He appointed twelve [designating them apostles] that they might be with him and that he might send them out to preach."

The word "ordain" is not used in the New Testament, but it is clear that some men were set apart for a special work. Jesus appointed the apostles as noted above. The church at Antioch laid hands on Paul and Barnabas (Acts 13:2–3), the Holy Spirit directed the church to send them to do His will. Paul in 1 Timothy 3:8–12 also tells the church to set apart elders and deacons to do the work of God in the churches. All who were set aside for such duties were men. No women were so designated at any time in the New Testament.

This is not to say that women did not take leadership roles in Scripture. Deborah in the Old Testament was certainly a leader and even judged over Israel for many years (Judges 4:4; 5:31). Philip's four daughters are described as prophets (Acts 21:8–9).

So, women had leadership roles, but are never said to be ordained by the laying on of hands as it says in the New Testament.

Jesus never says that we must do so and the example in Paul's letters does not include the setting aside of women as elders or even deacons.

There is thus no command from any New Testament figure that we are to ordain, lay on hands or designate women in such a role. Women are to respect their husbands or the leaders of the church but are nowhere told to take up a role as the apostles were called to do by Christ. Women's ordination is not a moral imperative.

But neither is there a command not to do such a thing.

ELLEN WHITE
October 25

Acts 9:15, "But the Lord said to Ananias, 'Go! This man is my chosen instrument to proclaim my name to the Gentiles.'"

The strongest argument for women's ordination is the ministry of Ellen White. We have no command, as I noted, in Scripture to ordain women. The Bible does not say that we must do so, nor does it give an example of such an act.

But it is also clear that God, on occasion, has called women to leadership. And this is particularly clear in the case of Ellen White.

She did not desire to take this role but was called by God to do so and the church at that time recognized her calling and respected her as a prophet or messenger from the Lord. And the church has been immensely blessed by her ministry and advice.

This signal to the church, this idea that women may be called to assume leadership and that they can be helpful to the church in such roles, is clear from Ellen's work among us. Her words continue to this day to inspire and encourage all who will take them seriously.

Her message to the church to step out in medical work and to educate its children has been a blessing to millions of people, Christian and non-Christian alike. Loma Linda alone has sent thousands to the underserved areas of the world. She has clearly been a help to those who are less fortunate. She has given a vision to the church that it could not have adopted without her ministry.[152]

It is a powerful example for women's ministry for the church that is not found in the Scripture itself. We should move wisely in this situation.

---

[152] Gerhard Pfandl, "Ellen G. White's contributions to the Seventh-day Adventist Church," *Ministry*, https://1ref.us/1j2 (accessed January 20, 2021).

WOMEN'S ORDINATION PART 2
October 26

1 Corinthians 13:5, "[Love] is not easily angered, it keeps no record of wrongs."

Can we address this conflict among us with grace and love? Is it possible to deal with one another regarding this issue in such a way as to bring praise and glory to God and His work here?

> During World War II, Hitler commanded all religious groups to unite so that he could control them. Among the Brethren assemblies, half complied and half refused. Those who went along with the order had a much easier time. Those who did not, faced harsh persecution. In almost every family of those who resisted, someone died in a concentration camp. When the war was over, feelings of bitterness ran deep between the groups and there was much tension. Finally they decided that the situation had to be healed. Leaders from each group met at a quiet retreat. For several days, each person spent time in prayer, examining his own heart in the light of Christ's commands. Then they came together.
>
> Francis Schaeffer, who told of the incident, asked a friend who was there, "What did you do then?" "We were just one," he replied. As they confessed their hostility and bitterness to God and yielded to His control, the Holy Spirit created a spirit of unity among them. Love filled their hearts and dissolved their hatred.
>
> When love prevails among believers, especially in times of strong disagreement, it presents to the world an indisputable mark of a true follower of Jesus Christ.[153]

---

[153] "Love," Sermon Illustrations, https://1ref.us/1j3 (accessed January 20, 2021).

EVE

October 27

Genesis 4:1, NIV 1988, "Adam lay with his wife Eve, and she became pregnant and gave birth to Cain. She said, 'With the help of the Lord I have brought forth a man.' Later she gave birth to his brother Abel."

When God spoke to Adam and Eve, they had no idea what the choice to take the fruit would mean. It seemed so good at the time. The fruit would make them wise.

But instead, they were cast naked from their garden home.

Eve became pregnant with Cain, whom she called a blessing from God. He toddled around their home, the first child ever seen on earth. His brother came along shortly.

But when they grew up, Cain in a fit of rage killed his brother. Then he left the home to live on his own, alienated from his family by his act of murder.

What a painful thing it must have been to find the body of her son in the field and know that her other son had done it and that he had left, at odds with God, on his own in the world, desiring to have nothing to do with her! The first family was dysfunctional in a most profound way. How the tears must have flowed! How sorrow must have wracked the souls of Eve and Adam! Torturing themselves with blame would have been natural. It was a terrible consequence of their sin.

Eve is a tragic figure. She brought sin into the world with her husband. She suffered terribly. But God did not reject her but gave her the promise of a Redeemer to come. Despair was tempered by hope. But the tragedies of life must have filled her life with nearly unbearable sadness.

SARAH

October 28

Genesis 18:10–12, "Now Sarah was listening at the entrance to the tent, which was behind him. Abraham and Sarah were already very old, and Sarah was past the age of childbearing. So Sarah laughed to herself as she thought, 'After I am worn out and my lord is old, will I now have this pleasure?'"

This is hardly a statement of faith. She laughed at God's promise and then when called out in the next verse, she lied about it!

Sarah's story has always amazed me. Hebrews says that without faith it is impossible to please God (Heb. 11:6). And here Sarah laughs about the promise and even worse she denies that she laughed.

But in spite of her lack of faith, Isaac showed up in the usual nine months and is called "laughter" when he is born (Gen. 21:6). So maybe she developed faith after all.

> *This story shows the grace of God in action. Sarah was not faithful. She did not believe that she could have a child at all, even laughing about it. But God did not take her unbelief to heart but blessed her anyway.*

This story shows the grace of God in action. Sarah was not faithful. She did not believe that she could have a child at all, even laughing about it. But God did not take her unbelief to heart but blessed her anyway.

Sometimes our faith is as weak as Sarah's was. We just can't wrap our minds around the promises that He has given us. It's just too much.

This story is for just such circumstances. You might even say Sarah is the mother of the faithless! But she had a baby, a gift of God for her and her faithful husband. We can have such blessings even if we only have little faith.

I love this story because it shows the grace of our God. He loves us in spite of ourselves. His love is not easily disturbed by our foibles. He allowed even for Sarah's laughter.

HAGAR PART 1
October 29

Genesis 16:2, 4, 6–8, 10, 13:

> *[Sarai said] "Go, sleep with my slave; perhaps I can build a family through her".... When she [Hagar] knew she was pregnant, she began to despise her mistress .... Then Sarai mistreated Hagar; so she fled from her. The angel of the LORD found Hagar near a spring in the desert .... And he said, "Hagar, slave of Sarai, where have you come from, and where are you going?" "I'm running away from my mistress Sarai," she answered .... The angel added, "I will increase your descendants so much that they will be too numerous to count." She gave this name to the LORD who spoke to her: "You are the God who sees me."*

Hagar was used and abused by the people of God to "build the family" that God had promised. But when she began to despise her mistress, she was beaten and then fled from her, finding herself abandoned in the desert between Canaan and Egypt.

But this slave girl received a promise just as amazing as the one Abraham and Sarah had received: unnumbered descendants, an unheard of gift to a slave and a woman at that.

Hagar responded in awe calling God with such assurance, "The God who sees me." What a wonderful observation of a slave girl fleeing, apparently abandoned by all who cared about her. Left alone in the desert, feeling that death was near and here God shows up, the same Jehovah who had visited Abraham at night telling him of his posterity. She receives the same promise! What a wonderful God we serve, One who has made a point to record this episode of an insignificant actor in the plan of salvation.

"The God who sees me." What a wonderful realization.

HAGAR PART 2

October 30

Genesis 16:9, "Then the angel of the LORD told her, 'Go back to your mistress and submit to her.'"

Hagar's life is instructive for another reason, and a reason that is more difficult to comprehend and accept: that of God's will for her after seeing her in the desert.

Besides giving her a promise as great as the one given Abraham, the father of the people of God, He commands her to return to her mistress, that is, the one who had just driven her away by her mistreatment. She is told to submit to Sarah. The word "submit" in Hebrew has the same root as the word "to beat," the word describing Sarah's actions against her.

Why did God command her to do such a thing? It seems rather severe.

1. Being in Abraham's house was apparently the best for her.

2. Though this home had drawbacks, there were at least legal and financial protection there for her and her son. If she went back to Egypt, she would be vulnerable to all types of predation by others.

3. Most importantly, her son would have the rights of a firstborn. Ishmael was loved by Abraham who could hardly let him go later when Isaac was born. A father's love has a beneficial effect on a boy and there is no substitute.

God's command seems harsh and unreasonable. But He knew all the characters involved and knew what would be best. His will is always best even when it is difficult.

REBEKAH

October 31

Genesis 24:66–67, "Then the servant told Isaac all he had done. Isaac brought her into the tent of his mother Sarah, and he married Rebekah. So she became his wife, and he loved her; and Isaac was comforted after his mother's death."

Genesis 27:5, 11–13, "Now Rebekah was listening as Isaac spoke to his son Esau .... Jacob said to Rebekah his mother .... 'I would appear to be tricking him and would bring down a curse on myself rather than a blessing.' His mother said to him, 'My son, let the curse fall on me.'"

And indeed it did. She never saw her son again after he fled to Paddan Aram. Isaac lived, but Rebekah died before Jacob returned.

What happened here? Why this scheming? Why this deceiving of Isaac?

The Bible does not tell us, only to say that as time went on, one parent favored one child and the other favored the other child. This is a strategy for division and alienation.

Favoritism in the family leads to trouble and differences among the children. And if parents do not resist such feelings—for one child will almost certainly be more attractive to a parent than another—jealousy will arise. Mothers particularly favor their children, often at the husband's expense. She can fall so deeply in love with the fruit of her body that she turns from the love of her husband to the children. It is a fatal error and divides the home, leaving all its members bitter and resentful.

God made a home by joining two adults who are to love and cherish each other, forming a bond of love. The children will be the result of that love but must never replace it. Parents must not fall into the trap that Rebekah did. It will most assuredly divide the home, hurting all.

JOCHEBED

November 1

Exodus 2:1–3, "Now a man of the tribe of Levi married a Levite woman, and she became pregnant and gave birth to a son. When she saw that he was a fine child, she hid him for three months. But when she could hide him no longer, she got a papyrus basket for him and coated it with tar and pitch. Then she placed the child in it and put it among the reeds along the bank of the Nile."

Moses was born to a slave woman. She was not the wife of a wealthy, respected Bedouin like Sarah was. She was the weakest; a woman of a despised people whose race Pharaoh had determined to destroy.

The child she bore is called "a fine child," or "a goodly child" as the KJV says. She determined to protect him and save his life. She hid him for three months, but as happens with children, his crying became louder and louder and could no longer be muffled. What would she do?

She devised a plan to save him from the Pharaoh by doing exactly what he had commanded. She cast him into the Nile.

Whether she knew the place where the princess bathed is unclear. She put her little basket with its precious cargo in the river among the reeds with his older sister as guardian nearby.

The princess came to wash and saw the infant crying and her heart went out to the mother who had put such a child in the river. Her mind was made up, she would raise him as her own.

> **What a faith was Jochebed's! She gave up the child to receive him back to raise as the future king. Her skill is shown in the life he lived.**

What a faith was Jochebed's! She gave up the child to receive him back to raise as the future king. Her skill is shown in the life he lived.

ZIPPORAH

November 2

Exodus 4:24–26, "At a lodging place on the way, the LORD met Moses and was about to kill him. But Zipporah took a flint knife, cut off her son's foreskin and touched Moses' feet with it. 'Surely you are a bridegroom of blood to me,' she said. So the LORD let him alone."

After Moses killed the Egyptian overseer and fled, he was taken in by the family of Jethro, marrying one of his daughters, Zipporah. He did not think he would be returning to his people in Egypt. So, his son, Gershom, was not circumcised as was required by the Abrahamic covenant. Apparently, Zipporah had refused to allow this rite to be performed on her son.

But now God had called Moses to lead Israel and the family began the journey back to Egypt. On the way, says Scripture, God appeared to Moses, threatening to kill him! Zipporah, knowing the problem, quickly grabbed what was near, a flint knife, and performed the necessary rite, touching Moses' feet with their son's foreskin, complaining, "Surely you are a bridegroom of blood to me." And God let him alone.

How hard it is to obey God when the peace of the home must be sacrificed for that obedience!

When we are called to do a work for God, it is important that we be careful to do all that God has commanded. Zipporah had refused to allow her son to be circumcised, an odious act in her mind. Moses, wanting to keep peace in the home, had gone along.

But Israel's leader could not be outside the covenant. His example of disobedience would leaven the whole nation to disobedience.

We cannot let even the most intimate of family ties keep us from our duty. God has a work for each of us and we must take His words seriously, though it might lead to family tensions.

MIRIAM

November 3

Numbers 12:1–2, "Miriam and Aaron began to talk against Moses because of his Cushite wife, for he had married a Cushite. 'Has the LORD spoken only through Moses?' they asked. 'Hasn't he also spoken though us?' And the LORD heard this."

We all are bundles of strengths and weaknesses, and Miriam was no exception.

She bravely watched over the basket in the Nile where Moses was hidden. Her courtesy and tact won the heart of Egypt's princess allowing her mother to care for the baby, who had been thrown in the river at Pharaoh's command, until he became of age. And she led the people in rejoicing, The Song of Moses and Miriam (Exod. 15:1–21), after the rescue at the Red Sea.

Yet just before the people were to enter Canaan, she chaffed at Moses' leadership and the fact that he had married Zipporah, a non-Jewish woman. She and Aaron began to be critical of his leadership and God had to intervene. God, noting that He spoke to Moses face to face, said, "Why then were you not afraid to speak against my servant Moses?" (Num. 12:8).

Apparently, Miriam was the main instigator for she was struck with leprosy from head to toe. Moses prayed for her and she was cured but had to spend a week outside the camp in quarantine (Num. 12:10–15).

God expects us to respect the leadership He has installed to lead His people. Even a relative is to treat a leader as one called by God. They may not be perfect, but still must be respected.

But she was still a chosen vessel in spite of her failings. Her death is mentioned and remembered by her brother in Numbers 20:1. She was a woman of talent and devotion. God was gracious to her.

MICHAL, SAUL'S DAUGHTER
November 4

1 Samuel 25:44, "But Saul had given his daughter Michal, David's wife, to Paltiel son of Laish, who was from Gallim."

2 Samuel 3:15–16, "So Ish-Bosheth gave orders and had her taken away from her husband Paltiel son of Laish. Her husband, however, went with her, weeping behind her all the way to Bahurim. Then Abner said to him, 'Go back home!' So he went back."

2 Samuel 6:20, "When David returned home ... Michal ... came out to meet him and said, 'How the king of Israel has distinguished himself today, going around half-naked in full view of the slave girls!'"

Michal fell in love with David, and Saul, scheming to destroy him, said she could be his wife if he brought 100 Philistine foreskins. David delivered 200 and they were married (1 Sam. 18:27). But when he fled from his father-in-law with her help, she was given to another, Paltiel, who apparently loved her deeply.

From the very beginning, she was exploited as a pawn in the politics of Israel. First, her father, seeing her love for David, used her to entice him into a trap. Then David, wanting to assert his power as king, made her return to his house. She became a bitter presence there until her death.

Where was God in all this?

God does not suspend the law of reaping and sowing when His people choose an evil course of action. Michal suffered greatly for her father's and David's choices to act selfishly. Our acts for good or ill are like waves spreading out as from a stone thrown in a pond. Her history is a sober reminder of this law of life. God will not be mocked; it behooves us to be careful how we order our lives here. Our acts have consequences.

THE LITTLE MAID IN NAAMAN'S HOUSE
November 5

2 Kings 5:2–3, "Now bands of raiders from Aram had gone out and had taken captive a young girl from Israel, and she served Naaman's wife. She said to her mistress, 'If only my master would see the prophet who is in Samaria! He would cure him of his leprosy.'"

I find the character of this child one of the most beautiful in Scripture.

She is torn from her parents and sold as a slave to a prominent family of her enemies. But after recovering from the original shock of her captivity, she harbors no ill will toward her captors! Instead of a morose bitterness, she displays a simple childlike love, desiring only good for her master.

And the open-faced faith of this child is rewarded with his healing and the revealing in Damascus that there is a prophet in Israel who can cure even an enemy of his illness.

This child's faith is a rebuke to our unbelief. She was stolen away to a foreign land separated from her family, but still believed in God as a Savior in spite of her circumstances. She was instrumental in bringing healing and salvation to one who was an enemy of her people. How could Naaman again war against Israel when one of them had cured him of that dread affliction?

We can teach our little ones to believe if we believe and put the kingdom of God first in our hearts. They naturally will turn to the One we love if His love is revealed in us.

Children can be witnesses of God's desire for the whole world: salvation to all. Let us be an example to them.

BATHSHEBA

November 6

2 Samuel 11:2–4, "One evening David got up from his bed and walked around on the roof of the palace. From the roof he saw a woman bathing. The woman was very beautiful and David sent someone to find out about her .... She came to him, and he slept with her."

Clearly David had no business taking Bathsheba to himself that evening. But it is also clear that Bathsheba had no business being out there bathing in plain sight of the palace. It is altogether possible that the whole point was to be seen. Perhaps she was dissatisfied with Uriah as her partner. Whatever their motives, the sordid affair was a blot on the character of David, the "Man After God's Own Heart" (1 Sam. 13:14)

Thereafter peace fled from David's household.

But Bathsheba appears to have become his favorite wife. Their "love child" died, in spite of David's pleas for his life, but their next offspring, Solomon, was so loved by God that Nathan was to tell the couple he should be named Jedidiah, "Loved by God" (2 Sam. 12:24–25).

How is it that at one point God punishes David and Bathsheba for their sin, but in the next submits a name for Solomon signifying His love?

David knew God and His willingness to forgive. He says in Psalm 103:8–10:

"The Lord is compassionate and gracious, slow to anger, abounding in love. He will not always accuse, nor will he harbor his anger forever; he does not treat us as our sins deserve or repay us according to our iniquities."

David knew this because he had sinned a great sin and had been forgiven. God loved even the issue from that adulterous relationship, calling it Jedidiah so that we might take courage when we fall deeply into sin. He is indeed slow to anger and plenteous in mercy.

THE VIRGIN MARY PART 1
November 7

Matthew 12:46–50:

> *While Jesus was still talking to the crowd, his mother and brothers stood outside, wanting to speak to him. Someone told him, "Your mother and brothers are standing outside, wanting to speak to you." He replied to him, "Who is my mother, and who are my brothers? Pointing to his disciples, he said, "Here are my mother and my brothers. For whoever does the will of my Father in heaven is my brother and sister and mother."*

For many who hold the virgin Mary in special regard, Jesus spoke the words recorded here. Did He really have to repudiate His relationship with her in this way? Was Mary special in any regard at all?

When the angel greeted her at the beginning before her pregnancy, he addressed her noting that she was "highly favored" (Luke 1:28). She was chosen to bear the Son of God and became a vehicle for the realization of God's will for the world in His birth. However, as Simeon said, a sword would pierce her own soul as well (Luke 2:35).

But Jesus' repudiation of His family ties and the instillation of His disciples as His true family is important for us.

God knew that Mary would become a very special individual for many of His followers. She would be exalted above her station: that of a willing servant of the Most High. She submitted to God's will and experienced the pain of the sword, even from the beginning.

But that did not make her a sharer in the redemption that Jesus alone could obtain for us. Even she herself needed His redeeming power.

So, to teach His followers her true position, He spoke on this occasion. His words are almost painful to read, but that is what was necessary for our redemption.

THE VIRGIN MARY PART 2
November 8

Mark 3:34–35, "Then he looked at those seated in a circle around him and said, 'Here are my mother and my brothers! Whoever does God's will is my brother and sister and mother.'"

Many Christians think that Jesus' relationship with His mother Mary was a special one. And of course, our experience with our own mothers colors that thinking. How could Jesus not have such a relationship with His mother that is similar to the ones we have with ours?

But Jesus in these verses reveals a profound truth: we may have an even closer relationship with Him than that which His earthly mother had with Him. He takes the family ties that we all have with our parents and tells us, "I can be closer to you even than that wonderful person that bore you and brought you into the world and nurtured you with her own body. I can be closer to you than that."

As God says in Isaiah 49:15, "Can a mother forget the baby at her breast and have no compassion on the child she has borne? Though she may forget, I will not forget you!"

In this instance when Jesus' family tried to exercise authority over Him (see Mark 3:21), Jesus decided to make clear His relationship to us. He is closer to us who believe than He was even to His own mother!

John stood in awe at what Jesus had done. 1 John 3:1, "How great is the love the Father has lavished on us, that we should be called the children of God!" And that is what we are!

That we might realize the depths of that love, Jesus said the relationship with even His mother fell short of it.

THE WOMAN AT THE WELL
November 9

John 4:15–18, "The woman said to him, 'Sir, give me this water so that I won't get thirsty and have to keep coming here to draw water.' He told her, 'Go, call your husband and come back.' 'I have no husband,' she replied. Jesus said to her, 'You are right when you say you have no husband. The fact is, you have had five husbands, and the man you now have is not your husband.'"

This woman, like the woman caught in adultery, had a checkered past. Ellen White describes her in the following passage:

"When Jesus sat down to rest at Jacob's well …. He was faint and weary; yet He did not neglect the opportunity of speaking to one woman, though she was a stranger, an alien from Israel, and living in open sin."[154]

Living in open sin! And yet our Savior asked her for a drink and revealed to her that He was the Messiah. The Pharisees and lawyers would not have tolerated such an announcement.

But this woman was open and accepted Him immediately. After a short conversation, one in which He had even remarked on her sinful life, she became a missionary to her town. She did better than the disciples!

How often we let outward appearances or behavior prevent us from lifting up Christ to our sinful neighbors and even strangers. We have no idea what is going on in their minds and hearts.

If we will give ourselves unreservedly to Jesus and be filled with His love for sinners, He will prepare us to meet those who so desperately need Him. He will help us reveal the charms of the Savior of the world.

It is the highest privilege He could give us.

---

[154] Ellen G. White, *The Desire of Ages* (Mountain View, CA: Pacific Press, 1898), p. 194.

MARY MAGDALENE, JOANNA AND SUSANNA
November 10

Luke 8:2–3, "[A]nd also some women who had been cured of evil spirits and diseases: Mary (called Magdalene) from whom seven demons had come out; Joanna the wife of Chuza, the manager of Herod's household; Susanna; and many others. These women were helping to support them out of their own means."

Mark 15:40–41, "Some women were watching from a distance. Among them were Mary Magdalene, Mary the mother of James the younger and of Joseph, and Salome. In Galilee these women had followed him and cared for his needs. Many other women who had come up with him to Jerusalem were also there."

It came as a surprise for me to learn that Jesus had an entourage of women with Him in Galilee who even made the final trip with Him to Jerusalem. Their number was large enough and their support important enough to be mentioned by Luke and Mark. Some had high social standing.

As an example of that support, His undergarment was spun as a single piece, showing special skill in preparation.

However, Jesus did not have them minister to the people as His disciples did but allowed them to serve from behind the scenes.

During the crucifixion, they stood afar off, to avoid embarrassment. Only His mother came near.

But some of their number were the first to visit the tomb on Sunday morning. Their intention to take spices to the tomb was frustrated by His resurrection. The devotion of these women enabled them to be the first to proclaim Him risen from the dead. Though performing humble tasks, Jesus honored them as the first to carry the good news to the world.

THE MOTHER OF JAMES AND JOHN
November 11

Matthew 20:20–22, "Then the mother of Zebedee's sons came to Jesus with her sons and, kneeling down, asked a favor of him. 'What is it you want?' he asked. She said, 'Grant that one of these two sons of mine may sit at your right and the other at your left in your kingdom.' 'You don't know what you are asking,' Jesus said to them."

> *Jesus cannot grant the request, but instead of belittling them for their selfishness, He turns their minds to the selflessness of His work, inviting them to join Him in it (Matt. 20:23). That is His way.*

This little episode shows the wonderful tact and grace of our Lord.

The crucifixion was but a few weeks away and a typical Jewish mother comes to Jesus kneeling, begging a favor for her two sons. "What is it you want?" He asks.

"Give them the two top positions in your coming kingdom," she boldly replies.

Our Lord is shortly to lay down His life, to experience the second death, to bear the sins of the whole world and this mother is scheming to obtain a political plum for her sons!

But His answer contains no sarcasm or rancor. Instead of a rebuke, He gently asks about commitment.

He has just told the disciples (Matt. 20:17–19) that He is going to Jerusalem where He will be crucified. "Can you drink the cup I am going to drink?" (Matt. 20:22).

He endeavors to deepen their understanding of His work and call them to a deeper commitment.

"'We can,' they answered" (Ibid.).

Jesus cannot grant the request, but instead of belittling them for their selfishness, He turns their minds to the selflessness of His work, inviting them to join Him in it (Matt. 20:23). That is His way.

In Matthew 7:7, Jesus tells us to ask, seek and knock. This mother was doing just that. Although He could not grant her request, He treated her with tact and grace. He will treat us the same.

SITTING AT JESUS' RIGHT AND LEFT
November 12

Matthew 20:24–28:

> *When the ten heard about this, they were indignant with the two brothers. Jesus called them together and said, "You know that the rulers of the Gentiles lord it over them, and their high officials exercise authority over them. Not so with you. Instead, whoever wants to become great among you must be your servant, and whoever wants to be first must be your slave—just as the Son of Man did not come to be served, but to serve, and to give his life as a ransom for many."*

The mother was not the only schemer. The other disciples coveted the top spots as well and were angry with James and John for seeming to gain the upper hand.

Was Jesus' band of followers about to fracture? Would three years' work all come to naught?

Jesus met the threat head-on. He must explain to them the nature of the kingdom and let them decide if living as servants was what they wanted. He gives them a chance to leave, knowing fully what following Him entailed.

He points them to His example of service, bidding them to see in Him the work they as His followers would be required to do.

"Not so among you." They were not called to rule at His right and left as overlords, but as servants. They were to be slaves!

The disciple's response is not recorded, but they were still arguing at the Last Supper.

Jesus trod the winepress alone, and none trod with Him.

Are we willing to lead as servants even in lowly capacities? Such who do this, drinking Jesus' cup, will sit at His left and right, places prepared by the Father for them.

Section 12

God and The Church

How is God involved with His church?

"The church has one foundation, 'Tis Jesus Christ her Lord;
She is His new creation, By water and the word;
From heaven he came and sought her To be His holy bride;
With His own blood He bought her, And for her life He died."[155]

---

[155]Samuel Stone, "The Church Has One Foundation," *The Seventh-day Adventist Hymnal* (Hagerstown, MD: Review and Herald, 1985).

GOD'S ETERNAL PURPOSE FOR THE CHURCH
November 13

Ephesians 3:10–12, "His intent was that now, through the church, the manifold wisdom of God should be made known to the rulers and authorities in the heavenly realms, according to his eternal purpose that he accomplished in Christ Jesus our Lord. In him and through faith in him we may approach God with freedom and confidence."

God's first purpose for the church was to reveal something utterly amazing: that we may freely approach God and may do it in confidence that we will be heard and received.

Paul says earlier in Ephesians that the Gentiles had been excluded from the covenants and from citizenship among the people of God. They were without hope and without God in the world (Eph. 2:12). He called them Gentile sinners (Gal. 2:15), for at that time, that is how Jews saw them. Their behavior, lust and debauchery indicated that that was indeed true.

But now God had revealed what had been kept secret through the ages, that He had a plan for even "Gentile sinners" that they might be brought near (Eph. 2:13).

Paul says, "Although I am less than the least of all the Lord's people, this grace was given me: to preach to the Gentiles the boundless riches of Christ, and to make plain to everyone the administration of this mystery" (Eph. 3:8–9). We all have free access to God through faith in Jesus.

What a vision for the church! We are called to reveal that the way to heaven may be trod by even the rankest of sinners through Jesus.

Oh, the amazing grace of God! We fix our eyes so low at the sins that we think exclude us, when the horizon is bright with the grace of God: freedom of access even by the worst.

CELEBRATING COMMUNION
November 14

Luke 22:15–16, "And he said to them, 'I have eagerly desired to eat this Passover with you before I suffer. For I tell you, I will not eat it again until it finds fulfillment in the kingdom of God.'"

When I was a youth the celebration of Communion was a very solemn service. We were memorializing Jesus' death and that was a solemn and sad occurrence. But now, as I have become older, the rite has become more celebratory in nature. There is less sadness and solemnity, and more joy at what God has done for us.

So, which is the more appropriate attitude? Should this be a day of solemn thought and even sadness, or should we joy in the love that the sacrifice of His Son has revealed of the heart of God?

I believe that we may experience both of these emotions when we come to the table of the Lord. Both are appropriate. In fact, tears of joy may be mingled with tears of bitter sorrow for the sin that made such a sacrifice necessary.

We so often fail to see the sinfulness of our actions and even the sin that is deeply imbedded in our souls. We have become calloused to its presence and a fresh revelation of the darkness in our hearts is needed. Like the disciples who were arguing about preeminence at the Last Supper, we often wound our Lord by our self-absorption. His supper awakens the memory of what had to be done that we might be saved.

But when we have realized our own sinfulness, we may rejoice in the sacrifice that has brought reconciliation. And such a gift is cause for great rejoicing.

Thus, the sorrow for sin and the joy at salvation are combined in the feast, a heavenly irony indeed.

JESUS EATING WITH SINNERS
November 15

Luke 15:1–2, "Now the tax collectors and sinners were all gathering around to hear Jesus. But the Pharisees and the teachers of the law muttered, 'This man welcomes sinners and eats with them.'"

There is something about sitting down and eating with someone that changes things. It is difficult to hate that individual, especially if they prepared the meal.

We are often afraid that Jesus does not accept us as we are because of the defects in our characters and the weaknesses we so profoundly know. We are too impure, too willing to follow our natural inclinations, too compromising with sin and thus feel that we are excluded from the presence of the Holy One.

But then we read what Jesus did while here on earth. He came to change that attitude. The verse says sinners were flocking to be in the presence of the King of the universe. He did not send them packing but seemed to enjoy their company. And when some criticized Him for this practice, He told the parables found in Luke 15, including His most beloved, the prodigal son.

Not only were they gathering around Him, He would accept invitations to their homes for dinner.

How open the King was with these sinners! He walked among them, spoke to them, even preferring to be with them over the teachers of the law.

He will treat us sinners in the same way. He has even said to us: "I am standing at your door, knocking" (Rev. 3:20, paraphrase). And He will come in if we wish, no matter if we are sinners or not.

Eats with sinners! What a Savior.

PETER AND EATING WITH "SINNERS"
November 16

Galatians 2:12, "For before certain men came from James, he (Peter) used to eat with the Gentiles. But when they arrived, he began to draw back and separate himself from the[m]."

The seriousness of this matter is easily missed from our perspective two millennia later. To us, it looks like another squabble between Jews and Gentiles; a problem that has been seen among them since Ezra's time (recall that when the Samaritans offered to help with the temple reconstruction, the Jewish leaders forbade them [Ezra 4:3]).

But this was more than just a squabble between two ethnic groups. It was a denial of the work that Jesus had come to do for the whole world.

From yesterday, we see that Jesus ate with sinners. He partook of the meals given by them. But here Peter is drawing away from fellow Gentile believers! He would not eat with them as Jesus had done, but instead showed prejudice.

It would not have been so significant if it had not been the leader of the apostles that dissembled. He was an example for the whole church and if this was the leader's practice, then the whole enterprise was lost, for doing so would show that the practice of Jesus was no longer accepted.

In fact, Peter was denying his Lord again. He probably acted hastily, not thinking of the consequences that his act would have on the group as a whole. But it was a denial nonetheless. Here was the same Peter seen in the Gospels, easily swayed by a critical look to deny his Lord.

But Paul, the one called after, not chosen by Jesus while He was here on earth, stood firm for the practice of eating with sinners.

We must all be thankful for his faithfulness in this situation that required a man of principle.

AN ILLEGITIMATE CHILD
November 17

Ephesians 1:5, "[H]e predestined us for adoption to sonship through Jesus Christ."

There was a young man who was born to an unwed mother. At that time this was considered a great shame. The shame and embarrassment that was shown toward the young woman was showered on him as well.

When he went to town with her, he would see people staring at him, trying to make a guess at who his father might be. The children at school would say cruel things to him so that he kept to himself at lunch and recess.

> *All of us are children of God. Don't let anyone tell you different. Now go out and claim your inheritance!*

As a teen he began attending a little church in the mountains. The preacher was both attractive and frightening. He had a chiseled face, a heavy beard and a deep voice. The boy did not know why, but his preaching did something for him.

However, he was not sure he was welcome there, so he would slip out before anyone could say, "What's a boy like you doing at church?"

One day, his exit was somehow blocked. The next thing he knew, a heavy hand was placed on his shoulder. He looked up and it was the preacher. He trembled with fear as the preacher turned him around and looked intently into his face. The boy knew what he was coming next. He was going to make a guess about his father.

The preacher said, "Well, boy, you're a child of …" and then paused. The boy's heart sank: his feelings would be hurt and he would never come back again.

The preacher continued: "Well, boy, you're a child of God! I see a striking resemblance!"

He swatted him on the shoulder saying, "Now go out and claim your inheritance!"

The boy left a different person. In fact, he said, it was really the beginning of his life.[156]

All of us are children of God. Don't let anyone tell you different. Now go out and claim your inheritance!

---
[156]Fred B. Craddock, *Craddock Stories* (St. Louis, MO: Chalice Press, 2001), p. 156.

WHOM SAUL PERSECUTED
November 18

Acts 26:14–15, "I heard a voice saying to me in Aramaic, 'Saul, Saul, why do you persecute me? ...' Then I asked, 'Who are you Lord?' 'I am Jesus, whom you are persecuting,' the Lord replied."

While living here on earth, we often feel far from God and many of us become discouraged with our lot. The world seems against us and the circumstances that surround us close in, causing deep distress. The family may be breaking up, the children rebellious. Our friends may stand aloof from us and we fall into despair. Where is God? Why is this happening to us?

These verses tell us of Saul who, being sent to Damascus to persecute the Christians there, was accosted by Jesus Himself and told who he was really persecuting. It was not Christ's followers he was trying to kill or imprison—it was Jesus Himself!

Jesus so closely identifies with us that He considers the afflictions befalling us to be directed at He Himself. He is being persecuted through us.

We sometimes think our woes and distresses, the result of those who are against us or wish to take advantage of us here, are of no interest to heaven. But in reality, the acts of our tormentors reach to the very presence of God and are felt by the Lord Himself sitting at His right hand. The pain and betrayal that we feel, He feels. Our distresses are His distresses. Our afflictions are His.

If we would but grasp this fact, that Jesus is with us in all that befalls us, we would not become so discouraged or despairing. The fact is our Lord is pained by every pain we experience. Our trouble is His.

Take courage, then, that you are not an orphan, but one that is of deep interest to Him who loved us and gave Himself for us. He knows you better than you think, for He actually feels your pain.

KICKING AGAINST THE GOADS
November 19

Acts 26:13-14, "About noon ... as I was on the road, I saw a light from heaven, brighter than the sun .... We all fell to the ground, and I heard a voice saying to me in Aramaic, 'Saul, Saul, why do you persecute me? It is hard for you to kick against the goads.'"

Some Christians have wondered why God has not spoken to them as He did to the apostle Paul. Why doesn't God meet me as He met him? Was God showing some kind of favoritism to this man to give him such a direct call?

I certainly would have been happy to receive such a revelation! But when you examine this carefully, it is clear why most of us do not have such visitations from Jesus.

Most of us do not need this kind of intervention to come to a knowledge of Jesus and the gospel. We listen to the Spirit speaking to our hearts and come under conviction and give ourselves to the loving Savior who gave Himself for us. The words of His ambassadors are enough to bring us to salvation.

But Paul would not give in to such pleadings of the Spirit. He was committed to the Jewish leaders and the Jewish faith. He was "kicking against the goads." He was under strong conviction, but his stubborn heart would not relent.

So, God gave him a last chance, by appealing to him directly. Most of us are not so stubborn. It really speaks to Paul's hardness of heart that God had to go to this length to deliver him from himself.

God does not deal with many of us in this manner because we have softer hearts. We are not so actively kicking as Saul was.

God was very merciful to Paul. He uses the means that He needs to gain us if He can. Most of us are much less stubborn than Paul. We should be thankful that that is so.

FAITH

November 20

Hebrews 11:6, "[W]ithout faith it is impossible to please God."

Some have complained that God has made faith the only way of salvation. It is just too simple, a childish way to do things. It strikes some as a sort of dependance on gullibility. It is no compliment to say that a person believes everything they hear.

But it was the great wisdom of God that made faith the thing necessary for redemption. For it is something that all have in some measure and that therefore all can exercise to gain heaven. In great mercy, God made faith the requirement.

There were other options:

Knowledge: God could have made knowledge the requirement for heaven, to know the innermost thoughts of God or some obligatory secret or practice. The Gnostics had this idea and said that the secret knowledge they had was what was really necessary to be a real Christian.

It is clear that this approach would lead to exclusion rather than inclusion. Some of us have a problem learning and cannot grasp difficult concepts. Some are completely unschooled and would suffer for their lack. God wisely rejected this way.

Great Acts: deeds of valor or bravery or feats of great strength could also have been the requirement for heaven. But again, the timid and weak, sickly and worn would have been without the gates.

Virtue or Sacrifice: God could have required such as this. But as the Bible says, our righteousness is as filthy rags (Isa. 64:6). Who then could have walked the streets of gold?

God chose to make salvation dependent on faith. Faith in Him. That is, trust that He can do as He has said and believe He will do as He has promised.

Any can do this. Even the smallest child understands what it means to believe something and act on it.

God made salvation dependent on a thing that any of us can do. He has chosen a wonderful way. A way of inclusion and not exclusion.

And because of this, all have an opportunity to be with Him in Paradise. Making faith the requirement was an act of sheer genius and great mercy.

A HUSBAND'S OBLIGATION
November 21

Ephesians 5:25, "Husbands, love your wives, just as Christ loved the church and gave himself up for her."

In Paul's letter to the Ephesians, he reveals to us the characteristics of the Christian household. He spends most of his time writing to husbands. The words he writes show the depths of his discernment of the government that is to rule in a Christian home: a husband is to love his wife as Christ loved the church, giving himself for her.

This is not the way of the world. Such sacrificial love is not a trait that most men bring to the marriage union. Often it is the wives that show such sacrifice.

How can a man, the ruler of the house, the house-band, be so humble as to give himself that the home may thrive under his care and yet receive the respect that he deserves? Is not such love a sign of weakness?

But God knows that if such love is revealed in the character of a husband, even if the wife does not obey God's command to respect, his love will be such a leavening influence that it cannot be gainsaid. There is something about a love that deep that touches the very soul of a woman and convinces her that such a one can be trusted with her soul. It is only then that she can reveal the true depths of her love.

Such a love allows a woman to be free with herself in such a way that is most engaging. There is then no reservation in the giving of herself. The true sweetness of feminine love can then be experienced in all its delight and profundity. When a husband demonstrates such love, a wife can be all that is possible to him—a rich reward.

A WIFE'S OBLIGATION
November 22

Ephesians 5:33, "[T]he wife must respect her husband."

There is little argument among Christians about the obligation of a husband to his wife: he must love her as Christ loved the church—a self-sacrificial love.

But there is confusion about the obligation of a wife to her husband.

It is surprising that God does not command a wife to love her husband. In fact, love is not mentioned at all! God gives two other commands. She is to respect him and then God says she is to submit to him. And to make it clear, he says she is to submit in all things (Eph. 5:24).

And it does not say that she may wait until he loves her as Christ loved in order to respect him. He does not have to *earn* her respect; she is just to respect him.

This command recognizes a profound truth about manly nature. Although men want love, they crave respect. Wives rarely understand how utterly important it is that a man be respected. If he is not respected, his very masculinity is called into question. And such doubt leads to all the evils that men are capable of. They need the respect a wife can give to really fulfill their duty toward her.

They are commanded to love their wives regardless. But if a wife wants to assist him in his duty to love in that way Christ loved, in the way a man can really love, she can help by giving him the respect he longs for. She will be amazed at the difference it makes.

Disrespect is poison. If wives only knew, they would turn from contempt and give their men the gift that would lighten their lives and brighten his, their respect.

THE OBLIGATION OF CHILDREN
November 23

Ephesians 6:1–3, "Children, obey your parents in the Lord, for this is right. 'Honor your father and mother'—which is the first commandment with a promise—so that it may go well with you and that you may enjoy long life on the earth."

Paul gives rather long instructions to husbands and to wives but is much shorter in his advice to children.

The instruction is only to obey the fifth commandment to honor their parents.

He could have said much more. But for children his only advice is to obey.

Obedience is an act that is very satisfying to a loving parent. Disobedience is such a difficult problem to deal with. If they have their children's best interests at heart, disobedience threatens the child's wellbeing and in some cases their very existence.

An obedient child removes the worry and fretting that disobedience engenders in the heart of loving parents. If children only knew the pain and distress they can inflict by their actions, they might take a more thoughtful course.

Paul notes the promise given in the fifth commandment, the promise of long life. Small children do not have the capacity to realize the magnitude of the promise, but older children do have the ability to appreciate it. And they are the ones most likely to benefit, as they have a harder time with their desire for independence and temptations that can lead to the shortening of life.

The promise is there for them if they will take it. Parents of teens have even a stronger wish for their wellbeing, knowing the pitfalls of youth that can ensnare them.

If the children have embraced their parents' wisdom, their chances of long life are excellent.

SLAVES AND MASTERS
November 24

Ephesians 6:5, "Slaves, obey your earthly masters with respect and fear, and with sincerity of heart, just as you would obey Christ."

These verses have been used by proponents of slavery to argue that the Bible does not condemn the practice of holding slavers. Paul even tells them to serve wholeheartedly as if to the Lord, not men (Eph. 6:6).

Why would God allow such words in Scripture?

The Old Testament and New Testament slaveries were different from the slavery practiced in the American South. In the Old Testament, the slaves were debt slaves. That is, when they could not pay their debts, they would voluntarily become servants of their fellow Israelites. They could only be a slave for six years and were then released (Exod. 21:1). If they felt their slavery was better than the life they could live on their own, they could become permanent slaves, in essence wards of their owners. There was no racism about it nor was there permanent servitude.

In the New Testament, slavery was governed by Roman law, not the law of God. Slaves in the Roman world were debt slaves, like in the Old Testament, though not treated as the Old Testament slaves were, or they were slaves because they had been captured during some military enterprise. These slaves could be educated people, teachers, doctors and other people that had unfortunately come under the rule of Roman conquest.

Christians had no standing to influence the slave laws and practices of the Roman Empire. Paul's advice is given so that the Christians, a small illegal sect, could avoid the accusation of encouraging slaver unrest, a real threat to the Empire. The egalitarian practice of the church, where all met together, masters and slaves, and where slaves could even lead a church with masters as members, struck a blow to the practice.

The Bible nowhere endorses the practice of racial slavery.

PREDESTINATION
November 25

Ephesians 1:3–5:

> *Praise be to the God and Father of our Lord Jesus Christ, who has blessed us in the heavenly realms with every spiritual blessing in Christ. For he chose us in him before the creation of the world to be holy and blameless in his sight. In love he predestined us to be adopted as his sons through Jesus Christ, in accordance with his pleasure and will.*

These verses describe God's will for us. And it is a high and holy will. Unfortunately, there has been great debate about them. Especially about that term "predestination." Are the saints chosen for heaven and the wicked for hell? Where does our will come in?

Calvinists, in thinking this verse was meant to avoid works by righteousness, declared that it was God that saved us, not ourselves.[157] He decreed our salvation, it is not something that we did, but He did (Rom. 8:29–30; Eph. 1:5, 11).

Luther, on the other hand, mustered scores of texts showing that we are saved by faith, we believe in the salvation offered to us by God through Christ.[158] We make a decision to put our faith in Him.

Arminius took a different view, emphasizing free will.[159] His influence was profound on Wesley, and the Methodist position which Adventists have inherited. But whatever position is taken, the wonderful truth of these verses cannot be hidden. God even from the beginning of time has had us in mind. We have been the focus from then. We can argue about how God saves us, and how He has put His plan together. But the Best is to put ourselves under His love and care. "Trust and obey, there is no other way."

---

[157] "Predestination in Calvinism," Wikipedia, https://1ref.us/1j4 (accessed January 20, 2021).
[158] Nathan W. Bingham, "Justification by Faith Alone: Martin Luther and Romans 1:17," Ligonier Ministries, https://1ref.us/1j5 (accessed January 20, 2021).
[159] Matthew Steven Bracey, "Jacob Arminius: On Predestination and Election," Helwys Society Forum, June 16, 2014.

THE PURSUIT OF GOD PART 1
November 26

Psalm 42:1, 2, "As the deer pants for streams of water, so my soul pants for you, O God. My soul thirsts for God, for the living God. When can I go and meet with God?"

"If with all your heart ye truly seek me, ye shall ever surely find me, thus saith your God." So Felix Mendelssohn put to music in his oratorio "Elijah."

Is God is hiding from us, and trying to keep his creatures from Him? Is all this need for seeking really necessary? Shouldn't it be obvious? So why is it that there is this idea of our seeking Him, and yet yearning after Him when He says He is even near everyone of us? (acts 17:27).

A.W. Tozer has written a small book, *The Pursuit of God*, telling of his experience.[160] The book is a best seller that has assisted many in their pursuit of the Most High. I can recommend it.

Tozer, a self-educated pastor from a poor family, himself was a pursuer. Converted at age fifteen, he began a life-long seeking after God. At this early age, he set up a private place in the basement of his parents' home where he could seek God alone. Desiring an intimate relationship with Him, he spent hours in prayer and worship. And he was rewarded with the ability to explain to others the process by which he had found God.

He tells of God's prevenient grace: the fact that before a man can seek God, God must have already sought him. This grace prompts seeking, and a man, if he will, may take advantage of all the means God has supplied that we might find Him: prayer, the Bible, spiritual meetings, Christian friends, etc. I recall this happening in my own life. It was a wonderful thing.

He gives many more insights, but it is worth reading that you, reader, may understand your own soul.

---

[160] A.W. Tozer, *The Pursuit of God* (Camp Hill, PA: Christian Publications, 1993).

THE PURSUIT OF GOD PART 2
November 27

Jeremiah 31:3, "I have loved you with an everlasting love, therefore with loving kindness have I drawn you."

Ellen White's book on pursuing God is *Steps to Christ*.[161] She tells of the process that Tozer describes, whereby we might find Him who is our soul's desire. This book gives the principles God has set in motion to bring us into His presence. It is a wonderful roadmap to the throne of God. And to have two mature Christians relate their ideas is twice the good.

But we have been given another resource that is invaluable: the written experience of one converted, who opened a window into her soul that we might see the self-doubt, fear of eternal loss before, and joy and peace after finally meeting Jesus. This is Ellen White's description of her own conversion in *Life Sketches,* pages 20 to 42.[162] I have read and reread these chapters many times to understand my own struggles. Hers is an opening of the heart that Tozer did not attempt.

Sometimes her heart was filled with the fear of hell. Nights are spent in agonizing prayer. Her reserved personality kept her from sharing her suffering with Christian friends, until she finally spoke to her mother. She encouraged her to talk to a trusted pastor who inspired her to faith. She says, that shortly thereafter:

> As I knelt and prayed, suddenly my burden left me, and my heart was light. At first a feeling of alarm came over me, and I tried to resume my load and distress. It seemed to me that I had no right to feel joyous and happy. But Jesus seemed very near to me; I felt able to come to Him with all my griefs, misfortunes, and trials...

Such a revelation is balm to a troubled seeker.

---

[161] Ellen G. White, *Steps to Christ* (Mountain View, CA: Pacific Press Publishing Association, 1892).
[162] Ellen G. White, *Life Sketches* (Nampa, ID: Pacific Press Publishing Association, 1943).

OUR FIERY TRIALS
November 28

James 1:2, "Consider it pure joy, my brothers and sisters, whenever you face trials of many kinds."

Joy in trial? Happiness in trouble? Rejoicing in persecution? What alien concepts are these! How seldom we see such reactions to our difficulties.

Ellen White says this: "Many who sincerely consecrate their lives to God's service are surprised and disappointed to find themselves, as never before, confronted by obstacles and beset by trials and perplexities .... Like Israel of old they question, 'If God is leading us, why do all these things come upon us?'"[163]

Then she writes this amazing statement: "It is because God is leading them that these things come upon them. Trials and obstacles are the Lord's chosen methods of discipline and His appointed conditions of success."[164]

Trouble is sent on purpose! It is God's very intention, His chosen method! His way of bringing success!

She goes on:

> He sees that some have powers and susceptibilities which, rightly directed, might be used in the advancement of His work. In His providence he brings these persons into different positions and varied circumstances that they may discover in their character the defects which have been concealed from their own knowledge. He gives them opportunity to correct these defects and to fit themselves for His service. Often He permits the fires of affliction to assail them that they may be purified.[165]

Then that famous statement: "God never leads His children otherwise than they would choose to be led, if they could see the end from the beginning and discern the glory of the purpose which they are fulfilling as co-workers with Him."[166]

The glory of our purpose. That is what trials are for—our glory. This will help remove the sting that trials often bring.

---
[163] Ellen G. White, *The Ministry of Healing* (Mountain View, CA: Pacific Press, 1905), p. 470.
[164] Ibid., p. 471.
[165] Ibid.
[166] Ibid., p. 479.

THE WORLD AND ITS GIFTS
November 29

John 2:9–10, "[T]he master of the banquet tasted the water that had been turned into wine. He did not realize where it had come from, though the servants who had drawn the water knew. Then he called the bridegroom aside and said, 'Everyone brings out the choice wine first and then the cheaper wine after the guests have had too much to drink; but you have saved the best till now.'"

As men set forth the best wine first, then afterward that which is worse, so does the world with its gifts. That which is offered may please the eye and fascinate the senses, but it proves to be unsatisfying. The wine turns to bitterness, the gaiety to gloom. That which was begun with songs and mirth ends in weariness and disgust. But the gifts of Jesus are ever fresh and new. The feast that He provides for the soul never fails to give satisfaction and joy. Each new gift increases the capacity of the receiver to appreciate and enjoy the blessings of the Lord. He gives grace for grace. There can be no failure of supply. If you abide in Him, the fact that you receive a rich gift today insures the reception of a richer gift tomorrow. The words of Jesus to Nathaniel express the law of God's dealing with the children of faith. With every fresh revelation of His love, He declares to the receptive heart, "Believest thou? thou shalt see greater things than these." John 1:50. [167]

Do you believe, dear reader? Then the promise is for you. The world is deceptive with its gifts, but not the Savior. The water of life and the joys of the Lord may be yours today.

---

[167] Ellen G. White, *The Desire of Ages* (Mountain View, CA: Pacific Press, 1898), p. 148.

PRAYER FOR THE SICK
November 30

James 5:14–15, "Is anyone among you sick? Let them call the elders of the church to pray over them and anoint them with oil in the name of the Lord. And the prayer offered in faith will make the sick person well; the Lord will raise them up."

This is a wonderful promise. But we must understand that there are certain conditions to healing. These are enumerated in the little book by Ellen White, *The Ministry of Healing*.[168]

Those praying for the sick must be faithful followers of Jesus, obedient to His Word, not regarding sin in their hearts and refusing to renounce it. Unhealthy practices must be abandoned. To disregard God's instruction is to prevent Him from placing His healing hand on us.

We must confess our sins to the Master Healer and He will bend over us to heal and restore.

The Lord may not choose to heal immediately; patience is necessary. The sick should not disregard their duties to friends and family who may survive them if God should not choose to heal.[169]

It is also necessary to take advantage of any remedies that may be within our reach. It is not a denial of faith to place ourselves in a position most favorable to recovery.

If we do these things, we can rest our future in His loving hand, giving ourselves again to Him who loves us with a sacrificial love.

God may not answer as we would wish. We may have to accept the bitter cup but must realize that it is the Father who holds it to our lips. Faith can grasp the hope beyond the promise.

If restored, we are placed under renewed obligation to our Creator and Redeemer. He will lead us in the way of life if we will allow Him to do so.

---

[168] Ellen G. White, *The Ministry of Healing* (Mountain View, CA: Pacific Press, 1905), pp. 227–231.
[169] Ibid., p. 231.

GOD'S WORK AMONG THE HEATHEN
December 1

Romans 2:14–15, "(Indeed, when Gentiles, who do not have the law, do by nature things required by the law, they are a law for themselves, even though they do not have the law. They show that the requirements of the law are written on their hearts.)"

When one looks out on the wickedness of the world around us, it is hard to see that there are any that might respond to the gospel. Paul was discouraged in Corinth when he realized how sinful the city was. But God told him He had many people in that city (Acts 18:10).

The Magi were heathen but responded to the Holy Spirit and followed the star to minister to Jesus, first making the announcement of His birth to Jerusalem and then providing for His escape to Egypt by their generous gifts.

Ellen White says this:

> The light of God is ever shining amid the darkness of heathenism. As these magi studied the starry heavens, and sought to fathom the mystery hidden in their bright paths, they beheld the glory of the Creator. Seeking clearer knowledge, they turned to the Hebrew Scriptures. In their own land were treasured prophetic writings that predicted the coming of a divine teacher. Balaam belonged to the magicians, though at one time a prophet of God; by the Holy Spirit he had foretold the prosperity of Israel and the appearing of the Messiah; and his prophecies had been handed down by tradition from century to century.[170]

We cannot see what God is doing through His Spirit. It is only He who has intimate knowledge. If we are called to work in an unpromising situation, seeking His guidance will lead to enlightenment. He may have multitudes where we see only a few.

---

[170] Ellen G. White, *The Desire of Ages* (Mountain View, CA: Pacific Press Publishing Association, 1898), pp. 59–60.

PREPARING TO DIE PART 1
December 2

Luke 12:20–21, "But God said to him, 'You fool! This very night your life will be demanded from you. Then who will get what you have prepared for yourself?' This is how it will be with whoever stores up things for themselves but is not rich toward God."

> *Not by painful struggles or wearisome toil, not by gift or sacrifice, is righteousness obtained; but it is freely given to every soul who hungers and thirsts to receive it.*

I was looking at my hands a few days ago and saw them as I had not seen them before. They were wrinkled and covered with age spots and I thought that I was getting older. The next morning, I thought of death and that it was getting closer and that I should prepare for it.

It is inevitable after all and I had planned for retirement and for many other things. It makes good sense to plan for this. In fact, it is an imperative. I thought for a while about what I must do to prepare and came up with a list of five things that I felt were important. I will go over these in the next two entries.

1. Lay up treasures in heaven. I have mentioned that the saying "You can't take it with you" is a lie of the devil. Jesus says otherwise, telling us to lay up for ourselves treasure in heaven (Matt. 6:20). It is not for others that we do this, but for ourselves. Jesus does not see that to prepare for heaven in this way is selfish.

2. I want to be more effective in prayer. Jesus taught us to pray to our Father in heaven, but His example of prayer is even more compelling. When crisis in His life came, He, though possessing a divine nature, would go to a quiet place and agonize in prayer for His disciples or the people He was teaching at that time. He knew of the temptations that would befall them; some they would not recognize as such. He prayed to prepare them. I want to have the prayer life He did.

PREPARING TO DIE PART 2
December 3

Acts 4:18–20, "Then they called them in again and commanded them not to speak or teach at all in the name of Jesus. But Peter and John replied, 'Which is right in God's eyes: to listen to you, or to him? You be the judges! As for us, we cannot help speaking about what we have seen and heard.'"

3. I want to work God's works. I have longed to do the work of God. At times, I have been convinced to speak or act on His behalf, but when the time comes, if I sense that some will take offense or that I might be shunned, I alter my behavior to keep the peace. But it has made me feel guilty and unhappy. I have resolved to do as He asks and though fearful at times, I have moved forward with good results.

4. I want to tell those I love that I love them. I have read many stories of regret when a loved one fails to tell their beloved of their feelings. When they pass, it is too late to do so. The present is the time to let our loved ones know how we feel about them.

5. I want to be covered with Christ's robe of righteousness rather than my own. In the parable of the wedding feast, Jesus tells us that all in heaven will possess a robe of righteousness (Isa. 61:10). Ellen White says this: "Not by painful struggles or wearisome toil, not by gift or sacrifice, is righteousness obtained; but it is freely given to every soul who hungers and thirsts to receive it."[171] It is a free gift for all who would take it as theirs. What a privilege is ours. A gift of surpassing worth given without price.

These actions on my part have given me peace. I pray that God will bless you as He has me.

---

[171] Ellen G. White, *The Faith I Live By* (Washington, DC: Review and Herald, 1958), p. 109.

Section 13

Satan And The Angels

What is our knowledge of God's dealing with supernatural beings—Satan and his angels?

"Though the cause of evil prosper, Yet 'tis truth alone is strong; Though her portion be the scaffold, And upon the throne be wrong; Yet that scaffold sways the future, And, behind the dim unknown, Standeth God within the shadow, Keeping watch above His own."[172]

---

[172]James Lowell, "Once to Every Man and Nation," *The Seventh-day Adventist Hymnal* (Hagerstown, MD: Review and Herald, 1985).

I WILL MAKE MYSELF LIKE THE MOST HIGH
December 4

Isaiah 14:14, "I will ascend above the tops of the clouds; I will make myself like the Most High."

Jean-Paul Sartre wrote, "the best way to conceive of the fundamental project of human reality is to say that man is the being whose project is to be God."[173]

The great existentialist philosopher perceives the point of human existence as the endeavor to carry out the will of Satan himself! "I will make myself like the Most High." Such hubris is astounding. How can man who has not even the power to call himself into existence make himself God? His very presence on earth is the result of someone else's will!

But that is the foolishness of our natural hearts and the thinking of the world in which we live. But as the title of Sartre's book hints, such thinking leads to nothingness.

Our desire to be in control, to be God, is a constant temptation. It is the motivating force of our natural hearts and our greatest danger. The desires of our inmost being can lead to our downfall and destruction.

But how to resist the temptation? We will fall to it if we do not make a concerted effort to do otherwise.

Jesus tells us. "Whoever wants to be my disciple must deny themselves and take up their cross daily and follow me. For whoever wants to save their life will lose it" (Luke 9:23–24). And, "Take my yoke upon you and learn from me ... and you will find rest for your souls" (Matt. 11:29).

Sartre does not offer rest but a "project" whose end is nothingness. Jesus calls us to humble ourselves, in a sense to become nothing now, that we might save our very selves eternally. An astounding paradox, but one from the soul of the Most High, who made Himself nothing (Phil. 2:7).

---

[173]Jean-Paul Sartre, *Being and Nothingness*, translated by Hazel E. Barnes (London: Methuen, 1957), p. 358.

THE ORIGIN OF EVIL
December 5

Ezekiel 28:12, 14–15, "You were the seal of perfection, full of wisdom and perfect in beauty …. You were anointed as a guardian cherub, for so I ordained you. You were on the holy mount of God; you walked among the fiery stones. You were blameless in your ways from the day you were created till wickedness was found in you."

Satan was created the covering cherub, that is, the one who stood next to the throne, shielding others from God's glory. And he was full of wisdom, until, yes, until wickedness was found in him.

How could such a being fail?

Genius is able to discern what others cannot see. Einstein, on pondering the problem of the movement of an electromagnetic field, became aware of an inconsistency. On pondering this, he realized that space and time changed depending on the relative speed of the observer. Two observers would see things differently, thus relatively. No one else had noted such a problem or solution.[174]

Satan, standing in God's presence, in a perfect creation, realized that God had withheld something from the angels. His massive intellect detected something that was not there, a stroke of genius. He realized that God had withheld all that was the opposite of good. There was nothing evil or destructive. All was good. And since God had not made it His own, Satan could make it his.

He could have revealed the wondrous good God had done for His creatures—the power of choice. But Satan, showing ingratitude, decided instead to become king of what God had withheld—the realm of evil. He would be king there and thus become king of the whole universe (Isa. 14:14).

God had given Satan the mind of a genius. What a privilege! But Satan used it to destroy himself and has taken myriads with him. A terrible consequence. We must watch and pray that we enter not into his path.

---

[174]John Stachel, "How Did Einstein Discover Relativity?" American Institute of Physics, https://1ref.us/1j6 (accessed January 21, 2021).

SATAN'S PROJECT
December 6

Galatians 4:8–9, "Formerly, when you did not know God, you were slaves to those who by nature are not gods. But now that you know God—or rather are known by God—how is it that you are turning back to those weak and miserable forces? Do you wish to be enslaved by them all over again?"

Ellen White describes the plan Satan has for us in the following words:

> Since the announcement to the serpent in Eden, "I will put enmity between thee and the woman, and between thy seed and her seed" (Genesis 3:15), Satan had known that he did not hold absolute sway over the world. There was seen in men the working of a power that withstood his dominion. With intense interest he watched the sacrifices offered by Adam and his sons. In these ceremonies he discerned a symbol of communion between earth and heaven. He set himself to intercept this communion. He misrepresented God, and misinterpreted the rites that pointed to the Saviour. Men were led to fear God as one who delighted in their destruction. The sacrifices that should have revealed His love were offered only to appease His wrath. Satan excited the evil passions of men, in order to fasten his rule upon them. When God's written word was given, Satan studied the prophecies of the Savior's advent. From generation to generation he worked to blind the people to these prophecies, that they might reject Christ at His coming.[175]

And he continues to do the same work today, striving to cloud our minds to the love and mercy of our Father who only desires our good.

But we need not heed his temptations or adopt his thinking. We may set our minds on God's Word, our strength in any temptation.

---

[175] Ellen G. White, *The Desire of Ages* (Mountain View, CA: Pacific Press, 1898), p. 115.

ARGUING OVER THE BODY
December 7

Jude 9, "But even the Archangel Michael, when he was disputing with the devil about the body of Moses, did not himself dare to condemn him for slander but said, 'The Lord rebuke you!'"

Envision the situation here: Moses has died and now Jesus (Michael) and the devil stand above the grave, arguing over the body. This seems a rather odd development. Why would such an argument even occur and to what end?

Clearly the devil feels that he has a right to Moses. This is the first resurrection recorded in Scripture and the devil is not going to let it go down without a fight. Jesus, on the other hand, wants to raise Moses then and there.

So, why is Satan even allowed to dispute and what would be his reasoning?

God's universe is open to all ideas and God does not silence by force those who disagree, nor does He do His will secretly, but in full view of all, allowing for airing of the issues. Satan is permitted to speak and give his reasoning.

Moses has sinned; he is a murderer and struck the rock in disobedience. The devil's point is that all sin must be punished. There is no place for anything but justice. What can Jesus say to that? He has the record books in heaven after all and they confirm the facts. It seems an open and shut case for the devil.

But Jesus has a deeper defense. It is *not* this: "Satan, you are a dirty rotten scoundrel and I don't have to listen to you." That would be an argument the devil would make. Rather, Jesus says, "The Lord rebuke you!"

What does this accomplish?

Satan has no standing. He cannot bring an accusation, for he is under condemnation himself.

Also, God's government is based not on justice only, but mercy. Ellen White says there is an atmosphere of mercy surrounding the planet, as real as the air we breathe. Since this is so, God can rebuke the adversary, for He does not take this into account.[176]

Thus, the argument is won. By grace. And Moses takes his place in heaven. Thank God for our Redeemer's rebuke.

---

[176] Ellen G. White, *Steps to Christ* (Mountain View, CA: Pacific Press, 1892), p. 68.

THE ILLEGITIMACY OF TEMPTATION
December 8

Genesis 3:4–5, "'You will not certainly die,' the serpent said to the woman. 'For God knows that when you eat from it your eyes will be opened, and you will be like God, knowing good and evil.'"

Satan tempted and deceived Eve with these words. He promised her that she would be like the Most High Himself. Like God!

But that is the strange part of this temptation. She was like God already! God had made her like Him.

God said at the Creation of man and woman, Genesis 1:26, "Then God said, 'Let us make mankind in our image, in our likeness.'" Eve was already like God, for God had made her in His likeness and image.

Satan did the same with Jesus when he tempted Him with the world's splendor. Matthew 4:8–9, "Again, the devil took him to a very high mountain and showed him all the kingdoms of the world and their splendor. 'All this I will give you,' he said, 'if you will bow down and worship me.'"

Although Satan is the prince of the air, he only usurped the rulership of the world from Adam. Jesus, the Creator, still ruled above him and the world was His. Satan actually had nothing to give that was not already Christ's.

Satan promises pleasure, wealth, fame and multiple blessings, but he actually has nothing that is actually his. God has pleasures at His right hand forevermore (Ps. 16:11). And any material blessing we might gain here is immediately surrendered at death.

But God has promised eternal life and the possession of crowns and mansions that will be ours forever.

Keeping this in mind can help us to resist when the great deceiver comes with his smooth talk. Our answer is, "Thus says the Lord."

THE ADULT IN THE ROOM PART 1
December 9

Job 1:6–7, "One day the angels came to present themselves before the LORD, and Satan also came with them. The LORD said to Satan, 'Where have you come from?' Satan answered the LORD, 'From roaming throughout the earth, going back and forth on it.'"

There are a few times in Scripture where God directly confronts Satan. Each instance, however, gives us insight into God's way of dealing with His great adversary.

In Job, the Sons of God present themselves to Him in a grand congress. But instead of Adam as earth's representative, Satan appears. But he has, like a loiterer, no fixed ambition or duty on the planet. He is aimlessly roaming the earth as a vagabond might. Since he is in rebellion against God, he has no duty to perform for the Most High. He is his own boss and thus is actually unemployed. It is God only who has a sense of real purpose.

So, God brings up one of *His* representatives on the planet, Job.

Satan of course takes umbrage. "Does Job fear God for nothing?" (Job 1:9). And so begins the testing of Job.

God does not dispute Satan's role as a representative from earth. He is also called the prince of the air (Eph. 2:2, KJV). His rule here, though under God, is not argued. God accepts it. This shows God's respect for Adam's choice and Satan's right to Adam's allegiance. There is a sense that we are indeed the sons and daughters of Belial. We have all rebelled and pledged loyalty to him. God has acted to woo us away, but we are rightfully his and God honors the choices we have made.

This encounter shows God as a fair and impartial ruler, not favoring or ignoring one because He might or might not be a favorite. God is fair in His dealings with even Satan.

THE ADULT IN THE ROOM PART 2
December 10

Zechariah 3:1–2, "Then he showed me Joshua the high priest standing before the angel of the LORD, and Satan standing at his right side to accuse him. The LORD said to Satan, 'The LORD rebuke you, Satan! The LORD, who has chosen Jerusalem, rebuke you! Is not this man a burning stick snatched from the fire?'"

In this second encounter, the Lord rebukes the devil who is standing at the right hand of the High Priest who is dressed in filthy garments.

That is no way to appear before the Lord of hosts and Satan's accusation seems legitimate. How can the Lord rebuke him for the obvious shortcomings of Joshua, the representative of all humanity? One covered with unlaundered and dirty linen has little basis for hope.

God can rebuke Satan for two reasons:

1. Satan has no standing. That is, he has no right to accuse anyone else because he has so transgressed that he will come under the most severe judgment. One so evil as he is has no right to accuse another. He is being presumptuous.

2. The Lord had something bigger than sin to use against Satan. The mystery of His sacrifice had not yet been revealed, but this would make his accusations irrelevant. Jesus was to take all sin to Himself, making Him able to forgive Joshua for his misdeeds. God rebuked Satan in advance because He knew what was to come.

God did not need to get into a petty tit for tat with Satan. He was the Adult in the room with the long view. He had the situation well in hand and rebuked the accuser appropriately. May His name be praised.

THE ADULT IN THE ROOM PART 3
December 11

Matthew 16:22–23, "Peter took him aside and began to rebuke him. 'Never, Lord!' he said. 'This shall never happen to you!' Jesus turned and said to Peter, 'Get behind me, Satan! You are a stumbling block to me; you do not have in mind the concerns of God, but merely human concerns.'"

Christ and the adversary are again face to face. Peter becomes the lips of Satan, striving to dissuade Jesus from the mission He undertook at the foundation of the world. Recorded here is the sternest rebuke of our Lord. He would have no broaching of His will to press on to the thing He came to do above all other things—to destroy the works of the devil by His death on the cross. He set His face as flint to it and determined to follow through to the end.

Ellen White says this: "[Jesus'] thought was for His disciple. Satan had interposed between Peter and his Master, that the heart of the disciple might not be touched at the vision of Christ's humiliation for him."[177]

"Get behind Me, Satan! No longer interpose between Me and My erring servant. Let Me come face to face with Peter that I may reveal to him the mystery of My love."

Yes, the rebuke was severe, but it allowed Peter to eventually see his Lord. It took many months before the veil Satan had made was removed. But Jesus knew the character of the man He was working with. Peter did become a leader in the infant church. He was one who could sympathize with the weak and sinful. His life has been a source of hope to so many.

---

[177] Ibid., p. 416.

THE ANGELS, UNCONVINCED
December 12

Revelation 12:7–8, "Then war broke out in heaven. Michael and his angels fought against the dragon, and the dragon and his angels fought back. But he was not strong enough, and they lost their place in heaven."

This war occurred after the crucifixion of Jesus and His enthronement in heaven. There had been a semblance of peace, but now war (Rev. 12:10).

Why not before this time? Why did the crucifixion stir the angelic hosts to battle in heaven itself?

The answer is because before then, the character of Satan had not been fully revealed, and there still remained some sympathy for him among the angels who had not joined the rebellion.

After 4,000 years, it was only the crucifixion that finally revealed Satan's true self.

When God created all things, He excluded the principle of deception from His government. But when sin entered, deception become the special study of the evil one. He honed it to perfection so as Jesus said, if it were possible, even the very elect could be deceived (Matt. 24:24). He cast doubt on God's character and presented evidence that seemed to show that God was not a God of love, but One who cared only for Himself. His arguments were so subtle that angels were unsure. Does God really love us or must we fend for ourselves?

But the crucifixion could not be gainsaid. Jesus had endured terrible suffering that He might save men, the most fallen, aside from Satan himself. Christ's self-sacrifice was astounding and showed how far God was willing to go for His creatures.

All doubt was removed. The mask was torn from the deceiver and they wanted nothing to do with him. God honored their desire and Satan was cast out.

And he may be cast from our lives as well if we will allow God to rule there.

Section 14

The End and the Consummation of All Things

What are God's thoughts about the end and the beginning of life eternal?

"O there'll be joy when the work is done,
Joy when the reapers gather home,
Bringing the sheaves at set of sun
To the New Jerusalem."[178]

---

[178] F. E. Belden, "Joy By and By," *The Seventh-day Adventist Hymnal* (Hagerstown, MD: Review and Herald, 1985).

WELL DONE THOU GOOD AND FAITHFUL SERVANT
December 13

Matthew 25:21, "'Well done, good and faithful servant! You have been faithful with a few things; I will put you in charge of many things. Come and share your master's happiness!'"

There is a paradox in the reward of the righteous. Why should they receive any reward at all? Every act, every power, every talent is a gift from God and they have nothing that has not been given to them. Even the ability to freely choose was a gift gained at great cost. And any return on His investment is only the sure result of their using their God-given powers in such a way as to realize that return. Their very existence is the result of an act of the Creator and they live only because of all that He has given and done.

When you think about it, the righteous have nothing at all whatsoever that they have not received as a gift already. EVERYTHING they have belongs to God.

So, how is it then that God will reward them? They have really done nothing deserving a reward. And yet we have the words of Jesus, "'Well *done* …. Enter into the joy of your lord!'" (Matt. 25:21, NKJV).

> *God is so full of grace; it is such a foundational part of His character that it just bubbles up from the depths in such acts as this, giving great rewards to the undeserving. It is just how He is and what He delights in.*

The first reason is grace. God is so full of grace; it is such a foundational part of His character that it just bubbles up from the depths in such acts as this, giving great rewards to the undeserving. It is just how He is and what He delights in.

Second is that God rewards acts that He really values. He loves righteousness and so rewards those that have done such things. Just as a boss will promote the workers who most invest themselves in the company, so God promotes those that please Him.

And finally, the righteous have emulated God's act at the beginning of all things by choosing good over evil at great expense to themselves. They have done what He did then, chose others over self. They are truly reflecting their Father. Any father knows what pride this brings to him.

So, the undeserving righteous receive what they have not earned. What a great God we serve.

THE BOOK OF REVELATION
December 14

Revelation 1:1, "The revelation from Jesus Christ .... to his servant John."

The book of Revelation or the Revelation of Jesus Christ was a controversial book from the beginning. Its vivid imagery and strange symbols have led to endless discussions on its actual meaning. What is God trying to tell us with all of this? Why has it not been made clearer? Why so much mystery? Some in the early church did not even accept it as a canonical book![179]

But think what the Bible would be without this book. It would end with Jude, a good little (really little) book no doubt, but quite an anticlimax for the New Testament.

Revelation, however, is a fitting end for the Bible and it would not have had the impact it does without that mysterious book of beasts and plagues.

The end where God wipes away all tears and death itself is cast into the lake of fire while all the creatures of heaven and earth worship and rejoice and praise God for the great deeds He has done fills us with hope and removes despair and depression from our souls when we face trial on this dark planet (Rev. 20:14; 21:3–7).

> *The message of Revelation is that love and good win in the end, even against great odds.*

The message of Revelation is that love and good win in the end, even against great odds. The souls of the righteous are seen under the altar, crying out for God to limit the suffering here. "How long, oh, Lord?" (Rev. 6:9–10, paraphrase).

They are rewarded with white robes and in the end enter the city of light where there is no night.

And the invitation at the end is so wide and broad! "Come, take the *water of life* freely. Freely!" (Rev. 22:17, paraphrase).

What a way to end the Bible, an invitation to all of suffering humanity.

---

[179]"Book of Revelation," Wikipedia, https://1ref.us/1j7 (accessed January 21, 2021).

WORSHIP IN HEAVEN PART 1
December 15

Revelation 4:8, "Each of the four living creatures had six wings and was covered with eyes all around, even under its wings. Day and night they never stop saying: 'Holy, holy, holy is the Lord God Almighty, who was, and is, and is to come.'"

The book of Revelation is full of worship, but in chapters 4 and 5, there is a vision of the throne room of God and the worship there. John tells of four creatures and twenty-four elders surrounding God's throne (Rev. 4:4, 6). How do the beings in God's very presence worship?

It is of interest in this instance that there is no singing, no petition for God to act or to grant a blessing. There is no thought of their needs. The creatures' total focus is on God and His character and person. When bowing before Him they mention three traits of God: His holiness, His eternal existence and His creative power.

What is this holiness?

When one is holy, they are uncorrupted, pure, free from defilement. Only God is holy.

When Isaiah was transported to heaven, and saw the creatures calling to one another, "Holy, holy, holy," he immediately realized his own sinfulness, and cried out in shame, "I am undone!" (Isa. 6:3–5, paraphrase).

After Moses saw God, his face glowed with such a light that the people, who were not holy, could not endure the sight (Exod. 34:30). They were able to endure the light of the sun, but not the light from the glory of God. The wicked can endure the light of the sun as well but call for the rocks to fall on them when Jesus comes again.

God's holiness outshines the sun. When unveiled, it is the quality of His personality that is most noticeable. The hymn says, "Oh worship the Lord in the beauty of holiness."[180]

If our worship does not include this, it is no worship at all.

---

[180] J.S.B. Monsell, "O Worship the Lord," *The Seventh-day Adventist Hymnal* (Hagerstown, MD: Review and Herald, 1985).

WORSHIP IN HEAVEN PART 2
December 16

Revelation 4:8, "Day and night they never stop saying: 'Holy, holy, holy is the Lord God Almighty, who was, and is, and is to come.'"

Besides declaring that God is holy, the heavenly beings also tell of God's eternal existence. He is not like us. We are contingent beings. That is, we depend on another for our existence, we are not self-determined.

But God is of a different sort.

The verse says, He was, is and is to come. He inhabits all time. The past, the present and the future are open to Him even now.

Psalm 90:2 says: "Before the mountains were born or you brought forth the whole world, from everlasting to everlasting you are God."

On the other hand, Psalm 103:15–16, speaks of us in this fashion, "As for man, his days are like grass, he flourishes like a flower of the field; the wind blows over it and it is gone, and its place remembers it no more."

When we realize our own ephemeral nature and how quickly we pass and are forgotten, and the profoundness of this terrible fact, we can appreciate the blessing that God is both holy and eternal.

It is a humbling realization. It compels us to bow before Him who has eternity in His hand, both past and future.

1 Timothy 6:15–16 states, "the King of kings and Lord of lords, who alone is immortal."

The beings of heaven worship the Immortal, Everlasting One who dwells in eternity. To humbly bow in acknowledgment of this is to share their worship.

WORSHIP IN HEAVEN PART 3
December 17

Revelation 4:11, "You are worthy, our Lord and God, to receive glory and honor and power, for you created all things, and by your will they were created and have their being."

The third quality of God that inspires worship is the fact that God is Creator of all reality, both physical and spiritual. All that we know and see are the works of His hands.

The wonder of the Creation has awed man from the beginning.

David said, "When I consider your heavens, the work of your fingers, the moon and the stars, which you have set in place, what is mankind that you are mindful of them, human beings that you care for them?" (Ps. 8:3–4).

> *True worship acknowledges the Creator, for He has given us life and all things pertaining to it and He gives it freely to us!*

But this existence is ours that we might know Him, the One who stooped to make us from the dust of the ground.

He also created the spiritual realm, the unseen realities of heaven, fellowship with Him and the ministry of angels.

True worship acknowledges the Creator, for He has given us life and all things pertaining to it and He gives it freely to us!

Psalm 145:16, "You open your hand and satisfy the desires of every living thing." Think what an evil god would do. He would create a desire and then not satisfy it so that his creatures might suffer want and privation. Our God feeds the birds and all creatures, even with abundance.

And because He loves us, He gives us freely. The air we breathe, the sunlight that brings life to all are freely given. The rain falls on the just and unjust to show His care for all. And there is also the possibility of communion with Him.

To confess God as our Creator, allowing Him to rule is true worship and worship as is done in heaven.

WORSHIP IN HEAVEN PART 4
December 18

Revelation 4:10–11, "[T]he twenty-four elders fall down before him who sits on the throne and worship him who lives for ever and ever. They lay their crowns before the throne and say: 'You are worthy, our Lord and God, to receive glory and honor and power.'"

This final act of the elders (redeemed saints)[181] shows the utter worthiness of God and His generosity toward us.

As I have lived here on earth, struggling with sin, but being called higher and higher by my Lord, I have realized that any righteousness that I may possess, even every skerrick is due to the work of God in me. My righteousness is as filthy rags, but He gives me a robe of righteousness as white as snow now and in heaven.

The saints, when they sit in God's presence, realize this as well. And to give honor to whom it is due, to show that the crowns that they have received at the hand of God are really due to Him, they place them at His feet.

Paul speaks of the crown he will receive: "Now there is in store for me the crown of righteousness, which the Lord, the righteous Judge, will award to me on that day" (2 Tim. 4:8). If God Himself gives such a thing to us, is it not legitimately ours?

They are indeed ours, for He gave them. But we know the truth of the matter, that we are the work of His hands and that all our goodness is because of Him. And yet He rewards *us*!

It is too much. So, we cast our crowns at the feet of Him who has loved us with His whole heart. That is where they belong.

---

[181] "Twenty-Four Elders," Wikipedia, https://1ref.us/1j8 (accessed January 21, 2021).

DESTROYING THE WORKS OF THE DEVIL
December 19

1 John 3:8, "The reason the Son of God appeared was to destroy the devil's work."

A reason for Jesus' visit to this planet was to destroy the works of the devil as this verse says. We often think of sin, death and disease as the things that Jesus came to destroy. And they are.

But we do not understand the depth to which the world has been molded by Satan. Every principle of action bears his imprimatur. Every action is colored by his rule.

> *We praise what appears to us to be great acts of sacrificial giving, but Jesus, with penetrating insight, noted that the poor widow who threw in two mites gave more than all of them (Luke 21:3)!*

Our societal system is based on the opinions of the elite. But Jesus rejected that criterion; the lowly and outcast were His companions. He ate with sinners and even a thief was promised the kingdom.

And what of competition? Will there be contending for the highest place as the disciples did at the Last Supper? No, the first will be last. We will all be loved by God and need not compete for it or struggle with one another for anything—no gas wars or lawyers advertising on billboards, for God's benevolence will supply our needs.

Then there is capitalism. It is a very successful system for creating wealth here. But there will be no money in heaven. No need for bargaining or haggling. God gives His best to all, freely.

John says, "Whoever is thirsty, let him come, and whoever wishes, let him take *the free gift* of the water of life" (Rev. 22:17, emphasis added). All that is necessary for eternal life will be provided.

We praise what appears to us to be great acts of sacrificial giving, but Jesus, with penetrating insight, noted that the poor widow who threw in *two mites* gave more than all of them (Luke 21:3)!

The principles of this world will be overturned. The devil's work will be completely undone. What a reason to rejoice!

OPENING THE BOOKS
December 20

Revelation 20:4, "I saw thrones on which were seated those who had been given authority to judge."

Revelation 20:12, "And I saw the dead, great and small, standing before the throne, and books were opened …. The dead were judged according to what they had done as recorded in the books."

During the Millennium the righteous go over the books in heaven (Matt. 19:28; 1 Cor. 6:2) and will determine the punishment that is to be meted out to the unrighteous. At the same time, I can imagine the saints will remember the part they played in the sins of the wicked, though the sins of the righteous are covered with the blood of Christ and will not appear in the record.

Let us say a son is born to a godly woman and she prays for him daily. But he rebels against God and starts living a wicked life. His mother prays and prays, but in her distress, loses faith in God because of her son and she too abandons God. Eventually she dies, but the young man comes to Christ, repents and is received into the kingdom. He remembers his part in the loss of his mother. What would you do after realizing your part in the loss of a soul, even your mother?

I think such souls might crowd to the throne room and plead with God that their relatives and friends be given another opportunity. Another chance, a "Second Chance" to accept the loving rule of Christ.

God knows that none would use a "Second Chance" to turn to Christ. The wicked have had lives full of chances, but what of the role the righteous played in sin? God, in His mercy, offers something for them to see. It is worked out on the plains surrounding the heavenly city when the New Jerusalem comes to earth.

THE PROBLEM OF HELL PART 1
December 21

Revelation 20:14–15, "The lake of fire is the second death. Anyone whose name was not found written in the book of life was thrown into the lake of fire."

Revelation 20 describes the final destruction of the wicked. God resurrects them after the Millennium; this is called the second resurrection. After they are raised, Satan deceives them in some manner and they go out to do battle, surrounding the city of God, the New Jerusalem, to take it by force.

At this point, fire falls from heaven, destroying Satan, his fellow angels and all his followers, those who had rebelled with him. All were judged out of the books of record. Each receives judgement according to what is written in the books.

The righteous, ensconced safely in the city, observe all that is happening outside. They see the wicked surround the city with evil intent. They see the fire fall from heaven utterly destroying all who are outside the city. They see their friends and relatives alike burned alive in the flames.

This seems a cruel act and some have criticized God for it. Why not let the wicked sleep for eternity rather than raise them, only to have them die a horrible death? Is God trying to prove a point? Is there some eternal consequence that must be meted out in this fashion? Is God a tyrant that must be appeased by the death of His enemies?

These questions deserve answers. In the next few entries these issues will be brought into focus. God is not a God of hate, but of love. Evil, however, is the opposite of love.

THE PROBLEM OF HELL PART 2
December 22

Revelation 20:5–6, "(The rest of the dead did not come to life until the thousand years were ended) .... Blessed and holy are those who share in the first resurrection. The second death has no power over them."

Jesus said in Matthew 25:41 that hell was not prepared for humans, but for the devil and his angels. God has no interest in us being in that place of torment but came rather to save us from it.

So, why raise the wicked only to destroy them after this resurrection? There seem to be two reasons.

The first is to mete out justice for the crimes that the wicked have committed. Jesus died, bearing the sins of the whole world. All such crimes were taken by Him and borne, if we would let Him take them. But some do not want to renounce sin. They love sin and refuse to comply with the requirements for salvation: to turn from evil and do right. They will not have Jesus as Ruler over them and they choose self-rule instead. They become so identified with sin that they are changed into sin itself. God cannot save them because they have chosen death over life.

And so, they appear before the judgement seat of Christ that each may receive what is due him for the things done while in the body (2 Cor. 5:10; Rev. 20:12).

Life on earth has been unfair. The wicked have committed wrongs that have not been righted. Injustice is rife. Murder, rape and theft on a massive scale have occurred without proper judgement being served.

Such injustice is resolved in the lake of fire. Jesus would have borne it all—ALL—but they would not have it. They therefore bear the judgement themselves against God's will. This is one reason for the second resurrection.

THE PROBLEM OF HELL PART 3
December 23

Hebrews 9:27, "Just as people are destined to die once, and after that to face judgement."

I believe there is a second reason for raising the wicked. It is to show that if they were given a second chance, such a chance would not result in a change of heart on their part.

At the end of the Millennium, the unrighteous are raised. The New Jerusalem descends from heaven. Since Jesus has died for all sinners, why would the wicked, if they wanted heaven, not be able to enter the city if the thief on the cross was allowed into Paradise?

So the gates of the city remain open that the wicked might come in. But because Christ reigns within, they will not enter. They have determined to be ruled only by themselves and will not have Christ rule over them (Luke 19:14).[182]

Satan sees this and goes out to deceive them (Rev. 20:7–8) with the idea that they can take the city by force. Jesus commands the gates to be closed and they surround it to storm the walls, a more agreeable prospect than to submit to Christ's loving rule. It is then that fire descends and devours them (verse 9).

It is not that Jesus would not save them and give them eternal life; it is that that life would only be used for evil. They have demonstrated this by their lives on earth. The "second chance" that the second resurrection gives them does not change their hearts. They remain wicked still. The gracious rule of Christ they reject, for it would be torture to them. The whole universe, the righteous and the angels of God see at once that their cases are hopeless, everything that could have been done has been done. Even a "second chance" has not helped.

So, fire descends and they realize they have forfeited the right to live forever. God did not deny them, but they refused to take the steps necessary to have eternal life. They chose evil instead and that evil must be removed from the universe.

---

[182]Ellen G. White, *The Great Controversy* (Mountain View, CA: Pacific Press, 1911), pp. 662–664. When the New Jerusalem descends from heaven, the gates open to receive the Righteous (p. 663). They are not closed until the wicked surround the city (p. 664).

THE PROBLEM OF HELL PART 4
December 24

Luke 2:34, "Then Simeon blessed them and said to Mary, his mother: 'This child is destined to cause the falling and rising of many.'"

In light of Simeon's message, Ellen White comments:

> In the day of final judgment, every lost soul will understand the nature of his own rejection of truth. The cross will be presented, and its real bearing will be seen by every mind that has been blinded by transgression. Before the vision of Calvary with its mysterious Victim, sinners will stand condemned. Every lying excuse will be swept away. Human apostasy will appear in its heinous character. Men will see what their choice has been. Every question of truth and error in the long-standing controversy will then have been made plain. In the judgement of the universe, God will stand clear of blame for the existence or continuance of evil. It will be demonstrated that the divine decrees are not accessory to sin. There was no defect in God's government, no cause for disaffection. When the thoughts of all hearts shall be revealed, both the loyal and the rebellious will unite in declaring, "Just and true are Thy ways, Thou King of saints. Who shall not fear Thee, O Lord, and glorify Thy name? ... for Thy judgements are made manifest." Revelation 15:3, 4.[183]

Everyone who is found in the lake of fire will know exactly why he or she is there. The excuses will have been swept away and the horrible truth will be revealed.

"I could have had it all! How foolish I have been!"

We can avoid this fate if we will listen to God's pleading now. Let us reconsecrate ourselves to Him.

---

[183]Ellen G. White, *The Desire of Ages* (Mountain View, CA: Pacific Press, 1898), p. 58.

THE PROBLEM OF HELL PART 5
December 25

Matthew 22:13, "Then the king told the attendants, 'Tie him hand and foot, and throw him outside, into the darkness, where there will be weeping and gnashing of teeth.'"

The Bible does not teach that the wicked will live forever in hell, but that they will be destroyed there, body and soul: eternal death. The punishment is forever, that is, it is final, there is no remittance from it, but the suffering ends at some point.

Jesus in several parables describes this suffering as "weeping and gnashing of teeth" (Luke 13:28, KJV). What does that mean?

Although there will be physical pain in hell, Jesus' words indicate that that will be the least of the suffering. Ellen White tells us that on the cross the physical suffering of Christ was hardly felt because the pain of His Father's separation was so intense. It was the psychological suffering that was most severe.[184]

It will be the same with the wicked. It is not the flames that will be so horrible. It is the realization that eternal life has been lost. They have just seen the joys and pleasures of the righteous in the New Jerusalem, an eternity of love and peace and joy, a life of wonder and delight! It could have been theirs!

And what did they exchange for this? The trifles and trivia of sin! The pleasures that endure but a moment, giving way in time to remorse and despair. They chose these! And the Spirit came to them time and time again, pleading to reconsider, but they would not listen.

Such is true suffering. Wailing and gnashing of teeth is an apt description. Let us choose God and His way and flee temptation that this suffering may never be ours.

---

[184]Ibid., p. 753.

THE WIPING AWAY OF ALL TEARS PART 1
December 26

Revelation 21:3–4, "And I heard a loud voice from the throne saying, 'Look! God's dwelling place is now among the people, and he will dwell with them. They will be his people, and God himself will be with them and be their God. He will wipe every tear from their eyes.'"

After the fire descends from heaven to destroy the wicked, there is not a time of rejoicing. In fact, it will be just the opposite.

Was the punishment just? Yes, it was. In fact, the saints, standing on the sea of glass sing the Song of Moses and the Lamb: "Just and true are your ways, King of the nations" (Rev. 15:3). It is not justice that is the problem.

No, it is the destruction of those they love.

Before the fire of hell descended, the righteous see their family and friends outside the city. There are mothers, fathers, children, friends and companions, wives and lovers there. Ones they so loved on earth. Ones they would even have been willing to give their lives for. But alas! The wicked would not choose God and life.

And so the fires of hell destroy them. The righteous are not celebrating this; rather the city is filled with the weeping saints, even in the presence of God! Sorry for the destruction that is justly meted out.

And how can they be made happy? Do the wicked by their wickedness have power over the joys of heaven? Can they make their families miserable for eternity by their rebellion?

It is not so. And the reason is only that God can wipe away their tears (Rev. 21:4). The Bible does not tell us how He does it, but He does.

It is the last act of mercy in His dealing with sin, comforting the righteous at the moment of hell.

Thank God we have this picture of His grace.

THE WIPING AWAY OF ALL TEARS PART 2
December 27

Revelation 21:4, *"'He will wipe every tear from their eyes.'"*

Why are the righteous crying in the Holy City? Why this weeping?

It is partially because they know of their part in the loss of the wicked. They know of their shortcomings, the weaknesses in their lives. They have not been faultless in their actions, even toward the ones outside the city.

> **Eternity is filled with the rejoicing of our Savior over His bride, the ones that He has saved from destruction.**

Does Jesus forgive and bear the consequences of their mistakes? Yes, most assuredly so. But there are still the consequences of those mistakes that have caused trouble.

The punishment for these mistakes has been borne by our Savior. He took all sin to Himself and there certainly is an issue of sinfulness in these acts of neglect or evil.

But God has the capacity to wipe all tears away, and He does so.

The realization that we have an influence for good or evil here on earth should bring us to sober consideration of our actions. They have eternal consequences. To realize this and to contemplate those consequences will give us motive for seeking the Savior that we might be constantly surrendered to Him. We will then have the assurance that we have done all that we could have done for those outside the city.

Eternity is filled with the rejoicing of our Savior over His bride, the ones that He has saved from destruction. That all would not so choose to be saved is a tragedy indeed. But free choice and the dignity of personhood are two of God's most wonderful and serious gifts. And to abuse the gift and destroy oneself is sad but cannot be blamed on God.

We would be wise to dwell on our part in the salvation of others. Such serious thinking will result in less remorse in the future.

THE HOME OF THE JUST PART 1
December 28

Revelation 21:1–3, "Then I saw 'a new heaven and a new earth,' for the first heaven and the first earth had passed away, and there was no longer any sea. I saw the Holy City, the new Jerusalem, coming down out of heaven from God, prepared as a bride beautifully dressed for her husband. And I heard a loud voice from the throne saying, 'Look! God's dwelling place is now among the people, and he will dwell with them.'"

The first surprising thing about the home of the just is that it is not heaven at all, but a remodeled, rather, newly-created earth. The just are not taken to live with God in heaven, but He comes to live with them on the earth made new.

Apparently, heaven, the present center of the universe, is left vacant so that God may come and live with His Son Jesus and the redeemed. The earth thus becomes the nerve center of the universe. That is the value God places on this little rock of a planet circling a so-so star two-thirds the way from the center of the Milky Way.

> **The redeemed are God's most precious possession. They are the ones for whom He gave His greatest Gift, His Son.**

Why would God do such a thing?

The redeemed are God's most precious possession. They are the ones for whom He gave His greatest Gift, His Son. All heaven was poured out, and so, in order to be forever with those He loves most, He comes to earth and takes up residence there.

And this place is where the depths of His love were shown to the whole universe. Just as lovers have special places that are dear to them because of associations they have with them, so this little planet, surrounded by an atmosphere of grace, is dear to Him.

It is so dear that there is no place He would rather be than here. How strange that this insignificant world should be so honored!

THE HOME OF THE JUST PART 2
December 29

Revelation 21:4, "He will wipe every tear from their eyes. There will be no more death or mourning or crying or pain, for the old order of things has passed away."

Although there are many wonderful things said about the New Jerusalem—the streets of gold, the walls of jasper and precious stones, the gates of pearl and the mansions fair—it is some basic characteristics that make it most desirable. John gives them primacy of place.

The first is the absence of death. This aspect of the heavenly abode is mentioned first, for it's the most important characteristic. No death! No more funerals or mortuaries or mothers being told of sons dying in some far-off land. It has been the ultimate process of separation from our loved ones. No dusk and twilight to annoy us with the thought of an end to it all. Oh, what a gift Jesus has bought for us!

This idea is almost incomprehensible. Our world is full of death and decay. Its lurking can take the pleasure from any action or relationship. Even the youth, often feeling they are immortal, realize it vaguely with the end of school or a job or a relationship. We cannot imagine what living without death is like. But there will be no death.

Without death a main reason for crying disappears. But if pain remains, crying would continue. So, pain is dismissed.

I have found pain a most useful instructor. It has taught me most effectively. It has prevented accidents and foolish actions. But in heaven there will be no need for its tutelage. It will not be necessary. Hallelujah!

Thus, no more death, crying or pain. What a wonderful place.

THE HOME OF THE JUST PART 3
December 30

Revelation 21:9, "One of the seven angels who had the seven bowls full of the seven last plagues came and said to me, 'Come, I will show you the bride, the wife of the Lamb.'"

The New Jerusalem is the bride of the Lamb. The wedding banquet occurs when Jesus comes to this planet to fetch her and take her home with Him.

But God then made a new home for His Son and the bride He had taken to Himself. That home is the renovated earth. And the Father, of course, denies no resource to make it the most beautiful and desirable of dwellings for His beloved Son and His wife. There are the streets of gold, the walls of jasper and a foundation whose builder and maker is God (Heb. 11:10).

There is a river of life and a tree that straddles the river whose fruit gives eternal life to all who eat. And the water and fruit are given freely to all who enter there. And the leaves of that tree heal the envy, hatred and animosity of the nations.

But the citizens of this city are its real attraction. The saints live there, but even they are overshadowed by God and His Son, the Groom whose "honeymoon" cottage this is. There is no night there and they are the light of the place. The humble of earth are allowed to enter.

And God makes His dwelling among them. His presence would light even the humblest of abodes with the blinding light of holiness and love. But in heaven, it shines in all that is done.

And we may be part of this if we will. Oh, the love and kindness of our Lord to give us such a gift!

THE HOME OF THE JUST PART 4: THE INVITATION
December 31

Revelation 22:17, "The Spirit and the bride say, 'Come!' And let the one who hears say, 'Come!' Let the one who is thirsty come; and let the one who wishes take the free gift of the water of life."

And so the last book of the Bible ends with a wondrous invitation. "Whoever is thirsty, let him come; and whoever wishes, let him take the free gift of the water of life" (Rev. 22:17, paraphrase).

There is no restriction on God's part. If any be thirsty, they may come. And amazingly, whoever wishes is invited to take of the FREE gift of the water of life.

God has made His kingdom available to all and it is free. We are not required to pay a price for there is no price that we could pay that would add to the price already paid—the death of God's Son.

What keeps us from accepting? Really it is our concentration on ourselves and our sin. We let these things separate us from God. But if we look to the Savior, who has taken care of it and us, we find that the way is open. He does not hold our sins against us, so we may freely approach the throne and find grace to deal with the very things that separate Him from us. He has made a way of escape so that He can say to us all, "Come! Take the free gift, the water of life."

Oh that you, dear reader, would realize how freely it is given to the unworthy and sinful, the high and the low, the good and the evil, and how He who is life itself has taken all our sin and alienation unto Himself that we might be reconciled! Oh, the wonder of it all!

Did you read that whoever wishes? Let that sink in. You, whoever you are, are not excluded.

May God give you understanding of the possibilities open to you by His grace. Amen.

Bibliography

Acton, Lord. "Lord Acton writes to Bishop Creighton ...." ONLINE LIBRARY OF LIBERTY. https://1ref.us/1g7 (accessed December 2, 2020).

Alexander, Cecil. "All Things Bright and Beautiful." *The Seventh-day Adventist Hymnal.* Hagerstown, MD: Review and Herald Publishing Association, 1985.

Alexander, Cecil. "Once in Royal David's City." *The Seventh-day Adventist Hymnal.* Hagerstown, MD: Review and Herald Publishing Association, 1985.

"Alexander the Great." Wikipedia. https://1ref.us/1il (accessed January 20, 2021).

Babcock, Maltbie. "This Is My Father's World." *The Seventh-day Adventist Hymnal.* Hagerstown, MD: Review and Herald Publishing Association, 1985.

"Babylonian captivity." Wikipedia. https://1ref.us/1ii (accessed January 19, 2021).

Behe, Michael J. *Darwin's Black Box: The Biochemical Challenge to Evolution.* New York, NY: Free Press, 1996.

Behe, Michael J. "Molecular Machines: Experimental Support for the Design Inference." Pitt.edu. https://1ref.us/1i5 (accessed January 19, 2021).

Belden, F. E. "Joy By and By." *The Seventh-day Adventist Hymnal.* Hagerstown, MD: Review and Herald Publishing Association, 1985.

Bergman, Jerry. "Why Abiogenesis Is Impossible." Creation Research Society, Quarterly 36 (2000).

"Biblical Magi." Wikipedia. https://1ref.us/1ip (accessed January 20, 2021).

Bingham, Nathan W. "Justification by Faith Alone: Martin Luther and Romans 1:17." Ligonier Ministries. https://1ref.us/1j5 (accessed January 21, 2021).

Bonar, Horatius. "I Lay My Sins on Jesus." *The Seventh-day Adventist Hymnal.* Hagerstown, MD: Review and Herald Publishing Association, 1996.

"Book of Revelation." Wikipedia. https://1ref.us/1j7 (accessed January 21, 2021).

Breining, Greg. "Are Darwin's Finches One Species or Many?" Discover. https://1ref.us/1hw (accessed January 19, 2021).

"Building Features." Supreme Court of the United States. https://1ref.us/1ih (accessed January 19, 2021).

Camus, Albert. "Quotable Quote." goodreads. https://1ref.us/1ig (accessed January 19, 2021)

Carnegie, Dale. *How to Win Friends and Influence People*. revised ed. New York, NY: Simon and Schuster, 1981.

"Chronology of the universe." Wikipedia. https://1ref.us/1hp (accessed January 19, 2021).

Collie, Alareece. "Strange. Not getting my fair share." *Adventist Review*, May 2017.

"Color vision." Wikipedia. https://1ref.us/1i3 (accessed January 19, 2021).

"Co-Redemptrix." Wikipedia. https://1ref.us/1gn (accessed December 2, 2020).

Craddock, Fred B. *Craddock Stories*. St. Louis, MO: Chalice Press, 2001.

"Darwin's finches." Wikipedia. https://1ref.us/1hv (accessed January 19, 2021).

Dembski, William. "Repeat After Me: 'This Has Nothing To Do With My Views On Religion.'" UNCOMMON DESCENT. https://1ref.us/1hl (accessed January 19, 2021).

"13.2 DEVELOPMENT AND ORGANOGENESIS." BC campus. https://1ref.us/1id (accessed January 19, 2021).

"Did Frodo fail at Mt. Doom by putting on the ring and refusing to destroy it?" Quora. https://1ref.us/1g8 (accessed December 2, 2020).

Douthat, Ross. "Opinion." *New York Times*, January 6, 2014.

Duran, Mike. "Why God Exists in Trinity." Mikeduran.com. https://1ref.us/1g9 (accessed December 2, 2020).

Ellerton, John. "Throned Upon the Awful Tree." *The Seventh-day Adventist Hymnal*. Hagerstown, MD: Review and Herald Publishing Association, 1985.

"*Epic of Gilgamesh*." Wikipedia. https://1ref.us/1i9 (accessed January 19, 2021).

"Evidence Supporting Biological Evolution." Science and Creationism. https://1ref.us/1gj (accessed December 2, 2020).

"Faith." Sermon illustrations. https://1ref.us/1im (accessed January 20, 2021).

Ferguson, Andrew. "The Heretic." *Washington Examiner*. https://1ref.us/1hm (accessed January 19, 2021).

Fieldsend, John. "Shepherds' character reference." *CHURCH TIMES*. https://1ref.us/1io (accessed January 20, 2021).

"From Sabbath to Sunday." United Church of God. https://1ref.us/1ib (accessed January 19, 2021).

"Fun Fact – Nonmetal Hydrides." Karl's Personal Web Site. https://1ref.us/1if (accessed January 19, 2021).

"German-Soviet Nonaggression Pact." HISTORY. https://1ref.us/1j9 (accessed January 25, 2021)

Gillette, Carolyn Winfrey. "On our search for meaning …." Wagga Wagga Uniting Church. https://1ref.us/1j0 (accessed January 21, 2021).

"Great Leap Forward." Wikipedia. https://1ref.us/1in (accessed January 20, 2021).

Heber, Reginald. "Holy, Holy, Holy." *The Seventh-day Adventist Hymnal*. Hagerstown, MD: Review and Herald Publishing Association, 1985.

"Herod the Great." Wikipedia. https://1ref.us/1iq (accessed January 20, 2021).

"hyperbole." Merriam-Webster. https://1ref.us/1i6 (accessed January 19, 2021).

Jennens, Charles. *Messiah libretto*: Part 3, 46 chorus: "Since by man came death," 1741.

"Joseph Merrick." Wikipedia. https://1ref.us/1i8 (accessed January 19, 2021).

"Joseph Stalin." Wikipedia. https://1ref.us/1gc (accessed December 2, 2020).

Karabinos, Paul M. and Thomas E. Krogh. "Dating." Encyclopædia Britannica. https://1ref.us/1gh (accessed December 2, 2020).

Kenyon, Dean and Gordon Mills. "The RNA World: A Critique." Access Research Network. https://1ref.us/1hz (accessed January 29, 2021).

"Korban." Wikipedia. https://1ref.us/1iu (accessed January 20, 2021).

Kuhn, Robert L. "Is Your 'Self' Just an Illusion?" Live Science. https://1ref.us/1hk (accessed January 19, 2021).

Lewis, C.S. *Mere Christianity*. New York, NY: Collier Books, MacMillan Publishing Co., 1952.

Lewis, C.S. "Quotable Quote." goodreads. https://1ref.us/1iv (accessed January 20, 2021).

"List of religious populations." Wikipedia. https://1ref.us/1gl (accessed December 2, 2020).

"Love." Sermon Illustrations. https://1ref.us/1j3 (accessed January 21, 2021).

Lowell, James. "Once to Every Man and Nation." *The Seventh-day Adventist Hymnal.* Hagerstown, MD: Review and Herald Publishing Association, 1985.

Luther, Martin. "Martin Luther." AZ Quotes. https://1ref.us/1ic (accessed January 19, 2021).

"Mary in Islam." Wikipedia. https://1ref.us/1gm (accessed December 2, 2020).

"Massacre of the Innocents." Wikipedia. https://1ref.us/1ir (accessed January 20, 2021).

"Mind-body dualism." Wikipedia. https://1ref.us/1hn (accessed January 19, 2021).

Monsell, J.S.B. "O Worship the Lord." *The Seventh-day Adventist Hymnal.* Hagerstown, MD: Review and Herald Publishing Association, 1985.

Montefiore, Simon Sebag. "DELANCEYPLACE.COM 11/8/11—FIVE HUNDRED JEWS WERE CRUCIFIED EACH DAY." Delanceyplace.com. https://1ref.us/1iy (accessed January 20, 2021).

"Myths about antibiotics, resistance." Awesome Investors. https://1ref.us/1hy (accessed January 19, 2021).

Nazareth, Pascal Alan. "Gandhi, Christ and Christianity." Mahatma Gandhi's writings and philosophy. https://1ref.us/1ix (accessed January 20, 2021).

Newton, John. "Amazing Grace." *The Seventh-day Adventist Hymnal.* Hagerstown, MD: Review and Herald Publishing Association, 1985.

"NINE VIEWS OF CREATION." BLUE LETTER BIBLE. https://1ref.us/1gc (accessed December 2, 2020).

"nirvana." Merriam-Webster. https://1ref.us/1ik (accessed January 20, 2021).

Olivers, Thomas. "The God of Abraham Praise." *The Seventh-day Adventist Hymnal.* Hagerstown, MD: Review and Herald Publishing Association, 1985.

"Panpsychism." Wikipedia. https://1ref.us/1i0 (accessed January 19, 2021).

Paul, Ian. "Aristotle and the Household Codes." Psephizo. https://1ref.us/1j1 (accessed January 21, 2021).

Pfandl, Gerhard. "Ellen G. White's contributions to the Seventh-day Adventist Church." *Ministry.* https://1ref.us/1j2 (accessed January 21, 2021).

"Physics of Music-Notes." Michigan Technological University. https://1ref.us/1ie (accessed January 19, 2021).

"Predestination in Calvinism." Wikipedia. https://1ref.us/1j4 (accessed January 21, 2021).

"Problem of evil." Wikipedia. https://1ref.us/1gk (accessed December 2, 2020).

"Radiometric dating." Wikipedia. https://1ref.us/1gi (accessed December 2, 2020).

Richards, Jay. "LIST OF FINE-TUNING PARAMETERS." Discovery. https://1ref.us/1ht (accessed January 19, 2021).

Rippon's A Selection of Hymns. "How Firm a Foundation." *The Seventh-day Adventist Hymnal.* Hagerstown, MD: Review and Herald Publishing Association, 1985.

Ritmeyer, Leen. "The Treasury of the Temple in Jerusalem." Ritmeyer Archaeological Design. https://1ref.us/1iw (accessed January 20, 2021).

Samaan, Philip. *Christ's Method Alone*. Joplin, MO: College Press LLC, 2012.

Sartre, Jean-Paul. *Being and Nothingness*, translated by Hazel E. Barnes. Methuen, London: 1957.

Schlosser, S. E. "Babe the Blue Ox." American Folklore. https://1ref.us/1i7 (accessed January 19, 2021).

Schorsch, Ismar. "Shabbat: A Temple in Time." Jewish Theological Seminary. https://1ref.us/1ia (accessed January 19, 2021).

"Second voyage of HMS *Beagle*." Wikipedia. https://1ref.us/1hu (accessed January 19, 2021).

Seventh-day Adventists Believe. Hagerstown, MD: Review and Herald Publishing Association, 1988.

Stachel, John. "How Did Einstein Discover Relativity?" American Institute of Physics. https://1ref.us/1j6 (accessed January 21, 2021).

Stennett, Samuel. "On Jordan's Stormy Banks." *The Seventh-day Adventist Hymnal.* Hagerstown, MD: Review and Herald Publishing Association, 1985.

Stone, Samuel. "The Church Has One Foundation." *The Seventh-day Adventist Hymnal.* Hagerstown, MD: Review and Herald Publishing Association, 1985.

Szalavitz, Maia. "Touching Empathy." *Psychology Today.* https://1ref.us/1i4 (accessed January 19, 2021).

"Temple Mount." Wikipedia. https://1ref.us/1it (accessed January 20, 2021).

Tozer, A.W. *The Pursuit of God.* Camp Hill, PA: Christian Publications, 1993.

"Triple-alpha process." Wikipedia. https://1ref.us/1hs (accessed January 19, 2021).

"Twenty-Four Elders." Wikipedia. https://1ref.us/1j8 (accessed January 21, 2021).

"Visual perception." Wikipedia. https://1ref.us/1i2 (January 19, 2021).

Waggoner, Ellet J. "Studies from the Gospel of John. Christ Risen. John 20:11–20." *The Present Truth,* June 1, 1899

Waggoner, Ellet J. "Waggoner on Romans." Ellen G. White Estate. https://1ref.us/1jc (accessed January 25, 2021).

Wells, Jonathan. "Second Thoughts about Peppered Moths." Discovery Institute. https://1ref.us/1hx (accessed January 19, 2021).

"What is the best evidence or argument for intelligent design?" compelling truth. https://1ref.us/1hr (accessed January 19, 2021).

White, Ellen G. *Christ's Object Lessons.* Washington, DC: Review and Herald Publishing Association, 1900.

White, Ellen G. *Education.* Mountain View, CA: Pacific Press Publishing Association, 1903.

White, Ellen G. *Faith and Works.* Nashville, TN: Southern Publishing Association, 1979.

White, Ellen G. *Life Sketches of Ellen G. White.* Mountain View, CA: Pacific Press Publishing Association, 1915.

White, Ellen G. *Patriarchs and Prophets.* Mountain View, CA: Pacific Press Publishing Association, 1890.

White, Ellen G. *Steps to Christ.* Mountain View, CA: Pacific Press Publishing Association, 1892.

White, Ellen G. "Steps to Jesus." Ellen G. White Writings. https://1ref.us/1i1 (accessed January 18, 2021).

White, Ellen G. *The Desire of Ages.* Mountain View, CA: Pacific Press Publishing Association, 1898.

White, Ellen G. *The Faith I Live By.* Washington, DC: Review and Herald Publishing Association, 1958.

White, Ellen G. *The Great Controversy.* Mountain View, CA: Pacific Press Publishing Association, 1911.

White, Ellen G. *The Ministry of Healing.* Mountain View, CA: Pacific Press Publishing Association, 1905.

White, Ellen G. *Thoughts From the Mount of Blessing.* Mountain View, CA: Pacific Press Publishing Association, 1896.

White, James. "John 1:1—Meaning and Translation." Alpha and Omega Ministries. https://1ref.us/1ga (accessed December 2, 2020).

Whittier, John G. "John Greenleaf Whittier Quotes." Brainy Quote. https://1ref.us/1gb (accessed December 2, 2020).

Wolchover, Natalie. "Physicists Debate Hawking's Idea That the Universe Had No Beginning." *Quantamagazine.* https://1ref.us/1ho (accessed January 19, 2021).

Wood, Paxton. *The Sunday At Home: A Family Magazine for Sabbath Reading.* Vol. 27.

"WORLD'S FIRST OPENLY ...." ORTHODOX CHRISTIANITY. *The Christian Post,* October 8, 2015. https://1ref.us/1iz (accessed January 21, 2021).

TEACH Services, Inc.
P U B L I S H I N G

We invite you to view the complete
selection of titles we publish at:
www.TEACHServices.com

We encourage you to write us
with your thoughts about this,
or any other book we publish at:
info@TEACHServices.com

TEACH Services' titles may be purchased in
bulk quantities for educational, fund-raising,
business, or promotional use.
bulksales@TEACHServices.com

Finally, if you are interested in seeing
your own book in print, please contact us at:
publishing@TEACHServices.com

We are happy to review your manuscript at no charge.

www.ingramcontent.com/pod-product-compliance
Lightning Source LLC
Chambersburg PA
CBHW071906230426
43671CB00010B/1492